You Hold in Y[our...] [...] to Being a Better Counselor

Noel Tyl: "For all of us, in all situations, at any age, we live by a point of view that is (positioned) very, very close to the Sun, to the essence of who we are, who we were, and who we may become ..."

Christian Borup: "The key to all astrological work is the fact that every moment has its own cosmic qualities—and so does the meeting between astrologer and client ..."

Haloli Q. Richter: "There must not be a discrepancy between understanding the client (through listening and through the horoscope) and the client feeling understood. The latter quality is called 'empathy,' and it might as well be labeled 'magic' ..."

Diana Stone: "I rarely, if ever, encounter a consulting situation that is not best worked through within the [communication] model. Something that works 99 percent of the time is justification enough ..."

Donna Cunningham: "One hurdle to getting the information needed for successful problem-solving is the belief that we shouldn't have to ask any questions ... "

Karen M. Hamaker-Zondag: "You've prepared your chart very well and now you're busy explaining it in comprehensive terms, but the client doesn't react as you expected or hoped. What can you do?"

Susie Cox: "By the time you understand Bottom-Line Astrology, you will be able to sum up your client's chart in one simple sentence ..."

Jeff Jawer: "We need to connect to the unconscious part of our clients if we want to be effective counselors. Without awareness of this level of communication, we not only miss opportunities to help, but may inadvertently damage the client's capacities for growth ..."

Wendy Ashley: "As a mythic astrologer it is my task first to identify the myth through the horoscope, and then to assist my client on the journey of self-discovery that the myth brings ..."

To Write to the Authors

If you wish to contact the authors or would like more information about this book, please write to the authors in care of Llewellyn Worldwide, and we will forward your request. Both the authors and publisher appreciate hearing from you and learning of your enjoyment of this book and how it has helped you. Llewellyn Worldwide cannot guarantee that every letter written to the authors can be answered, but all will be forwarded. Please write to:

Llewellyn's New Worlds of Mind and Spirit
P.O. Box 64383-K866, St. Paul, MN 55164-0383, U.S.A.
Please enclose a self-addressed, stamped envelope for reply, or $1.00 to cover costs. If outside U.S.A., enclose international postal reply coupon.

Free Catalog from Llewellyn

For more than ninety years Llewellyn has brought its readers knowledge in the fields of metaphysics and human potential. Learn about the newest books in spiritual guidance, natural healing, astrology, occult philosophy, and more. Enjoy book reviews, New Age articles, a calendar of events, plus current advertised products and services. To get your free copy of *Llewellyn's New Worlds*, send your name and address to:

Llewellyn's New Worlds of Mind and Spirit
P.O. Box 64383-K866, St. Paul, MN 55164-0383, U.S.A.

Llewellyn's New World Astrology Series—Book 15

Communicating the Horoscope

edited by

Noel Tyl

1995
Llewellyn Publications
St. Paul, Minnesota, 55164-0383, U.S.A.

FIRST EDITION, 1995
First Printing

Cover Design by Lynne Menturweck

Library of Congress Cataloging-in-Publication Data
Communicating the horoscope / edited by Noel Tyl. — 1st ed.
        p.   cm. — (Llewellyn's new world astrology series: bk. 15)
        Includes bibliographical references.
        ISBN 1-56718-866-4 (alk. paper)
        1. Astrology. 2. Counseling—Miscellanea. 3. Horoscopes.
    I. Tyl, Noel, 1936–   . II. Series.
    BF1729.C67C65   1995
    133.5′4—dc20
                                                                    95-2097
                                                                    CIP

Llewellyn Publications
A Division of Llewellyn Worldwide, Ltd.
St. Paul, Minnesota 55164-0383, U.S.A.

The New World Astrology Series

This series is designed to give all people who are interested and involved in astrology the latest information on a variety of subjects. Llewellyn has given much thought to the prevailing trends and to the topics that would be most important to our readers.

Future books will include such topics as astrology and sexuality, astrology and counseling, and many other subjects of interest to a wide range of people. This project has evolved because of the lack of information on these subjects and because we wanted to offer our readers the viewpoints of the best experts in each field in one volume.

We anticipate publishing approximately four books per year on varying topics and updating previous editions when new material becomes available. We know this series will fill a gap in your astrological library. Our editor chooses only the best writers and article topics when planning the new books, and we appreciate any feedback from our readers on subjects you would like to see covered.

Llewellyn's New World Astrology Series will be a welcome addition to the novice, student, and professional alike. It will provide introductory as well as advanced information on all the topics listed above—and more.

Enjoy, and feel free to write to Llewellyn with your suggestions or comments.

Other Books in this Series

Forthcoming

Contents

Noel Tyl

For over 20 years, Noel Tyl has been one of the most prominent astrologers in the western world. His 17 textbooks, built around the 12-volume *Principles and Practice of Astrology*, were extraordinaily popular throughout the 1970s, teaching astrology with a new and practical sensitivity to modern psychotherapeutic methodology. At the same time, Noel presented lectures and seminars throughout the United States, appearing in practically every metropolitan area and on well over 100 radio and television shows. He also founded and edited *Astrology Now* magazine.

He is one of astrology's most sought-after lecturers in the United States, and internationally in Denmark, Norway, Germany, South Africa, and Switzerland, where for the first three World Congresses of Astrology he was a keynote speaker.

Noel wrote *Prediction in Astrology* (Llewellyn Publications), a master volume of technique and practice, and has edited Books 9 through 15 of the Llewellyn New World Astrology Series, *How to Use Vocational Astrology, How to Personalize the Outer Planets, How to Manage the Astrology of Crisis, Exploring Consciousness in the Horoscope, Astrology's Special Measurements* and *Sexuality in the Horoscope*. In the spring of 1994, his master opus, *Synthesis and Counseling in Astrology—The Professional Manual* (almost 1,000 pages of analytical technique in practice), was published. Noel is a graduate of Harvard University in psychology and lives in Fountain Hills, Arizona.

Noel Tyl

One's Point of View: So Close to the Sun

Through continuous study of the extraordinary symbolic ties between planets and people, astrologers build a keen sensitivity for empathy. Caught up in an Olympics competition, for example, we can feel the jumping push of a competitive dance skater's legs against the ice and share tears of fulfillment with the victor on the medal podium; we can be stirred in concert with people whose lives are shattered by accident and circumstance; we see client after client living life-dramas, with the feelings of which we can easily identify from our case experience and/or, indeed, from the vantage point of our own personal life.

We don't know *exactly* how someone else feels, but we can *appreciate* that feeling, the circumstances of a situation, and the philosophical adjustments used to assimilate it, regulate life, and keep life going. We recognize *patterns* of feelings, the structure of situations—including their timing significances—and we recognize the points of view that focus our self-image for ourselves and others.

The point of view we have about life probably embodies the most fundamental dimension of who we are as individuals. It is constructed through the conditioning of childhood. It is tested and seasoned in adulthood, and it is evaluated in our later years. How should I behave and pattern who I am to please my parents

1

and my teachers; how do I fit in to earn a living, cultivate a family, and establish personal significance; how has my life fared within the scheme of things, what has it all meant, will I be remembered? These dimensions of the point of view include many facets such as the behavioral patterns we use to manage insecurity, to cope with fear, to love ourselves, to love others, to continue to learn the ways of cooperation, and to relate somehow to the unknown. In terms of time, the point of view embraces the past, focuses the present, and projects the future.

The point of view is very much a part of the *persona*. The persona is the Latin word for "mask," that which was worn by actors in early times *(Dramatis Personae)*. In literary usage, it has come to define the "I" created by an author through whom the author shares points of view about characters and events. Jung embraced the concept of the persona as the mask, the portrait (my word) of ourselves we present to the world.

Every person portrays him or herself to the world through a constantly developing and articulated point of view. The point of view is founded on a structure blasted into being at birth and molded by events, relationships, and learning throughout life. Optimally secure in the personal point of view, one can feel, "That's the way I am (i.e., who I am), take it or leave it," which in turn is evaluated by others with their points of view, with the responses of tolerance, acclaim, or ostracism. Insecure in the personal point of view, one can feel, "I simply don't know who I am or what I'm supposed to do." In between, caught within the developmental pressure to adjust the point of view, one feels alarm, "Why, you're asking me to change my philosophy, everything I stand for! You're saying I've been a failure up to now!"

The point of view is the lens through which we see the world and react to it. We bring ourselves to the world *through* our point of view, through our points of view about many things, which are, at one and the same time, intrinsically fragile and necessarily robust: we can be extremely sensitive to criticism because we feel personally attacked and devalued; we can bluster defensively that we don't care what others think, in order to protect who and what we have become.

We encounter a point of view with every client. We suspend our own point of view in order to give full focus to the client's point of view and progress in development. We speak, we listen, learn, and teach *through* the client's persona, *about* the client's persona. For client realities to be clear to us, we need to be aware of this lens in our preparation of the horoscope and in our choice of communication style.

The astrology of one's point of view: the fundamental purpose of the point of view, to establish identity, interact with life, and give it meaning, must be linked first and foremost with the Sun. Astrologers feel the different life energies of the Fire signs, the Water signs, Earth, and Air. We can speak volumes about the expression of these zodiacal archetypes and their balance in the horoscope. Although Sagittarius and Capricorn are neighboring signs, there is no debate about the fact that Sagittarian energy is different than Capricornian, that Piscean energy is different than Arian. That's the miracle of astrology and that's *its* point of view!

We know that this Sun-sign energy permeates the entire horoscope, that the Sun's light, as it were, is reflected off each other body in the horoscope in different ways (distance, aspects) to energize certain attitudinal dispositions and behavioral resources. Purpose, needs, sensibilities, and actions all thrive on the Sun's energy to one degree or another. The other symbols in the horoscopic system establish their own presence, and synthesis begins.

Closest to the Sun are Mercury and Venus, never more than 28 and 46 degrees away from the Sun, respectively. These two planets, which we know symbolize the dynamics of mind and relationship in every individual, are tied to the Sun. They can not go far away. They are kept close. They need to be close. They feel the light and heat of the Sun more than any other planets do. They are nearest to the core of a life drama in which the mind is activated and social awareness is explored. Communication and the sharing of selfhood, in the main, are established by the Sun's energy expressed through Mercury and Venus. The Moon is not far behind, indeed, but here with the Sun, Mercury, and Venus is where one's point of view must begin.

This is not a "new view" of things. It is a reinspection of fundamentals, which must continuously take place in our studies for us to learn more about our subject and how we express it. The wise astrologers long ago had quite a rigid concept about planets that were close to the Sun, Mercury and Venus in particular (because of their greater frequency of solar conjunction). The extraordinary thirteenth century astrologer Guido Bonatus (or

Bonatti) still influences astrological practice, with so much of his work brought forward by William Lilly, 400 years later. With regard to the Sun's inner circle, if you will, Bonatus said that a conjunction with the Sun is the greatest misfortune that can befall a planet. Many astrologers throughout history followed the lead of this deduction.

The ancients and, indeed, we moderns, especially in horary astrology, observe the rules of Cazimi ("in the heart of the Sun," within 17 seconds of arc of solar conjunction) greatly strengthening the planet; Combust (between 17 minutes and 8.5 degrees from the Sun and in the same sign) burned, harmed, weakened; and Under the Beams of the Sun (between 8.5 degrees and 17 degrees from the Sun) less effect, diminished, depleted.

What this means for us in this discussion is that nearness to the Sun *emphasizes* a planet. Before we make an objective judgment of the emphasis—harmful or not—we should simply recognize that, in the cases of Mercury and Venus, *nearness to the Sun calls attention to the mind and to social awareness.* For better or for worse, the faculties of thought and relating are brought center stage in full illumination.

In our daily work with astrology, we know that the conjunction of Mercury and/or Venus with the Sun, or Mercury and Venus in conjunction with each other close to the Sun, say, 9 or 10 degrees away, or in conjunction quite a distance from the Sun but in the same sign as the Sun, registers as a strong focus on *idealism.* The energy of the Sun enflames the mind and the social antennae. All that characteristic energy potential is powerfully focused, often dominatingly. It leads the life in mental awareness (perception) and interrelationship. A perfectionism emerges from the core heat of the particular sign. The Sun and its tie to Mercury and Venus establish the primary stuff of the persona, the foundation of the life point of view.

Even when Mercury and Venus are *not* in the same sign as the Sun nor in conjunction with the Sun or each other, the manifestation of idealism, of a strongly distilled point of view of the world that often transcends reality can be immediately obvious. For example, Martin Luther King (January 15, 1929 at 11:21 A.M. in Atlanta, GA) had the Sun in Capricorn, Mercury in Aquarius (16 degrees away), and Venus in Pisces. But, Venus was exactly semisquare the Sun and tightly semisextile Mercury, accentuating the tie among these planets clearly. When we note that the Sun was in Capricorn, Mercury was in Aquarius, and Venus was in Pisces (along with the Moon), we feel the point of view quite dramatically focused: administrative power, humanitarian thought processes, and self-sacrificing relationship.

Mother Theresa (August 27, 1910) has the Sun in Virgo, Mercury in Libra, and Venus in Leo (the sense of service, the need to think for social good, a noble and dramatic social outreach). No clear aspect connects any two of these planets, but the Sun is at the midpoint of Mercury-Venus (Sun=Mercury/Venus), and this dimension of synthesis is most telling. Again, the meaningful triumvirate is brought into strong focus.

Karl Marx (May 5, 1818, 2:00 A.M., LMT, Trier, Germany) had Mercury in Gemini conjunct Venus in Taurus (with the Sun and Moon both in Taurus as well). Here, Mercury and Venus are in their own sign, as dominant as planets can be intrinsically; *and in conjunction besides.* Is it any surprise that this was the person to give idealized economic structure a quasi-religious intellectual framework and social imperative?

A survey of the Popes of Rome over the past 60 years shows pronounced idealist structures among the Sun, Mercury, and Venus or through Mercury or Venus being singled out strongly *in every papal case.* For example, Pope John Paul II (May 18, 1920 at 1:00 P.M. in Wadowice, Poland) has Mercury conjunct Venus, conjunct the Sun and Moon, all in Taurus, all in the 9th House (the first Pope to internationalize Catholic religious structure). John Paul I (October 17, 1912 at 11:30 A.M. in Canale, d'Agordo, Italy), who reigned for 33 days, had his Libra Sun conjunct Mars and Mercury, with Venus ruling the Midheaven and tightly semi-square the Sun. Administrative ascetic Pope Paul VI (September 26, 1897 at 11:00 P.M., Concescio/Brescia, Italy) had his Libra Sun conjunct a Libra Moon widely conjunct a Jupiter-Mercury conjunction in *Virgo,* with Venus also in Virgo square an exact Saturn-Uranus conjunction.

Other planets rush to the light, as it were, modify and extend the point of view. Mars involvement seems to tighten considerations into a focused force: opinionation, nervous drive, assertion, aggression. Jupiter often adds a dimension of religious rationale to the point of view. Saturn can show a depression; or a frustration in idealistic structures, a difficulty in working them out, a delay, often related to early family conditioning and/or social circumstances. Uranus, of course, impassions the mind and social outreach, exacerbating anxiety as well. Neptune adds mental mists, spiritual support or camouflage, introduces double meanings and hidden significances. Pluto empowers the thrust and lifts it to prominence (politician Jerry Brown has an Aries Sun with Mercury conjunct Venus in Taurus square Pluto), especially when an angle of the horoscope is involved.[1]

These other planets do not necessarily have to be involved with the Sun-Mercury-Venus complex. Neptune "oriental," for example (rising last before the Sun in clockwise motion), corresponds to a manifestation of idealism: Nelson Rockefeller (July 8, 1908 at 12:10 P.M. in Bar Harbor, ME) had Sun-Mercury-Venus all conjunct in Cancer with Neptune as well, with Neptune oriental!

The 3rd-9th House axis comes into consideration through the planets placed there and through the condition of the planets ruling the cusp signs of the two houses. Rockefeller and Pope John Paul II show their intense planetary complex in the 9th House. Mother Theresa has Neptune ruling her 3rd, opposed Uranus, with this axis squared by *Jupiter!* David Ben-Gurion, founding statesman of Israel, had Sun-Jupiter and Venus-Uranus, two conjunctions in Libra in the Libran 9th, with Mercury in Scorpio peregrine.

Normally, when the point of view—its bare-bones symbolic profile—is put together with even rudimentary "key words," the premise fills itself out from the Sun's inner circle through planets in aspect with that area, the manifestations of the "mental" axis through tenancy and rulership, and the dominant aspects elsewhere in the horoscope. All this helps us ascertain the person's point of view, its intensity, its directions. We study how it fits with the individual's employment, i.e., what he or she does *for a living*. We study Solar Arcs, Progressions, and transits in the early developmental time of life to suggest parental and social conditioning, and we put this together with the focus of the consultation that is going to take place, its stated purpose, the purpose that may be hidden, or the purpose lodged in the point of view of life that may be languishing out of circulation and nearly forgotten. The

1 Please see "The Profile of Prominence," Tyl, *Synthesis & Counseling in Astrology,* Llewellyn, 1994.

point of view—often vaunted in idealism—is compared with reality. The meaningful portrait, the persona, emerges.

Ralph Nader (February 27, 1934 at 4:52 A.M., Winsted, CT) has the Sun in Pisces opposed Neptune. Immediately, we *feel* the archetypal essence of Pisces, accentuated extremely. Mercury is also in Pisces and conjunct Mars! Again, this intensifies all the Piscean dedication to ideals. Mars rules the 3rd House. This is a channel of intense cerebration, a thinking process dominant in the Piscean dimension. The social outreach of it all is shown through Venus in *Aquarius*, which is peregrine (without major aspect, though exactly semisquare Sun) at the Ascendant while ruling the 9th! Pluto rules the Midheaven and trines it as well as the Mercury-Mars conjunction, leading it all to prominence, without any doubt.[2]

The heroic ideals of the knight errant and his life-dedication to idealistic romance and impeccably pristine relationship were embodied by Don Quixote, the "Man of LaMancha." The author of the extraordinarily popular tale, the allegory of idealism appreciated only after death, which has permeated cultures throughout the world, was Miguel de Cervantes (September 29, 1547). Cervantes had a Sun-Mars conjunction in Libra with Mercury in Libra trine Pluto in Aquarius; Venus was in Virgo (passionate chastity) conjunct Uranus.

Dr. Jack Kervorkian (May 26, 1928), the Michigan doctor persistently assisting patients ready to die to commit suicide, has Mercury in its own sign of Gemini at the midpoint of his Jupiter-Neptune trine, i.e., Mercury=Jupiter/Neptune, which is a classic suggestion of the mind working overtime within idealistic constructs.[3] His Venus is in Taurus, also the sign it rules, and is square Neptune, which adds the surreal, the idealized, aesthetic rationalization, fascination with the emotionally adventurous in relationships, and anesthesia to the mix. Of course, the focus upon death/suicide comes from other dimensions in the horoscope and personal life-experience. The point here is that Dr. Kervorkian has an

---

2   Ibid, see case #74.

3   The full text-image for this midpoint picture that I suggest (see Tyl: *Prediction in Astrology* [1992] or *Synthesis & Counseling in Astrology* [1994] for all possible midpoint pictures analyzed) reads, "Idealism; grand spirit; feeling quietly special; looking ahead to nice times; self-indulgences; rumor and scandal; active imagination, inspiration."

extraordinarily cerebral and convicted point of view that is highly idealized and adventurous.[4]

We humans are particularly susceptible to idealistic projections. Our points of view lead us there. They free us from upset,
they reinforce personal formulations, and they make us feel individually significant, worthwhile, and, most important, *justified*.
We talk of the Garden of Eden, Shangri-La, El Dorado, Camelot,
Heaven on Earth, Mom's apple pie, Home Sweet Home, "Jeannie's
light brown hair," and the thousands of ideal-life images that bom-
bard our senses every day through the public media. We espouse
religions to explain life. We internalize wisdoms to help us understand the complications of living. We pick and choose in relation to
our personal disposition. We become what we believe. People of
any family, any community, any country *are* their culture.

All of these considerations comprising the point of view that
is a person's badge of identification alert us astrologers to *how we
should listen and what we should listen for during a consultation.* In
our preparation of the horoscope, we get ready to address a particular point of view, to experience it directly from the person, to
give it respectability and measure its interaction with reality.

I will always remember a particularly tense consultation I
had many years ago with a very well-known and powerful man
in Germany. He was reclusive in his power, distant in his person,
hard to read in any way. His office where we met at 9:00 at night(!)
was a third-door, inner inner office, with a bustling staff in the
outer offices even at that hour. The room was dark; only a small
desk lamp illuminated where we sat together. I could see the
man's shadowed face but not his eyes. It was quite a 12th House
experience for this young astrologer.

The consultation went along well, all things considered: the
chart appeared accurate, the man and I communicated effectively
with each other; difficult developmental times in the past, especially during World War II and my client's prison-camp confinement, had been assimilated productively. About two-thirds of the
way through our meeting, this powerful, successful, cultivated

---

4   It is fascinating to note that Elizabeth Kuebler-Ross (July 8, 1926 at 10:45 P.M. at 008E32,
47N23), the modern hospital-services pioneer of humane care for the dying, including
management of the death experience, has a Sun-Pluto-Node conjunction in 15 Cancer (a
rare occurrence), with Pluto ruling her 8th House which holds Saturn in Scorpio trine
the triple conjunction in Cancer, and that Dr. Kervorkian's Pluto is in 15 Cancer as well.

man of many, many life experiences leaned forward and closer into the light on his desk, as if to reveal himself all the more to me. The change of position and the tone of voice indicated trust and a deeper level of intimacy. I expected a revelation, but what he asked me was simply, "Herr Tyl, now tell me: is this a . . . a . . . is this horoscope here a *good* horoscope?"

In spite of all his accomplishments, his seniority in life, and his personal conviction, this man had seen astrology as an important *evaluation* of who he was. He saw it as a scrutiny of his decisions and his reactions to extraordinary circumstances. He knew where he stood in his life, *but he wanted to impress me, the astrologer.* Perhaps astrology and I were another world to conquer, but this man wanted to be special. He wanted his point of view about life to be evaluated and respected, and to prevail into the future.

I think it's safe to say that practically *everyone* feels this way when they go to an astrologer. On that first visit, during that first meeting with the astrologer, a lot of self-regard is at stake. I think the astrologer has to stand back a bit and let the client get settled, to look the client over with eyes and ears to find certain strong points, and to compliment and assure the client about them sincerely and naturally.

The appointment chart for my consultation yesterday morning—which I prepared about 15 minutes before the scheduled appointment, knowing my client would be on time—was an easy read [See Christian Borup's chapter leading this volume—Ed.]: we would surely be discussing relationship factors (Pluto at the Descendant, squaring Mercury, Sun, and Saturn), job upset (Neptune conjunct Uranus, ruling the Midheaven), and probably, underneath it all, pains about lovableness (Sun-Saturn conjunction in the 11th, love needed, expected, hoped for, with Neptune, ruler of the 11th, conjunct Uranus). The client would look to me (the astrologer, the 7th House) as a source of power and leadership. Emotional security on all these fronts was dominant in the picture (Moon in Cancer in a Grand Trine with Jupiter and the 11th House group, defensively).

The client's natal horoscope corroborated these anticipations perfectly (see page 12): the Saturn retrograde phenomenon keyed an enormous well of unfinished business with her father; the ruler of the self-worth 2nd House was peregrine, dominating all concerns, and was at the Midheaven; Neptune ruled the relationship 7th and was retrograde in the 2; Saturn retrograde ruled the 5th, and difficult love-sex-giving-response concerns came out in our discussion, as well as a platonic marriage and a yearning for separation. Her Midheaven showed duality, potential job shift; transiting Pluto was approaching conjunction with the Moon (transformation of values and self image) and opposition with that Midheaven . . . and so it went.

My client was smart, articulate, polite, and not obviously hurting. Mention of the father immediately triggered tears of recogni-

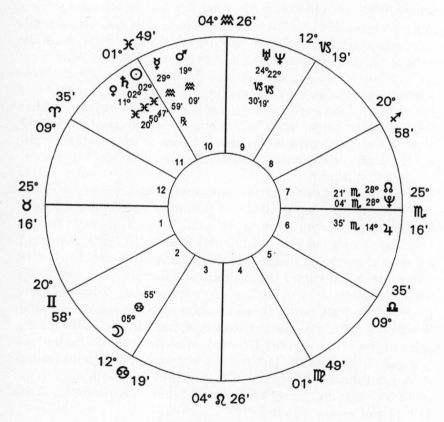

Example 1
Appointment Time
Feb. 21, 1994, 10:30 A.M. EST
Alexandria, VA
77W03 38N48
Placidus Houses

tion. The platonic marriage was presented and discussed as a matter of course. The point of view of settled patience, reserve, and perseverance dominated her life and our discussion (Sun-Mercury-Mars in Taurus; Venus in Gemini, *in mutual reception with Mercury*).

One more observation is important here for our discussion: my client was considerably overweight.

Note that Mercury is retrograde. This always suggests some counterpoint in the thinking process, some other line of concern behind the prevailing point of view, as if the mind is serving two masters or two themes. Often, there can be a completely different world of considerations than is presented to the world routinely day-to-day. In this case, I gave great importance to this signal since Mercury ruled her Ascendant as well. What was behind the prevailing point of view of patience, reserve, and perseverance, with a "some day my prince will come" idealization, which she voiced to me tying all her concerns together?

When my client told me she had just moved back with her husband, it was as if a bus had just pulled up to the corner to take on another passenger: "Well, he begged me to come back. I'm like a mother to him."

"Might this be making you feel loved?" I asked. "We've talked about the tremendous need you have for that."

Unemotionally, she replied, "But I don't *feel* loved by him. I feel his dependency."

"We've talked about your longing for that real-life, true, soul-mate love, and we've agreed that not everyone has that experience and . . . remember, that that doesn't mean one won't come your way. But I think, now, that it's first things first: you've got your pension secured in the next few months and you're resolved to relocate. You're working on a program that will help you bring your weight down. We're looking at a "new you," aren't we? And for all of that we have a schedule that's pretty clear astrologically."

"Right, I've got that down, and it makes sense."

"But there's something else here: it's your terrific need to know, to be in control of things (the Moon in Scorpio trine Jupiter in Aries, the pressing need and hope for ego-recognition at the Aries Point)."

As I began to talk about this other dimension, I consciously began to seek out the other level of her point of view and her way of acting in life, most likely the controlling attitude *that usually covers over emotional vulnerability*. At the same time, my client raised her hand up to her mouth, very slowly, supporting her head and masking a half smile.

Covering her mouth as she spoke, she said—the "other level" said— "You're so right. I even tell my boss what to do, and he does it!"

"Well, this is a part of you I don't see here, but I'm sure it's how you run most of your interpersonal relations. It's understandable, isn't it, as a cover-up for the emotional vulnerability you feel, the weight problem, not feeling attractive. This bluster and control tell us who you are. It's an understandable defense . . .

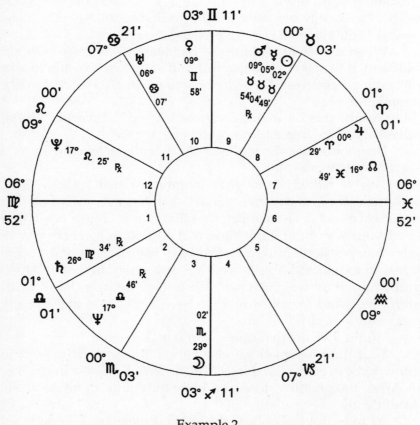

Example 2
Female

but what if we *change* this point of view? What if we convert this capacity you have of knowing, opinionating, and leading *into something you get paid for* (the Moon rules the 11th, the second of the 10th)! What if we see your assertiveness and leadership as hidden assets . . . coming out now as a 'new you,' divorced, relocated, into a new profession?"

"You mean running my *own* business? Maybe in fashion, as a buyer, as . . . ?"

"Yes, remarketing yourself into a new future. Let's talk . . ."

With more discussion of course, we were able to *understand* her point of view, her patience, reserve, and perseverance—really a quiet obstinacy—with her familial baggage, her overweight situation, the long government career that bored her, and appreciate the emotion hidden behind it all. Then we were able *to take the defensive measures and convert them into assertive action.*

I felt strongly that we satisfied the counterpoint of the retrograde Mercury. We altered her point of view by linking it to a new start, leaving job, husband, and excess weight—the past— behind. With the inexorable Pluto transit coming to her Moon and opposing her Midheaven, I recalled the consultation chart in which Pluto signified me the astrologer! I felt everything working together as it was somehow supposed to.

My client was changing. And so was her point of view.

All of us need to know where we stand in life. There are times when, even with all the conspicuous trappings of social security, we aren't so sure, as my German client reminded me. There are times when we are deluding ourselves—mid-life crises, drugs and alcoholism, repeated patterns of self-destructive behavior, depression and withdrawal, routinized denial—and there are times when we clear-headedly make strategic changes in how we present ourselves to the world. For all of us, in all situations, at any age, we live by a point of view that is very, very close to the Sun, to the essence of who we are, who we were, and who we may become.

With our talents for life, with our courage to practice them, and with our conviction to evaluate them for efficiency and permanence, we approach personal fulfillment. In Ralph Waldo Emerson's point of view, "To believe your own thought, to believe that what is true for you in your private heart is true for all men— that is genius."

Christian Borup

Christian Borup has studied astrology since 1968, and has a diploma from Denmark's I. C. Astrology Institute (1978) and a professional diploma from The American Federation of Astrologers (PMAFA, 1983). He was chairman of SAFA (the organization of professional Danish astrologers) 1983–1986, and ISAR International vice president for Denmark 1991–1992. He has been head of the teaching faculty of the I. C. Astrology Institute since 1978.

The I. C. Astrology Institute was founded by the Danish astrologer Irene Christensen in 1956, continued by Birthe Kirk. Since 1987, Christian has been its owner and director. He is also the chief editor of the well-known astrological monthly *Stjernerne* (The Stars) which has been published without interruption since 1956.

Christian has lectured widely in Denmark, England, France, Germany, Norway, Sweden, and the former Soviet Union, and has presented lectures at UAC'95 in Monterey, California.

Christian Borup

The Magic of the Consultation Time

Astrologers work in mysterious ways, and when describing the use of consultation charts, very personal statements and examples can not be avoided!

 What is the *raison d'être* of the consultation? It is quite simply the quality enhancement of the client's life! Period. Therefore, the astrologer's first and most significant task must be to obtain the client's acceptance, in order to establish the necessary trust between client and astrologer. To do this, the astrologer has to be able to communicate his or her knowledge of the client's chart in a manner relevant to the client, in a way that the client both recognizes and understands.

Astrology lives and breathes only in the consultation. Here astrology is put to the most difficult test of all: the client's unconditional acceptance of the content of the chart as real, as acceptance of the Self.

This is where the magic of the consultation chart enters astrology.

The Consultation Chart

A consultation chart is a chart erected for the date, time, and place of the meeting between astrologer and client. The consultation chart shows not only the general atmosphere of the consultation but also *the client's subconscious reason for wanting the consultation in the first place.*

Such consultation charts are not a new fad, but date back a long way in astrological tradition, where consultation charts have been used at all times. This especially applies in India, where a *Prasna* (consultation chart) has practically always been used to serve the general population astrologically, since so many do not know their birthday, nor often, even the year of birth.

In Eastern astrological tradition, consultation charts might even be more significant and potent than the birth chart! During a conversation I had with the Dalai Lama's personal astrologer, Professor Jampa Gyaltsen Drakton, in 1991, he mentioned that in certain cases it is in fact even possible to *replace* a person's birth chart with the consultation chart! That means, if certain conditions in the chart are fulfilled, a consultation horary can cancel the significance of a birth chart, making it obsolete. A thought undoubtedly too radical for a Western humanistic astrologer. But still . . .

The key to all astrological work is the fact that every moment has its own cosmic qualities—and so does the meeting between astrologer and client. What astrology actually does is measure a person's biological and subjective *experience* of time and space. While it looks like cosmic magic, it's just cosmic timing!

The Chart as a Map

We can compare the birth chart with a map: on a map, lakes, woods, roads, houses and fields are clearly marked, but a map can not describe whether or not the lakes are polluted, whether the woods consist only of tree trunks stripped by acid rain, whether the roads are riddled with holes and lack striping, whether the houses are well-kept or uninhabited, or whether cows or horses graze on the fields.

Similarly, the birth chart shows the client's static potential, but we cannot express an opinion about the dynamic "degree of maintenance" of the various signatures on the map. Neither can we know if the client at some time in his life has decided to make a complete tour of the "neighborhood," and therefore gained deep insight into himself and his own chart. In the chart, *we* see all the possibilities, but we have no way of knowing whether or not the client sees these possibilities. Even the transits and progressions are laid down at birth. Even the future of the "birth map" is fatally determined.

But when doing consultations, it's imperative and all-important to ascertain how *the client* experiences the birth chart. Otherwise we would be interpreting the chart at some inappropriate level. So, gradually, as our experience with consultations increases, our intuitive sense of the client's way of using his chart deepens. We begin to know intuitively how many "tours" of the chart the client has embarked on, i.e., how the client uses the chart.

We use two highly subjective terms to explain what we do: "experience" and "intuition." But is this enough to explain how we choose the right interpretation, i.e., the interpretation that fits?

Does a Mars-Neptune conjunction in the 12th House in a given chart show a person who punishes himself in masochistic fashion, or a person who derives great pleasure from helping others? The same energies are involved, but a totally different lifestyle can emerge.

Is a person with Mars in the 3rd House in square Pluto in the 7th House a renowned, efficient, crisis psychologist, or is he an equally renowned boxer or street-fighter with several people's lives on his conscience? How shall we measure these energies on the "map"? How can we know what the lake looks like and what the farmer has planted in his field? How can we be more specific in our interpretations when the client is sitting in front of us in the consultation room?

Most astrologers would say that the choice of the right interpretation can only be learned through experience and intuition. This is partly true, but if you let it, the consultation chart can be your knowledgeable, inspirational guide to a rewarding consultation.

Subjectivity and Objectivity

When I began my serious study of astrology in the mid-70s, it was usual for my teachers—and the books they had read—to use the term "level" to explain how it could be that one person used some aspects in a more "highly-developed" way than another person.

For instance, it was generally regarded as more highly developed to be a therapist or a charitable person than to be a street-fighter or a masochist. According to Western-Christian thought, aggressive Mars energies have always had to be suppressed, if development to higher levels of spirituality were the aim.

The thought that a human being should set himself up as a judge of another human being's spiritual level has always been foreign to me. Any evaluation of this kind must be made on the basis of extremely subjective attitudes and views about life, which every human being derives from his culture and the age in which he lives. A Chinese person will obviously have quite different values than a European. I feel that no one can advance completely objective views.

The Vicious, Subjective Circle

If you're a practicing astrologer, this problem begins to assume absolutely horrible proportions. The astrologer has his own personal, subjective chart. The client has his or her own personal, subjective chart. One day, one of these two subjective characters makes an appointment for a consultation with the other one, in order to have a thorough and rewarding discussion about personal life.

But, can the astrologer disengage himself from his own chart? Is the astrologer able to use objective intuition and objective experience? If not, the astrologer is at the mercy of the forces which the client triggers off in the astrologer's chart. If the astrologer doesn't like homosexuals, red-haired women, or male neurotics, for example, this will obviously be reflected in the consultation in an unfortunate manner, if the client should fall within the sphere of one of the astrologer's favorite aversions.

We are situationally in a "vicious circle," where one subjective system has to measure another subjective system; an experimental set-up which would never be approved in any high school science class. The sources of error wholly overshadow the possibility of the system measuring anything relevant. The two charts affect each other to such an extent that it is no longer possible to say who is "interpreting" whom!

We often hear astrologers say that, oddly enough, they keep getting clients who reflect their own personal situations or problems: "Imagine, I've just got divorced, and all my clients are getting divorced too." Now we can conjecture why!

This truth of subjectivity manifests in many disguises. When we've just bought a new yellow car, we see yellow cars all over the place. When we've just begun to get interested in postage stamps, we always get to sit beside philatelists on the bus. When I've just discovered that there's something called astrology, I see astrological symbols and charts everywhere. I think that the whole world is experiencing the same thing; that the whole world is finding out about yellow cars, postage stamps, and astrology.

It is all a question of subjective omens. If I say to my wife that I think we should move to Malta, and at the same instant the chandelier falls down from the ceiling, then maybe the chandelier is trying to tell me something. It *says:* "It's definitely not a good idea to move to Malta." But the chandelier only says anything if I *choose* to connect the fall of the chandelier to my urge to move to Malta. Otherwise the chandelier says nothing.

I choose to read (project) a subjective meaning into the chandelier's fall; a meaning which perhaps is not there; a meaning that only has meaning for me. (Maybe this is exactly what we do when we interpret the symbols in the chart?) There is nothing wrong with projecting, you just have to project the right things, i.e., choose to give the chandelier importance.

So the chandelier and Malta are subjectively connected in the person's mind, but they are also objectively connected in Time and Space, i.e., via the astrological chart of the moment.

"Well," a serious teacher of astrology would reply, "the thought of moving to Malta and the fall of the chandelier share the same time/space continuum, and therefore the same chart. Your statement about Malta contains the same form of energy that made the chandelier let go of the ceiling. Is it because you're about to give up here that you want to move to Malta?" And the astrologer can even elaborate on his interpretation of the omen and say something like: "Moving to Malta will turn out to be a hard physical strain for you, you'll feel older and a move like this will be likely to exhaust all your power resources." The astrologer is really saying that gravity will have a stronger effect on me if I move to Malta now. Saturn must clearly be activated in the horary erected for the time of the chandelier's fall and the formulation of the question.

Exactly this same principle can be applied to an astrological consultation.

The Client's Choice—the Consultation Chart

Each moment in time contains objective planetary positions for which we can erect a chart. When client and astrologer meet, they do so in a specific space and at a specific time. These two birth charts have a third chart in common: *the horary for the beginning of the consultation.* This third chart is the factor tying the two persons together within the present reality they share.

This consultation horoscope is created by the client's unconscious decision/desire to come for a consultation at a precise moment in time. This can be used by the astrologer to obtain insight into the way in which the client uses his or her birth chart, and into the expectations the client has from the consultation.

I maintain that the consultation chart is always subconsciously *willed* by the client.

The client "decides" to come 10 minutes early, and by doing so, tries to tell us that he or she is reacting to the energies being intercepted at exactly that moment. By means of the consultation chart we get a "second (or third) opinion" about the birth chart. By using it as such we better our odds of being objective in the consultation.

The way out of our subjective dilemma then is the introduction of this third element, which enables us to rise above the situation and obtain a degree of objectivity about what we are doing.

Because the consultation chart is *willed*, it also expresses the *degree* of free will possessed by the client at this point in time, and provides us with clues about the level at which the client is using the birth chart right now. The client's birth chart becomes a living entity.

Charts for the First Consultation

Since I have long been fascinated by this dilemma between objectivity and subjectivity, I have made it a habit always to work out consultation charts when I had clients, whether I used these charts or not. I just felt I had to work them out, and after the consultation I would continue to think about how they could be interpreted.

Today I would feel quite lost having to do a consultation without a consultation chart. It gives me a list of subjects that I just *have* to discuss with the client. Like the scent of a hunted animal, the consultation chart can keep you on the right track, giving the freedom and confidence to interpret the birth chart at the level where the client is in the here and now.

Early in the 1980s, very little literature was available about horary astrology, and the few books available gave no directions regarding the interpretation of consultation charts.

The following consultation took place in 1985 and involved one of my first VIP-clients: Joe.

Joe's Chart

Joe was 45 years old. He had just been contacted by a personnel "head-hunter" to take over a position of great responsibility as head of a large Government-subsidized organization which for a long time had faltered. The firm was notorious for its tense atmosphere, slander, and lack of trust between the different collegial groups. Since his appointment, Joe had regularly appeared in the media, and, with his previous record as a tough manager, he was expected to tidy up the organization and bring it to its feet again. He had stated in public that no-one would be laid off.

Joe's wife, Janis, had called to make the appointment for a consultation, which was to take place on October 8, 1985 at 1 P.M. in Copenhagen. As newly-appointed head of his organization, Joe was so harassed and stressed that the astrological consultation could only take place during his lunch hour.

He arrived at my office 5 minutes late, i.e., at 1.05 P.M. (see the consultation chart, page 25). It was as though he had deliberately tried to avoid the MC sextile with Neptune and square to the Moon. He could have come at 12.50 P.M. instead, making these aspects exact—but he didn't). It was as though, like a magnet, Pluto pulled the MC toward a conjunction with itself: he consciously sought the prominent position in the limelight which is precisely what this Pluto describes.

Although Joe's choice occurred at a subconscious level (unless he were an astrologer, and knew his daily transits by heart), it often seems as though the client has planned to come when a planet culminates the formation of an exact aspect to one of the angles. These aspects to the angles always show what energies have "driven" or "forced" the client to come to the astrologer. Therefore, the same aspects also describe *the lasting impact the consultation will have*. One might say that these aspects measure the transforming power of the consultation.

Even for a beginner at reading consultation charts—or horary charts on the whole, for that matter—Joe's chart clearly shows that considerable changes and readjustments will have to be made in connection with his job (Pluto on the MC). The Moon, which is always a triggering factor in any horary chart, first triggers the square to Pluto, and then moves on toward the opposition with Jupiter, which rules the Ascendant. There is no doubt that Joe will very shortly meet violent opposition, and enter into a deep personal dilemma. His public promise that nobody will be laid off can not be reconciled with the applying Moon-square-Pluto: he is approaching one of the biggest crises in his life. We are seeing this in horary terms, not in the real time of transits, of course.

Just for the record: in Joe's birth chart at the time of consultation, transiting Saturn was conjoining his Ascendant, which was at 3° Sagittarius 33. I have found that when the Ascendant of the consultation chart falls in the same sign as the Ascendant in the birth chart, the consultation chart is particularly reinforced, and thus can be ascribed greater significance and power. Simultaneously with the Saturn transit, transiting Neptune was square his MC for the first five months of 1986, while Pluto was sextile to the Sun and Mars. In the Secondary Progressions, Mars was conjunct the MC, Mercury opposed Saturn and the Sun squared natal Venus! All of these aspects indicated the work problems this man had at the time—and would later experience to an even greater degree.

By just looking at the consultation chart alone, there could be no doubt that Joe would no longer sit in his present job in seven months time. A severe crisis was on its way, and the Moon's position in the 7th House square to Pluto indicated that, even though he had promised on television that no-one would be fired, Joe would be forced to fire employees within the next couple of months, whether he wanted to or not.

This horary chart is extremely convincing, and this period in Joe's life could in fact be described solely on the basis of the influences shown by the horary chart. We shall return to this chart later.

In the two months following the consultation, I had ample opportunity to follow Joe's story in the media. He seemed stern and self-assured, some employees were fired, and, sure enough, he encountered violent opposition and personal criticism.

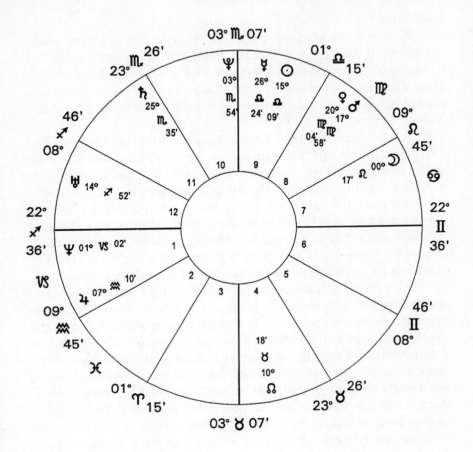

Joe
Oct. 8, 1985, 1:05 P.M. CET
Copenhagen, DK
12W35   55N42
Placidus Houses

Janis' chart

Two months after the consultation with Joe, his wife, Janis, called me. It was the end of November, 1985. This time she called to make an appointment for herself. She was worried about Joe's state of mind and about her marriage, and therefore wanted a consultation. We agreed on a consultation on Monday, December 2, 1985, at 2 P.M.

When that day came, Janis arrived 16 minutes late. A delay such as this can not be regarded as coincidental when working with horary astrology. Her excuse was that she had been unable to find a parking space. While this is a common excuse, her delay (see the chart) resulted in Pluto being placed exactly on the Descendant in exact square to the Moon! No wonder she was worried about her marriage. Suddenly I realized: Janis had more or less the same angle and Moon aspects as Joe had had! Her consultation chart repeated that of her husband in the strangest way.

Joe's Pluto had been on the MC, his crisis being connected with his profession, and now Janis, with Pluto on the Descendant, regarded *him* as the problem. In these two consultation charts, the aspects support and emphasize each other to such an extent that it is possible to predict an almost lynching atmosphere, which Janis in particular will experience, because she reacts much more personally than he does (Janis' aspects are to the personal Axis: Ascendant/Descendant). Even now—at the time of the consultation—she is harassed by journalists who invade her home, and who do not respect her and her family's privacy. In short, Joe's career is breaking up her whole family.

These two, surprisingly revealing consultation charts are so clear that it is unnecessary to go further with the classical rules for interpretation of a horary chart. These two charts gave me the starting signal for more intensive work with consultation charts in my future astrological practice. The two charts put me on the track of the rules for interpretation of consultation charts given below.

Here it should be pointed out that a complete description of the procedure to be followed in the interpretation of consultation charts would fill several books. The "Consultation Menu" shown on page 28 is thus merely a short resumé of the most important factors to which attention should be paid in such charts, and it is my hope that these rules will lead to an increased interest in consultation charts—an interest which they well deserve. In this chapter, I shall limit the interpretation factors to the main rules laid down by classical horary astrology.

It is important to be aware that, in this study, I have not included the clients' birth charts, which are the cornerstone of the best work with clients, but I regard consultation charts as extremely important aids for further insight. Read on, please, in this spirit.

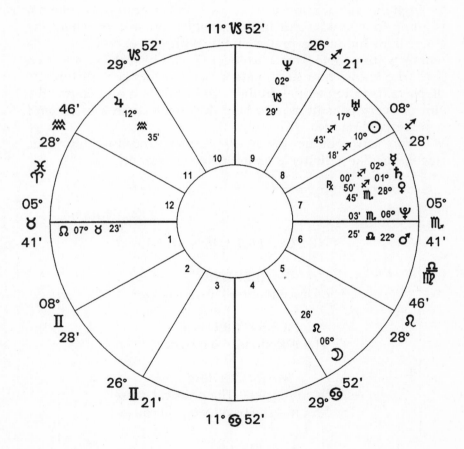

Janis
Dec. 2, 1985, 2:16 P.M. CET
Copenhagen, DK
12W35   55N42
Placidus Houses

The Consultation Menu

Imagine that throughout the consultation, the client and astrologer share a meal together (hopefully not the Last Supper!). When going through the various items given below, I shall return often to the two charts we have just examined, and study them in further detail.

I think it is also important not to make the whole thing more complicated than necessary. What is most important is to obtain, through the consultation chart, a quick and clear preview of what is going to/should occur in the consultation, and of where the client is in life at the present time. With our experience as "a worker with people," the astrologer should be just like a French chef who knows how to prepare a menu so that each dish really displays its full potential. In the final instance, it is of course the aim of every consultation to help the client attain a better and more rewarding life.

You can split up the interpretation procedure into four stages, just like a dinner at an exclusive restaurant:

THE CONSULTATION MENU

APERITIF
The Descendant—The Astrologer

HORS D'OEUVRE
The Ascendant—The Client

MAIN COURSE
Aspects to Angles—The physical cause
The Moon—The psychological cause

DESSERT
Aspects to Angles—The Impact

APERITIF—The Descendant

One of the most important factors the astrologer should be aware of is the expectation held by the client for the consultation. You can save a lot of time by becoming aware beforehand of the projections entertained by the client about you and the astrological consultation. The astrologer therefore has to enjoy the Aperitif alone—in a quiet moment prior to the consultation.

When we have ascertained the client's attitudes and antipathies/sympathies in relation to the astrologer, we can more rapidly create an atmosphere of trusting tolerance, which enables true communication and real trust between astrologer and client. Research in psychology has shown us that it is of no significance which form of therapy and psychological school the psychologist adheres to, as long as the client trusts and accepts the therapist. The same goes for astrological consultations.

In a consultation chart, the Ascendant always indicates the client, while the Descendant indicates the astrologer, and the expectations the client has from him/her. It is not just a question of expectations, it is also, at a deeper level, a question of real demands which the client wishes fulfilled before the necessary trust can be established between astrologer and client, i.e. before the consultation rises above the ordinary and becomes magical. The client pays the astrologer hard-earned money for the consultation and is therefore entitled to obtain satisfaction of his need for knowledge about and insight into himself, in the same way he would expect it of any other product in which he might choose to invest.

On the one hand, the astrologer has a duty to fulfill the reasonable wishes the client is entitled to have fulfilled, but on the other hand, must at the same time make a decision with regard to the unreasonable, unrealistic, or pathological demands with which an astrologer, or any other person who works with people, can be confronted. The 7th House is the house of projection. Backed with a knowledge of the 7th House in the consultation chart, we are no longer unprepared for the client's demands. The consultation chart thus gives us the chance to react more quickly when the client begins to project too much or makes demands we can not fulfill.

Let us look more closely at our two example charts.

Example 1: Joe's Descendant

If we look at Joe's consultation chart (recall page 25), the Descendant is placed in Gemini and, as always in horary astrology, we must look to the ruler of the house, in this case, Mercury, which is in the 9th House in Libra. Joe wishes to use the astrologer's statements as inspiration for later decisions. This same Mercury is a fine indication that the client accepts the astrologer as a professionally competent person (Mercury in 9th House = education), and probably chose the astrologer in the first place because of his diploma or other educational merits. Therefore, no power-conflict will arise in this consultation (particularly since the Ascendant is moving into a sextile with Mercury). We shall always be able to discuss things (Mercury/Libra) in a light-hearted manner. As you can also see, the Moon has separated from the square with Mercury.

At the same time, Mercury is in mutual reception with Venus (Mercury is placed in Libra, Venus' sign, and Venus is placed in Virgo, Mercury's sign), which provides a considerable freedom of choice (and free will) for the astrologer and for the client. The client will feel free to make personal decisions. The client seems to have come to hear the astrologer's professional opinion of how things stand, but the astrologer should not expect the client to follow his advice blindly, or even to take the advice seriously! Mercury in Libra asks *everybody* for their opinion, and then later makes his or her own decision. Joe here wishes to hear the astrologer cast light on his personal situation on the basis of his knowledge of the subject. And that's it!

Example 2: Janis' Descendant

Recall Janis' chart on page 27: Here Pluto lies exactly on the Descendant, which indicates Janis' great expectations from the astrologer's abilities in the deep, psychological sphere. In this case, it turned out that Janis worked in the field of alternative medicine and therefore had quite fixed ideas about how astrology could be used, and how it should be practiced. Having heard the tape from her husband's consultation, her expectations were high, and she explicitly asked for a consultation "of the same kind"— which of course is impossible.

This should be apparent to the astrologer on the mere basis of four planets in the 7th House, which make it clear that considerable demands are being made on the astrologer's abilities. The exact Mercury-Saturn conjunction (Mercury even being retrograde and approaching a conjunction with Saturn) makes it important for the astrologer to express himself in a traditional manner, preferably slowly.

The client expects the astrologer to give the impression of being a highly developed philosophical being (Mercury-Saturn in Sagittarius), who at the same time has charisma (Pluto on the Descendant). In this consultation, the astrologer has to play many different roles. If this demand is not met, a Plutonian power struggle will result.

If the astrologer wishes to have more control over the situation than the client (i.e., if the astrologer himself/herself wishes to make use of Pluto), then the astrologer should, early on in the consultation, mark off personal territory or, at least, give the impression of being aware of the infinite depths contained by the human mind. In short: I should say something general about the boundless and menacingly deep inner caverns encompassed by each human being. With a consultation chart like this, a good Pluto lecture on destruction and regeneration comprising also the main features of the principle of transformation can convince the client of the astrologer's excellence. This results in both respect and trust. The astrologer has to say: "I know what it's like, I've been there!"

Then, we can proceed to the ruler of the Descendant, which through its sign and house position shows the astrologer. As always in horary astrology, the "old" sign rulers are used: the ruler of this 7th House in Scorpio must be Mars. Mars is situated here in the 6th House in Libra, a sign position where Mars is in exile and therefore weak (as far away from Aries as possible), but this particular Mars is in mutual reception with Venus in Scorpio. Just as in Joe's chart, there is considerable freedom of choice (owing to the reception).

With all the planets in the 7th House and with this 6th House Mars, which with the help of the mutual reception can be transferred to the 7th House, it is again emphasized that the client has great expectations from the powers of the astrologer. What the astrologer says will be taken *very* seriously (Mercury conjunct Saturn). Advice given in a consultation such as this will therefore be followed slavishly. It is therefore advisable to emphasize that it is the client herself who must reach the decisions. With a consultation chart like this, there may otherwise be a tendency for the client to disclaim responsibility. Janis has placed responsibility (Saturn) in the house of "others" (the 7th House), and therefore prefers others to express the responsibility for things rather than herself.

The chemistry between astrologer and client is in this case good, the mutual reception between Mars and Venus being a reception between the rulers of the 1st and 7th Houses, between the client and the astrologer. The basis for a long cooperation between astrologer and client is therefore created. The mutual reception also warns the astrologer to look out for a tendency in both client and astrologer to get too personally involved (in some cases fall in love)—an occurrence which would be harmful to the work to be carried out together by client and astrologer.

HORS D'OEUVRE—The Ascendant

The Ascendant's sign position in consultation chart shows the client's mood and attitude. In a more simplified form, the ruler of the Ascendant shows the physical and psychological state of the client here and now. The house position of the ruler of the Ascendant shows what the client is preoccupied with at the moment, in the physical world, while the position in sign (with aspects) shows the psychological inner reality of the client.

Example 1: Joe's Ascendant

Here we see a client (see chart, page 25) who is very absorbed in his own situation (the ruler of the Ascendant, Jupiter, is placed in the 1st House in Aquarius). At this point in time, Joe considers himself to be a special, chosen or distinctive person (Aquarius again). Joe is nervous and quick in his movements (Jupiter in Aquarius), but also extremely uncertain (Neptune in the 1st House), an uncertainty which he is better at concealing in connection with his job (Neptune sextile Pluto-MC) than in more personal contexts. There seems to be a split in his personality between being a public figure (Jupiter square Pluto-MC) and withdrawing into isolation (Neptune and Jupiter in the 1st), a withdrawal I also experienced in him during the consultation. This kind of split must be discussed in the consultation.

When Joe arrived, he gave the impression of being under considerable stress and somewhat self-absorbed. The first thing

he asked me was whether he might eat his lunch while we discussed his chart. When I answered yes, he produced a home-
packed lunch and a bottle of mineral water from his impeccable
diplomat's briefcase: he opened the packed lunch, unwrapped a
sandwich, and leaned back, sandwich in hand, while he sig-
naled that I could begin to talk, a posture finely described both
by the Ascendant ruler Jupiter (Joe) and the descendant ruler
Mercury (astrologer).

Example 2: Janis' Ascendant
    In Janis' consultation chart (page 27), the Ascendant is
placed in Taurus. The Ascendant ruler Venus is in Scorpio; on the
face of it, a weak position. The woman (Venus) is situated in the
partner's house and is worried about him. She must think that the
partner is becoming so run down that his mental health is endan-
gered. Remember that, with this consultation chart, we have
reached December, when Joe's matter had already developed in
an unfortunate direction. Because of the Venus and Mars mutual
reception, Janis feels that she can help Joe home to his own sign
(Venus-Mars reception) and thereby save him. Her worries about
the durability of the marriage are especially shown by Pluto and
the Moon.
    Shouldn't the astrologer discuss the marriage with this
client? It is also important to get the client to concentrate more on
her own needs instead of being so focused on the partner's present crisis that she can practically see nothing else.

MAIN COURSE, Part 1—Aspects to Angles
    The aspects to angles show us the *physical cause* of the client's
coming for a consultation. Very often, the aspects to angles directly describe what the client says brought him or her to the
astrologer. The planets involved, and often their rulership, show
what the client sees as the problem area. The astrologer must tackle these subjects in the consultation. The client may beat us to it,
because these aspects are used as conscious explanations for coming to the astrologer in the first place.
    Here we also have the opportunity of measuring the way the
person uses the birth chart, that is, the level at which it operates.
The more exact the aspects, the more important the issue, and the more
stress the client feels about the subject. Aspects to angles show

where the client has "chosen" to experience the current transits and progressions to the birth chart.

Applying aspects (where the MC and Ascendant are moving into an exact aspect) are stronger, and show that the tension will continue to grow, even after the consultation. Separating aspects (where the MC and Ascendant are moving out of the exact aspect) show tension that has been activated and is now on the decline. As with all horary work, no fixed orbs are used, instead the last separating and first applying aspects are examined.

Conjunctions/oppositions to angles should be rated as more serious and stronger than the other aspects because the planet can place its energies directly on the Angle. I only use the classical five aspects: conjunction, sextile, square, trine, and opposition.

Example 1: Joe's Aspects to Angles
In this chart (page 25), it is clear that a crisis-situation is approaching. The MC is moving into the conjunction with Pluto, indicating considerable changes within the job sphere. This aspect is a most potent one. Joe's reason for coming for a consultation is the growing tension he feels about the press and the mass media (also Pluto). Somehow, he must be anticipating even more tension in the future. Just look at his situation: he has been hired to be the hangman, and he will have to quit the job when there are no more employees to execute!

I'll return to the important Moon square MC in a moment, but please note that the Ascendant has just left the square to both Mars and Venus, indicating problems with other people (Ascendant-Descendant) and his job/home-situation (Mars rules the 10th House, Venus rules the 4th).

The Ascendant is moving into the sextile to Mercury (ruler of the 7th House, the astrologer), providing optimum possibilities for the words of the astrologer (Mercury) to be taken in by the client (Ascendant). His physical explanation for coming to the consultation would be to have a talk about things. Mercury is in Libra: the astrologer should avoid self-important and pompous remarks in this consultation if trust is to be built between astrologer and client. Instead, the astrologer should stress that the interpretations given are inspiring possibilities from which to choose. Joe is already under sufficient stress. He doesn't need a conceited astrologer's advice on top of it!

Example 2: Janis' Aspects to Angles

Here again we have a strong Pluto aspect to an Angle (Pluto opposition Ascendant, page 27). The Ascendant is very close to Pluto, indicating that the tension has been building since I had Joe in consultation two months before.

There are no aspects to the MC/IC, only to the Ascendant/Descendant, so the physical reason for this woman coming to the astrologer has to do with herself, her partner (Pluto in 7th House) and her home (Moon, ruling 4th House), all being under considerable stress. The Moon being in the 5th House (squaring Pluto in the 7th) could very well indicate a sexual standstill in the marriage at present. Janis fears she will lose contact with Joe, probably because he shuts her out of his problems. She can not help interfering, caring, and mothering him too much, which Joe feels does not help him, but makes him vulnerable instead (Moon/Pluto again). This issue of mothering should be addressed in the consultation. (Why can't Joe even make his own appointments with the astrologer?).

The Pluto position indicates a partner wanting to be strong and powerful, but Janis' Moon will not let him. The classical way for Pluto to cope with crisis is to shut off all irrelevant contacts that are not part of the problem and concentrate on solving the problems at hand. Janis is right: Joe is drifting away from her at the moment and if she continues to criticize him for it, he will drift even further. She must accept his need to cope with the situation in his own way.

MAIN COURSE, Part 2—The Moon

As always in horary astrology, the Moon takes precedence over all the other factors in the chart. The Moon is co-significator of the client. Where The Main Course, Part 1 (Aspects to Angles) dealt with the physical, practical and mundane reasons for coming to the consultation, the Moon shows the deeper psychological, often subconscious, reasons. These reasons are not always obvious to the client, but they are the forces in the psyche that drive the person to the astrologer in the first place. They should be addressed with great caution, as the sphere of the Moon often contains very vulnerable and sometimes repressed psychic material.

The Moon very often shows a subject that the client subconsciously wishes the astrologer to address, a subject with which the client is unable to get in touch on his own. The Moon here acts as the midwife of the psyche.

As always in horary astrology, the Moon—being the fastest moving "planet" in the chart—also measures time. The separating aspects the Moon has already made show matters or events *that have already occurred*. The applying aspects show future developments.

As in ordinary horary astrology, one degree of Moon-movement equals one time-unit, a time-unit being either one year, one month, one week, one day, one hour or one minute. Many different rules have been listed in horary literature to calculate which time-unit to use in each case, but very often common sense— practical assessment of reality—is the best guide to the measurement of time. Let's look at Joe and Janis again.

Example 1: Joe's Moon

Joe's Moon is in the 7th House (page 25). When asked why he came into consultation, he bluntly said: "My wife sent me." This we could term the superficial explanation. Remember that the Moon always shows the subconscious reason for coming, and this reason must be pursued in the consultation.

The astrologer therefore has to talk about Joe's way of handling relationships with other people—an area to be heavily tested in the months to come. The Moon's square with Pluto shows that his subconscious concern is his problem with dealing with *many* people at one time.

A Moon in the 7th very often feels trapped by circumstance or by the needs and demands of other people. In this case both interpretations are true. For the first time in his life, this extremely successful businessman is being watched by the public and the media, i.e. the whole country; a totally new situation for Joe, who has been used to forms of leadership much more behind-the-scenes. Even at consultation time, he knows he has some nasty, tough decisions to make, which will both make him unpopular and turn him into a public scapegoat responsible for the whole unfortunate situation in the company. The ruler of the 7th House (Mercury) is in Libra, i.e., not desiring confrontation. He feels weak and undecided (Neptune in 1st) and, on top of this, the Moon has just entered Leo, showing that he is only beginning to learn to use his inner power of Self in this new situation. When the Moon will travel 2°50′ it will square the MC, at 3°38′ it will square Pluto and at 6°53′ it will oppose Jupiter in the 1st House.

The astrologer has to minimize the guilty conscience this man is already beginning to feel, even before it becomes necessary for him to fire people. It must be made clear to Joe that his feeling of being used and exploited (as a corporate clean-up man in fact = Pluto) is real, and not a sign of weakness. The Sagittarius Ascendant (with Jupiter in Aquarius) shows high ideals and a great need to justify his actions with law and ethics (which is not possible now). It is therefore important to make clear to Joe that he should see himself primarily as a businessman and not as a public figure, and that this particular situation is a crisis situation only because he is continually in the public eye. When the crisis is over, he can return to a more secluded position, probably in a privately owned company.

In this case, it seemed obvious to use the time unit 1° Moon-movement = 1 month. It just seemed logical to do so. This means that in 3–4 months' time (3°38′ till the square to Pluto) problems will have peaked, and he will stand alone with the decision he has had to make; probably being accused of being a monster and a tyrant. In seven months' time, opposing Jupiter (6°53′ = April/May 1986), he will have to leave his job because of problems with cooperation. At that time, it will even seem the right and proper (Jupiter) thing to do!

The Moon has to pass through a lot of hard aspects to reach her void period, the last aspect being *the square to Saturn,* and so does Joe. His transits and Secondary Progressions concur with this development.

Example 2: Janis' Moon

In the chart of Joe's wife, who came into consultation two months later, the Moon was in the 5th House, showing concern about her own creativity and sexuality. At that point in life, she was 43, probably experiencing early onset of menopause and needing a consultation dealing with sex and the question of still being attractive as a woman. As I mentioned earlier, a change in her sex life had probably already occurred, maybe less than two weeks earlier (Moon squared Pluto 21′ in the past), the physical reason or explanation being her partner's stress (Pluto opposition Ascendant).

Maybe she had even thought about having another child (number three), before this is no longer possible (Moon in 5th). With Moon squaring Pluto the partner does *not* of course want a child. Does she think she wants the child because she fears losing her femininity, or is there a real urge to become a mother again? With the aspects from the Moon to Pluto, it seems to have been a deep-rooted fear of change that brought on this dilemma. This issue should be handled with great caution, grace, and knowledge.

Very often, the Moon in the 5th House indicates a time to think about how happiness can enter into the person's life. How come all grown-ups are so serious compared to children? What do we lose in the process of growing up? What is life-quality really about?

In the consultation, Janis expressed her worry directly. She felt that Joe had changed and was not letting her participate in his problems. She talked about him like a concerned mother, already foreseeing the problems that would be surfacing in the months to come. She already felt paranoid about journalists besieging her house, telephone, and front door the moment Joe made a public announcement. Intuitively she knows that this is only the beginning of the process. Her husband has not "cleaned out" the company yet. The many planets in the 7th House (and Moon-Pluto) make her interpret the environment as exceedingly threatening, a position which could have become paranoiac.

With the upcoming trines to the Sun and Uranus I could promise Janis that—for her part—the crisis was over and done with (the Moon is separating from the square to Pluto) and that in the months to come she would feel better about the whole situation.

The next aspect the Moon would make was a trine to the Sun at 3°54' (April-May 1986), indicating freedom from the influences felt at the time of consultation. It was approximately the same period as when Joe's Moon made its final aspect to Jupiter.

DESSERT—Aspects to Angles

The last part of the menu is the dessert. This part of the menu—like the Aperitif—is only meant for the astrologer. Here the astrologer can estimate the impact the consultation has made on the client. That is, if the consultation has made an impact at all.

When you do a lot of consultations you realize that some consultations just do not make a difference and when you check with the consultation charts you will find that *those charts with no aspects to angles have very little impact*, while charts with many angular aspects do make a difference! Clients with many aspects to angles in the first consultation chart are sure to return again for consultation.

Joe's and Janis' Aspects to Angles

Both charts have very strong angular aspects. Both the husband and wife were to become regular clients of mine for the next six years!

Since 1985, when Janis and Joe started consulting me, they've had several consultations, mostly dealing with normal every-day decisions. Every time Joe wanted a consultation it was always Janis who called to make the arrangement, but when Joe called himself in April 1991, I knew that something special had happened. He asked for a consultation as fast as possible. By then Joe held a good and very well-paid job as managing director for a private company.

Last Consultation with Joe

The last consultation chart (page 41) has a lonely Saturn in the 7th, a position which, according to old horary rules, shows an incompetent or disqualified astrologer (Saturn even rules the 7th). There are no exact aspects to angles (the consultation will have only little impact) and the Ascendant (Joe) has just entered a new sign: Leo. Joe is beginning a new chapter in his life. The Sun (Ruler of the 1st House = Joe) is stressed by the applying square to Jupiter (0°48') and to Saturn = the astrologer (2°43'). The astrologer is stressed too. I had to book Joe into a break between two other clients that day.

Joe (Sun) is in a choice/dilemma situation. Should he choose Jupiter or Saturn? The young (Jupiter) or the old (Saturn) *partner*? In this consultation, he talks more than he has ever done before. He wants to share his secret with me, and he is being very honest about himself and his inner thoughts. He has met a new woman (probably on Moon trine Sun), and has moved away from Janis, telling her he needs some time to himself. The Moon (Joe) is in the 3rd House, approaching the square to Venus (partner) in the 11th.

He is talking very openly with the astrologer but is not telling his partner the truth. Joe is happy with the one room he has rented and feels like a young man again. His sexuality is increasing every day. But he has to make a choice between Saturn and Jupiter.

The Moon has left the trine to the Sun, 6 degrees and 6 minutes ago, indicating a great period for boosting the ego (Sun rules Ascendant). He met the new woman for the first time about *six years ago*. She had worked in the Government-subsidized organization which brought Joe to me for the first time in 1985. Actually Joe engaged her himself in the first half of 1986. He liked her already then, but because of the age difference he did not think he had a chance of winning her affections. She is 14 years younger than he. But they only met again 6 months ago—at a party. A week ago (almost 6 days ago) he moved away from the old flat where he lived with Janis into the small rented room where he now lives by himself—when he's not staying at his new girl friend's house. Here we have a rare case of the Moon describing several time-units at once.

Joe wants to know the chances of this new partnership turning into a marriage. Judging from the consultation chart the Moon only has to pass the square to Venus, the end of his old 4th House matter (Venus rules 4th House = end of the matter), after which the Moon "can come out to play." This gives a favorable prognosis.

During the consultation, we were crudely interrupted by my secretary, who otherwise has strict orders never to interfere. Knowing that Joe was in consultation, Janis had called, demanding he should call her back, and she also wanted to make an appointment for a consultation. My secretary reserved a consultation for Janis exactly one week later at the same time, resulting in almost the same angles as this interrupted consultation with Joe.

Joe phoned Janis from my office before leaving. Janis is worried about him, since he had not called her for two days. She seems not to have stopped mothering him! Before he leaves, Joe makes yet another appointment, this time for his new girlfriend Lydia to have a consultation. The Sun (Joe) is trying to balance the Saturn/Jupiter-opposition by giving both his women the same opportunity for astrological advice!

Clearly, this situation puts me, the astrologer, in an awkward predicament. I'm now truly disqualified (as Saturn in the 7th House predicted) and also caught in the web between two—or rather three—people who are playing a serious game of who-is-cheating-on-whom.

This was probably my last consultation with Joe. I don't think Joe will consult me again. By now, I know too much about his private life and his inner predicaments, and this embarrasses him. The Sun has to choose between Jupiter (the young) and Saturn (the old). And I'm shown by the Descendant too. He'll probably kick out both his old wife and his old astrologer!

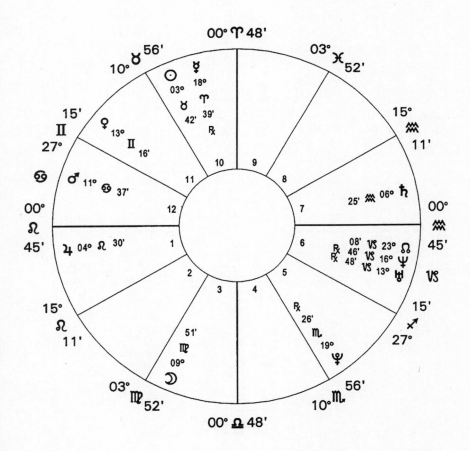

Joe's "Last Consultation"
Apr. 24 ,1991, 11:05 A.M. CET
Copenhagen, DK
12W35 55N42
Placidus Houses

Last Consultation with Janis

When Janis comes for her consultation a week later, the family situation is still not completely clear. I can understand that Joe still has not told her about Lydia. But Janis has a *very* strong suspicion that another woman is involved. She is getting ready to fight for Joe. The Jupiter/Saturn-opposition is massively activated by the Ascendant in the chart, and in this chart (compared with Joe's) the impact of the consultation is strong, but with dis-

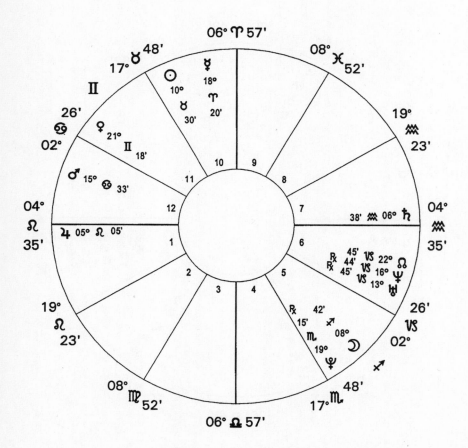

Janis' "Last Consultation"
May 1, 1991, 11:00 A.M. CET
Copenhagen, DK
12W35 55N42
Placidus Houses

with disruptive energies between astrologer and client. The sextile from Saturn and the trine from the Moon to the MC show the bond and the help extended by the current consultation. The astrologer is even more weak and disqualified than in Joe's chart the week before! As in Joe's consultation chart—exactly a week ago—the Sun rules the Ascendant, has by now passed the exact squares to Jupiter and Saturn, and is moving into a trine to Uranus, sextile to Mars and trine to Neptune while still in the 10th House, indicating great business opportunities coming up.

Janis wants the astrologer to break his moral code (Astrologer = Saturn, moral/ethics = Jupiter) by telling her if Joe has another woman—*and who it is!* She tries with all her might to make the astrologer tell the personal details that Joe had divulged in the consultation last week, which the astrologer—of course—declines to do. The situation calls for a balancing act on a knife edge, so aptly shown by the Jupiter-Saturn-opposition on the Ascendant/Descendant. A major power-struggle is taking place.

Again, Janis' real psychological reason for coming had to do with womanhood, and the probability of her being attractive enough to get a new partner if Joe leaves her (Moon in 5th). This more than anything else is what is actually bothering her, more than the fact that Joe might be leaving her. The consultation ends with her having a more optimistic outlook on the future, getting ready to do something about her own life. I tell her to start mothering herself and focus on her career until Joe knows what he wants. Janis is obviously in a crisis situation (Jupiter-Saturn-opposition), and the astrologer (Saturn) is unable to free himself with his knowledge. Janis will be highly-strung until Joe decides to let her in on his little secret.

The Moon shows the emotional support Janis gets from the astrologer, and she leaves the consultation more decided and ready to accept that Joe might not be coming back. This is again shown by Jupiter-Saturn directly on the Ascendant-Descendant: she also has to lose the old partner, but does she also have to lose the old astrologer?

First Consultation with Lydia

Because of summer vacations and her business travels and excessive workload, Lydia's first consultation was cancelled and moved several times, until finally we met in August. She had a very demanding job as a legal consultant in the company Joe headed in 1985. Lydia's main concern is herself and her life in general (Moon in the 1st House) and the balance between her personal and professional life (Moon square Midheaven).

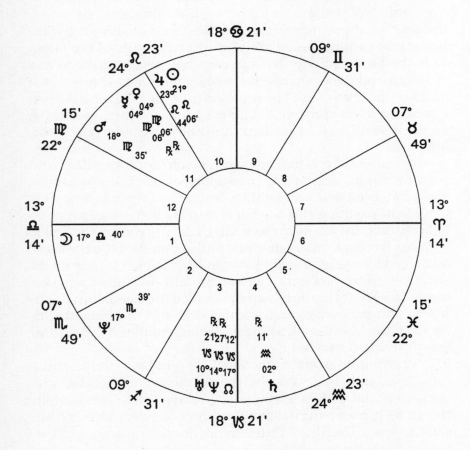

Lydia's First Consultation
Aug. 14 ,1991, 11:00 A.M. CET
Copenhagen, DK
12W35 55N42
Placidus Houses

Note the exact Venus conjunction with Mercury, both retrograde—Venus ruling the Ascendant. They are taking each other's hands and slowly going backward into Leo together. The fact that the Venus-Mercury conjunction does not form any aspects while retreating into Leo indicates a need for a quieter and less stressed life, and Lydia and Joe are indeed contemplating buying an isolated farmhouse where they will have space for all their creative plans and projects—and more time to be together. The square from the Moon to the MC indicates her job problems at this time (the Moon rules the 10th House).

Joe left Janis several months ago, but the fact that Joe used to head the company she works for gives Lydia a feeling that her colleagues have difficulty being honest with her. The company still has staff problems, and the atmosphere in the company is just as bad now as it was in 1985, although by now the financial situation has stabilized.

Maybe she will have to find another position in another company very shortly. A choice which she will have no problem making—when the Moon reaches the sextile to the Sun in the 10th House (in 3°26')—in probably 3 months time. This might also be the time when they find their new house.

The End of Joe's and Janis' story

In the spring of 1992, I received a letter from one of my astrologer colleagues. It stated that Janis had asked her to procure her birth chart from me because she wanted to change astrologers. The letter stated, "You have been *disqualified* due to your sex. The client wants to try a woman. Please fax me her chart." Saturn was indeed in the 7th House in my last consultation with Janis. The previous trust in our relationship could not exist again.

It is always a problem to have been the astrologer of a married couple, when they then later get divorced. One of the clients will of course have to change astrologers. So I sent the papers to my colleague, and since then have heard nothing from Janis or Joe. The Saturn in the last consultation charts meant that both my clients had changed astrologers.

At the time of writing, Lydia and Joe are disappearing from the public eye and settling into a satisfying home situation, which has resulted in the decline of their need for worldly success. Janis is currently involved in a very ambitious, pioneering and daring experiment at a hospital trying to introduce alternative medicine into the daily treatment of long-term patients. Janis is making a career for herself! She now has a new partner who is an artist— and ten years younger. She still lives in the old flat.

Epilogue

Even without the consultation chart, the astrologer is from the outset equipped with a complete map of the person's inner reality, and therefore is able to perceive the world through the client's own eyes. One might say that the astrologer crawls underneath the client's skin, and senses and perceives the outside world via the client's birth chart. The astrologer sees the world through the client's "spectacles." This is the main difference between an astrological and a psychological consultation. This perspective is what distinguishes an astrologer from a psychologist.

The psychologist can only process and take into consideration whatever the client—consciously or subconsciously—has chosen to signal. The psychologist can only see the client's wholeness "from the outside in."

To exaggerate somewhat: in the astrological consultation the client does not in principle need to cooperate or even be present. The astrologer's "key" to the client's psyche is the generally accepted methods and rules of interpretation which he shares with his past and present colleagues. The astrologer sees the client's wholeness "from the inside out."

Here another difference between astrologer and psychologist becomes obvious. It is generally agreed that a psychologist should be as objective as possible, giving the client the best possible means to communicate the inner reality to the therapist, thereby avoiding the projection of personal problems or preferences onto the client.

To a therapist, the ideal consultation is an objective consultation, where the therapist has no (or at least as few as possible) projections. Because the therapist has to rely on the messages he or she gets from the client, a no-projection situation is a must— but is of course extremely difficult to achieve.

For astrologers, the situation is different. We already have at our disposal the "map" of what the person—fully developed—*could be*, and therefore we must project an interpretation into the aspects, positions and glyphs in the chart. There would be no interpretation without our projecting meaning into the symbols of the "map." The interpretation of the chart is not there from the beginning, but is subjectively read into the chart by astrologers. So, therefore, it is most important that we not only project, but also project the *right* thing.

And the consultation chart can guide the astrologer to do just that!

Haloli Q. Richter

Haloli Q. Richter is a professional astrologer in the Washington D.C. area. Over almost 30 years, she has been student, teacher, translator, lecturer, writer, and book-reviewer. For a degree in psychology she bridged mythology, astrology, and Jungian psychology toward a deeper understanding of the human condition within cultural and cosmic parameters.

Haloli Q. Richter

Creative Listening
and Empathy

 When my mother died, I experienced congruent yet disparate feelings: a great sense of relief that her suffering had ended and a bottomless void of having lost the person who had listened to me unconditionally, totally, joyfully, for 45 years.

• I had experienced my self from the very beginning of life, through every step of development and growth, because my mother had given me not only love, but attention. She was interested, involved, supportive; she was caring about me. She shared my hopes and dreams, my anxieties and losses and, yet, she also gave advice from her wise woman's life experience. She was my nurturer and my counselor. She believed in me, and I felt cared for and cared about.

• Today, in my work as a wise woman—an astrologer—I instinctively and also consciously approach my clients the way my mother gifted me. I deeply, totally care about the human being, the client, who has come to me to trust and to share. I listen with my whole being to the quality of the voice, to the words, the nuances and beyond, to the vibration of the soul expressed through the voice. The voice is carried by breath, which is connected to the emotions, to consciousness, to life itself. My inspiration about the human being comes from his or her spirit, imbuing the air with a vocalized personal quality and soul expression.

• In turn, I am aware that *my* voice has a similar, if not as conscious, effect on the client. Often, I am told that my voice on the answering machine gives an apprehensive caller a sense of trustworthiness and warmth. They feel easier about this scary step of meeting an astrologer for the first time.

Listening is a very large part of an astrological counseling session. The traditional view is that the astrologer talks and the client listens. This makes for an outdated model based on the assumption that the astrologer knows more than the client does. On the other end of this polarity is psychoanalysis where the analyst listens and the patient talks, often for years, five times a week.

It seems to me that the most effective communication between astrologer and client is dialogue, where both parties share in the talking and listening. The important difference is that the astrologer should be a *professional* in both modes, i.e., listening with greater economy, gaining information and insight in a fraction of time and sharing it efficiently.

• There must not be a discrepancy between understanding the client, (through listening and through the horoscope) and the client feeling understood. The latter quality is called empathy, and it might as well be labeled "magic." When the person leaves after a session and predictably says in parting, "I feel so much better now," it is the empathic quality of the counselor, not the technical brilliance, that has brought about the client's feelings of connectedness, both to her/himself as well as to the world-at-large.

Empathy only appeared in the dictionary in 1903. This Greek word, meaning affection, but coming from the root *en* (in), and *pathein* (to suffer, feel), is closely related to the German "Einfuehlung" (to feel within, to feel into). Studies have shown that this non-specific quality can be learned, just as children can learn to be kind to others. So, listening with feelings for the other, is a learnable skill, if valued early by parents and teachers. It can be later applied to life in general and the helping professions specifically.

• Astrology is a helping profession, indeed. Therefore, helping skills should be equally as important as technical skills. In the long run, when the mechanics of astrology are securely applied, the psychological and spiritual dimensions need continuous building and growing. This process must not stop as long as we are alive and we interact with others. R. D. Laing said, "a therapist should be a specialist in attentiveness and awareness."[1] Substitute astrologer for therapist in this and all future quotes from thoughtful philosophers, priests, artists and counselors through the ages. Because *to be listening*—to God, to saint or sinner—is an age-old subject connected to human consciousness.

The Spiritual Traditions

The inner state of being and listening is closely connected in spiritual and philosophical traditions to a state of attention. The Latin word *attendere*, to turn one's mind to; *ad* (to) *tendere* (to stretch, to be present), means literally to stretch one's body when standing at attention and displaying awareness of a person or an ideal, but, it also means to stretch one's awareness, to pay attention to one's being and one's beliefs. "In spite of different names, what is described as highest attention is quite clearly the same inner state. All (traditions) agree that real, liberating attention can not come exclusively from the mind as we are usually taught, but must be generated from feeling and entered into with the body; it is an activity of the whole person, and closely allied with conscience."[2]

• So, the practice of attention is called meditation, prayer, or as G. I. Gurdjieff called it: "self-remembering," fundamentally an attempt to develop sustained, undistracted, observational attention both outwardly toward experience and, simultaneously, inwardly toward the experiencer. This particular aspect of Gurdjieff's work is similar to the "bare attention" exercise of Buddhist *vipassana* meditation. Krishnamurti teaches that

---

1. *Uncommon Wisdom: Conversations with Remarkable People*. Fritjof Capra, 1988, Simon & Schuster.
2. *Parabola*, Summer 1990: D. M. Dooling, "Focus."

the practice fundamental to psychological transformation is "choiceless awareness." It is again the cultivation of sustained, observational, nonreactive attention to inner and outer experience."[3]

If we pay attention to a voice singing beautifully about love or sorrow, passion or devotion, we attend with our ears, our hearts, our own memories. The step to listen equally empathically to a voice *speaking* of such human matters, should not be different in quality. If we know how to become still and centered through meditative practices or through knowing how to observe a portrait, sculpture, or the beauty of a flower, the step toward attentive awareness is more secure.

Truly to give attention, truly to listen, is a gift of respect and love. In that process, awareness is shifted from the self to the other. In prayer, attention is centered on a higher consciousness. The deepest meaning of prayer is to be still, to listen and to feel atuned to a higher truth. Out of such a state of active stillness comes the creative process, the spiritual consciousness, the intuitive knowing. These are the power tools of astrological practice.

I am a human being first, then an astrologer. Inner work, which in turn is reflected in the substance of astrological interpretation, is necessary. Inner work is reflective of external behavior. In other words, I can not teach, preach or advise anyone of anything I have not been willing to experience myself. In order to be listened to by the client, the astrological counselor has to have earned that status. Nadia Boulanger, the revered French musician and teacher, spoke also for our field when she said, "The more I try to think about the essentials of music (substitute astrology), the more they seem to depend on general human values. It's all very well to be a musician, it's all very well to be a genius, but the intrinsic value which constitutes your mind, your heart, your sensibility, depends on who you are. I only exist in my own eyes if I pay attention to myself."[4]

So it seems that in order to know how to give attention to God through listening, to another person through listening, we must also learn how to hear ourselves, indeed to pay attention to

3. Ibid., Phillip Novak, "The Practice of Attention."
4. Ibid., Nadja Boulanger, "Crystalline Moments."

who we are, where we came from and where we are going. True attention is rare in this age when we are overwhelmed with information, assaulted by meaningless messages, and not taught how to listen to anything or anybody very well. No wonder, then, that the empathic astrologer who gives total attention to the client's existence becomes a figure of honor, respect, and affection for the person who is also asking the very same questions: Who am I, Where did I come from, Where am I going . . . ?

William Segal puts it this way: "Cleared of all internal noise, conscious attention is an instrument which vibrates like a crystal at its own frequency. It is free to receive the signals broadcast at each moment from a creative universe in communication with all creatures."[5]

The intent of the astrologer to listen consciously and fully to the client must reflect his or her own journey. If I have never learned to listen, and, therefore, value myself, how can I truly know how to listen to and value the person who is seeking insight, and perhaps even *insound*, from me?

Soren Kierkegaard represents the Western awareness of attention with this poem:

As my prayer became more attentive and inward
I had less and less to say:
I finally became completely silent.
I started to listen—which is even further removed from speaking.
I first thought that praying entailed speaking.
I then learnt that praying is hearing,
not merely being silent.
This is how it is.
To pray does not mean to listen to oneself speaking.
Prayer involves becoming silent,
and being silent,
and waiting until God is heard.[6]

It seems a very good beginning to prepare for the listening part of the client session with a prayer, or with becoming quite still and asking not only to find the right words to say, but also

---

5. *The Structure of Man:* William Segal, 1987, Green River Press, Vermont.
6. *The Third Ear:* Joachim Berendt, 1988, Element Books.

to hear the words and feelings shared on the most intuitive level possible.

The Clinical Approach

Few people other than psychiatrists and women have had much training in listening.

—S. I. Hayakawa[7]

What can the astrologer learn from the psychiatrist? (A question that most likely is a long way from being asked the other way around.) The literature about listening and empathy as separate and distinct subject matters is not abundant. The wonderful library of the Jungian Society of Washington D.C., for example, had very little to offer. Jung's vast writing did not make note of those terms.

Two more recent publications, *Clinical Empathy* by David Berger, M.D., and *The Listening Process* by Robert Langs, M.D., are representative of the post-Freudian approach. The key words are *clinical* and *process*. Listening is dissected into methodologies and reconnected to therapeutic terminologies and techniques devoid of any sense of humanity. The psychotherapists' myth seems to be that they know all about listening and the clarification process because there is a basic system to apply and hide behind. Dr. Langs offers the following table.

The Intaking Process:
a. Entering each session without desire, memory, or understanding.
b. An openness to the unknown, the nonsensuous, and the neurotic.
c. The use of free-floating attention, role and image responsiveness.
d. Allowing each session to unfold and be its own creation.
e. Permitting the patient to generate all formulations and interventions.

---

7. *Talking Between the Lines:* S. I. Hawakawa, 1979, Viking Press, New York.

f.   The application of each aspect of the listening process to all communications from both patient and therapist.

g.   Additional tools:

1. Unconscious sensitivities
2. Empathy
3. Intuition
4. Trial identifications and limited introjections
5. Limited and controlled use of projections and projective identifications
6. Conscious fantasies—processed toward understanding of latent contents.[8]

The clinical-mechanical approach lists the most important tools as "additional," which has the ring of optional. One can not help but wonder how psychotherapy would be changed if the first three "additional tools" would get top billing. Without doubt, there are psychiatrists who have made that adjustment in their work because of their own mind-spirit awareness. The Association for Humanistic Psychology, with Rollo May as one of its founders, is proof of such awareness and development. Yet, after twenty-some years of existence, it still has difficulty gaining full acceptance.

The main difference between the mechanistic and the inner-aware approach to listening is in part style, in part philosophy. The psychoanalytic system of listening entails conscious and continuous categorizing, generalizing, and particularizing. This is all done with the left brain, with the learned knowledge skills, and by definition, exclusive of the intuitive process. Is it any wonder then that a well-known psychiatrist consults an astrologer to get a different viewpoint on particularly difficult patients? The astrologer approaches the horoscope of the patient as an ensouled human being (without a diagnostic label) to bring forth issues and values of being and becoming within a realistic framework, and to find existential meaning. Dr. Langs writes that "Therapists tend to generalize painful and specific material as a means of detoxifying it and rendering it essentially without meaning."[9]

---

8.   *The Listening Process:* Robert Langs, M.D., 1978, J. Aaronson, Inc.
9.   Ibid.

So, perhaps somewhat simplistically, the difference in listening is partially determined if we listen with the left or right ear (brain). A counterargument would be that there are situations that require the left-brain approach, but this writer-listener believes that the right-brain professional arrives at the truth in a far more direct way, and then has the freedom to superimpose left-brain skills on the subject.

An article comes to mind stating that mixing medicine with humanities will bolster the quality of the man underneath the doctor, and, in turn, make for a better surgeon (and therapist, astrologer, et al). "This type of cultural exposure will bring to the medical profession a better understanding of the society in which its members tread. Literature, history and the arts offer to the practitioners of the medical profession the right match for the impersonal and austere world of the basic and clinical medical sciences."[10] Of course, this is true and a way to a right-brain awareness, through the creative and/or through the spiritual path. Doctors, as well as other helping professionals, can become more conscious and, therefore, more effective with the human issues by cultural conditioning.

In the Middle Ages and the Renaissance, doctors were also astrologers—and there are even some today who understand and practice a clinical-spiritual approach to helping and healing. It is hoped that their number will increase, that science and the humanities will join forces to serve the human being holistically, regardless of medical or scientific specialty.

The learning for the astrological profession from the clinical-medical discipline has more to do with creating a structural frame of reference from which to start, and depart, in the process of helping the client: listening is one important ingredient, and the astrological model has the opportunity to take the best and then improve what the "listening" profession has accumulated in the last 100 years, by connecting millennia of wisdom teachings with a new consciousness tool.

---

10. *The Washington Post*, April 1, 1989.

The Person-Centered Path

In the 1950's, when behaviorism and psychiatry were still the leading models, a voice from within broke rank and left the "garage approach" behind. No longer was his motto, "you bring in the problem, we fix it." Carl Rogers developed a new paradigm based on genuineness, acceptance, and empathic understanding. In time, he had the courage to talk about multiple realities, mystical experiences, and altered states. He also operated from a humble heart. Rogers had a lot to say about listening: "To simply listen understandingly to a client and to attempt to convey that understanding were potent forces for individual therapeutic change."[11] He believed that when persons are empathically heard, it becomes possible for them to listen more accurately to the flow of inner understanding. His self-directed, person-centered way of helping emphasized the right brain and the heart over clinical structures. Of course, he was ridiculed by his peers, but the public identified with him and bought the books he had intended for fellow therapists.

I checked the indexes of his books for the word "astrology" and curiously came up empty. If not consciously, he nevertheless wrote for our profession when he stated his belief that the next frontier is the area of the intuitive, the psychic.

He is one of us when he makes the connection between the universe and the human being in different variations throughout his work! "The universe is always building and creating as well as deteriorating. This process is evident in the human being too."[12]

But, for the purpose of this subject matter, he is most moving when talking about being heard and listening—deeply. He has a short list and simple words to convey powerful principles for the helper—the therapist and the astrologer alike:

1. The ideal therapist (astrologer) is, first of all, empathic.
2. Empathy is correlated with self-exploration and process movement.
3. Empathy early in the relationship predicts later success.

---

11. *A Way of Being*: Carl Rogers, 1980, Houghton Mifflin Company.
12. Ibid.

4. Empathic understanding is provided freely by the therapist, not drawn from him or her
5. The better integrated the therapist is, the higher the degree of empathy he or she exhibits

Rogers touches on several all-important qualities in the listening-and-being-heard exchange. Empathy is not possible without self-reflection first, being in touch with one's own feelings and processing. Gender may have something to do with how well we deal with this quality. I am reminded of a statement my own therapist made years ago: "Men replace relationships, women mourn them." Perhaps the feminine, reactive, reflective, responsive core must be first awakened and then valued by the masculine consciousness.

Empathy is also very much connected to life experience. How real or valid would be the empathic understanding of an untested 25-year-old in matters of loss, for example? I have a client who has lost two sons to AIDS. What right or authority would I have had to counsel this woman for years between the past and future loss of a child if I had not experienced losses myself? To have experienced loss would not be enough unless those painful events were processed through all stages of consciousness, evolving and ripening until an essence of wisdom was distilled from the bitter fruit.

I believe this is what Rogers means by being genuine and real. He also adds the term "transparent" which I have practiced in sharing with clients relevant details of my own life. One client, for example, had tremendous difficulties in accepting the black husband of her daughter. She felt ashamed and betrayed and at the same time she wanted to be a good human being. When I shared with her that I was in a relationship with a black man myself, her whole attitude changed. She had accorded the astrologer a special place of respect over the years. Learning of such a shocking aspect about this person she revered broke a stereotypical image held with destructive intensity.

It would have been very easy to let that moment pass without revealing my personal story, but the effect for change through acceptance on her part would very definitely have been also lost. She allowed for an opening in that emotional wall of shame and rejection no theoretical technique in the world could have created. My unconditional positive regard for her primal feelings and my personal transparency created a way for her to change consciousness.

If the reader only wants to accept one pearl, may it be the seemingly simple Rogers person-centered approach: Being genuine and real and transparent; creating a climate for changes through acceptance; unconditional positive regard and Empathic understanding.

The Astrologer's Unique Position

The astrologer's role falls in between the therapist who listens and the psychic or channeler who talks. We do both and, we hope, both equally well. Eastern philosophy stresses that the sound of the bell is as important as the empty space between rings. The astrologer must be master of sound and silence. Wisdom is expressed through both, but knowledge more through sound. So, perhaps phrased differently, it takes both knowledge and wisdom to meet the client's needs and expectations. The astrologer is part messenger, part artist, part sage, part healer, part parent, and full-time fellow traveler. Each one of these parts or roles should have within themselves the full dynamics of sound and silence, speaking and listening, giving and taking, hearing and being heard. Through this polarity then flows the real essence of each part's purpose.

* The messenger has technical information to convey. Many astrologers stop at that level. To become technically ever more proficient is their total consciousness. Information is proudly presented without digression, in a fundamental fashion.

  Astrological cookbooks deliver such knowledge, as do computer analyses. The messenger talks but does not know how to listen. The messenger can only connect to someone who has a similar messenger mentality.

  The artist approaches the horoscope creatively, internalizing and interpreting the different components of the chart as a painter sees a portrait or a landscape. Not only does the artist's eye see the shades of colors, dimensions, perspective and golden mean, but also intuitively grasps the unspoken story, the drama behind the picture. Art is specific and non-specific. There is a quality about a work of art that defies words.

So often, the observer talks around that essence, because there are no direct words or names for it. The observer must see and feel that unspoken quality on a personal level. Like any object interpreted by different artists, the horoscope is painted by different astrologers in different styles, according to their creative talent. Creative interpreting and creative listening are part of the artist-astrologer's skills in bringing out many hues of the portrait.

- The sage knows solitude and has earned distance from desire and mundane issues. There is a motionless and emotionless quality in the approach to the chart. The client receives a cosmic viewpoint, lifted from the day-to-day concerns, focusing on issues of consciousness, transformation and the attempt to answer unanswerable questions. The sage's quiet eloquence is sought out by seekers, by clients who have chosen a path, or are looking for the road less taken, but the sage first listens to the sounds of consciousness, to the words indicating that there is a quest in progress. For the sage only speaks when there is mutual recognition.

  The healer gives unconditional empathy and projects an energy of hope and harmony. The client is understood and comforted for past events, carefully researched beforehand, for present-day angst, and for the universal wound that we all have in one form or another. The healing astrologer is very quiet, listening to the outpouring of pain and helping on several levels by understanding, by explaining how a situation was brought about, and by what the deeper meaning of the matrix is. *By understanding why there was a specific mode of experience,* releasing and healing take place miraculously. The use of metaphors is a tool of the healer. An open heart is a tool of the healer. A selfless attitude is a tool of the healer. The healer should always be part of the counseling astrologer.

- Being the parent is a complex function. The inner child of the client, the childhood memories, reexamined with the astrologer, often evoke feelings of intense mixed emotions. The parent speaks very calmly, soothingly. There must be awareness and avoidance of transference and countertransference. If the client is not in therapy, it is not advisable to bring up possible issues of abuse because the astrologer is not equipped to open up a wound and send the person out the door without proper support in place. The parental role is one of assurance, support and, if necessary, to give permission to let go of guilt, shame, needs for revenge, and other destructive thought forms. The parent hugs the client at the end of the session.

There are probably many other parts to the astrologer, some dependent on personal talents and strengths. But one who needs to be always present and apparent is the "fellow traveler." We are all pilgrims of one form or another, which needs to be recognized and respected in each other. I may be a little further along on the path or I may not be. What counts is that we are alive, more or less awake and aware, and walking toward a greater degree of understanding, of loving, of contributing to our own growth and through service to others. We are journeymen and women on the way to find meaning in our existence.

All parts of this astrological profile have to do with hearing and being heard. One can not exist without the other. We must have mastered the yin and the yang to expect a whole. Listening to another in any role is precious, but for the professional helper, it becomes a sacred task. In times past, the priest listened to the confession of sinners and they were absolved of their burdens. We have come a step further along by not presuming guilt or sin but by offering an understanding ear and heart to shift and dissolve emotional trauma and anxiety in order for the client to move freer and with more self-awareness, self-worth, and self-belief into time.

How to Integrate Technique and Consciousness

The importance of a professional framework and uniformity in the preparation and application of knowledge to the individual situation and circumstance focuses on the following factors:

- Initial contact and preparation
- Crucial first minutes of meeting
- The dialogue-enrichment process

- Positive resolution
- Files and memory

These segments are further divided into two equally important arenas, the *doing* and the *being* level. What has been stated earlier in different ways now becomes part of what we know as well as who we are. What we know is the sum total of academic and life experience learning—all the thousands of books on astrology and other subjects, the scores of conferences and seminars we have absorbed over time. The other factor is expressive of who we have become and whether we have developed an opened heart and an awakened spirit.

Technique "Doing"	Consciousness "Being"
Initial phone contact	Projecting accessibility
Preparing chart	Passive expectation
Study chart	Absorb chart with awareness
Welcome client	Non-intrusive observation
Give full attention	Be in attentive state
Conduct dialogue	Have positive regard
Avoid ego	Use spirit
Apply:	**Generate:**
Technical skills	Intuition
Knowledge	Wisdom
Experience	Empathy
Intellectual approach	Heart approach
Pace session and segments	Feel what client needs
Invite questions and re-statements by client	Hear what is important; how clearly you've been heard
Verbalize understanding	Project genuine understanding
Be in charge of material	Project inner authority
Come to conclusion with end of tape naturally	Leave time to avoid abrupt ending
Part with warm gesture	Part with authentic feeling
Keep notes for file, research, or future recall	Absorb experience into your consciousness

Each physical or mental activity has an underlying emotional and awareness level attached which will be the deciding factor if an interaction will either be helpful, meaningless, or destructive.

The client also applies different degrees of listening. Some people who are in crisis or deep pain can only hear that which is directly related to their problem. Other information is not even registered. Others have a very short attention span. Everyone has selective hearing, entering the session with preconceived expectations. For these reasons, it is important to tape the dialogue, because information is heard in layers. Frequently, I receive a phone call six months later only to be told that the client heard something for the first time on the tape. The tape becomes a source of repeated learning and healing, not only because of the varied levels of sending and receiving, but also because the healing is reinforced with every replay.

Reassurance and hope are important pillars of the dialogue, and when that message can be received over and over again, the benefits are multiplied unendingly. Also, just as a child wants to hear the same story over and over again, the client is fascinated with being the center of attention and relishes that total attention in an emotionally comforting way.

Often, a client will relisten to the tape just before coming for an update and relay specific events from the astrologer's predictive point of view as well as from the actual experiential purview. How wonderful for both to share that moment of reflection and reassessment before repeating the process for the year to come. The effect is that the client lives more awarely, is more in touch with the cycles of her or his life, and enjoys the ritual of sharing intimate information with the astrologer. There is that same quality of attention present that my mother had given to me, listening and reliving a portion of experience with me.

At such a moment, the astrologer not only listens to the actual description of events, but also to the quality of the experience, the feelings, the choices made, the imprint left on the person on a deeper level. Just as a parent should respond with the same degree of enthusiasm to a child's excited retelling of an experience, so should the astrologer respond with the same degree of enthusiastic attention to the client's retelling of the year's experiences. The client will feel heard, and therefore valued. The client will be aware in a larger sense that future life experiences will be of the same degree of interest to the astrologer. Often during the year, letters full with information, photos, and other proof of the need to share happenings will arrive from a client and find a place in the astrologer's heart and in the client's file. It is what Martin Buber calls the need to have our existence confirmed by another.

This means that the client not only listens at the time of the appointment, but over and over again thereafter. The influence continues. When the client is also in therapy I encourage the sharing of the tape with the therapist, who will find much useful information for the therapeutic process. As a side effect of this encouragement, I have gained many psychotherapists as clients who are so intrigued with this wisdom tool of astrology that they make an appointment for themselves. In turn, I refer many clients to therapists, who recognize and bridge the common boundary between spirituality and psychotherapy.

The consciousness of the astrologer is expressed through the technical tool astrology offers, as well as through its philosophical prism, but just as with the Bible, many philosophical approaches and interpretations are possible. It is important that we, as the practitioners of this art and science, are clear about ourselves, the power and influence we hold, and the effect we have on others. Listening well at all times will help in avoiding mistakes that cannot be corrected.

Intuition and Empathy

"To learn an art it involves the mastery of the theory and the mastery of practice. The essence of the mastery of an art is intuition and ultimate concern."

Erich Fromm authored this deep insight, which should be the guiding mantra of artist and helping professional alike. One does not really exist without the other. In order to be in a deep intuitive state, it takes going inward, listening to that inner voice and opening the heart. There is a shift in vibrational frequency, of connecting with a universal force.

For years, clients have said to me that I must be psychic. I always had a negative inner reaction because it has taken me many years and extremely hard work to reach this level of knowledge. Also, without the horoscope, I would not be able to offer insight. I do not believe at all that I am psychic, but I have stopped being offended by such a "compliment." I admit, however, that I am highly intuitive and empathic, using this "frequency" to get in touch with deeper levels of meaning of the horoscope symbols as well as intuiting the emotional state of the human being before me.

I use this same frequency when I observe and absorb a work of art or music. It has more to do with sensuousness than with psychicness. A pewter plate with three pomegranates affects and inspires me by its dynamic beauty and symbolism. Memories of mythological implications cross my mind, the symmetry and symbology of the number three floats through my consciousness; I observe and enjoy and remember and transform this experience into something meaningful to me. This ritual is no different than relating the beauty and symbolism of the horoscope to the person who lives it. As a result he or she will understand perhaps something about themselves that they have not yet discovered, not yet known is there.

The astrologer needs to practice these skills. Again, truth and beauty are closely aligned. Cosmos means harmony, and by referral, also beauty, as in "cosmetic." By being sensitive to the arts, which are an expression of creativity and beauty, we are also close to creation and cosmic connectedness. Take an art and music appreciation class, and learn to see and listen for the first time. Learn to listen to a symphony, to the movements, the moods, colors. With repeated listening, the different instrumental sounds will become individual expressions within a whole. The horoscope is also a symphony of many instrumental sounds, movements, moods and colors, which nevertheless, work together more or less harmoniously, to give life its own sound and its own silence. Music and astrology are based on the same mathematical principles. Transfer, then, what you know about one to the other.

Carl Jung describes intuition as one of the four functions of consciousness (thought, feeling, and sensation being the others). The scientific mind distinguishes empathy as a function of the experiencing ego, and intuition as a function of the observing ego.[13] I believe that intuition and empathy come from the same source. Webster's dictionary states that intuition is the capacity to perceive truth without apparent reasoning. To me it means that one is listening within rather than thinking without; to "know" by feeling, not having to learn from an external source. Intuitive knowing, or the German *Gefuehlswissen*, is another word for wisdom.

Carl Rogers writes "I find that when I am closest to my inner, intuitive self, when I am somehow in touch with the unknown in me, when, perhaps, I am in a slightly altered state of consciousness, then whatever I do seems to be full of healing. Then, simply my presence is releasing and helpful to the other. There is nothing I can do to force this experience, but when I can relax and be close to the transcendental core of me, then I may behave in strange and impulsive ways in the relationship; ways which I cannot justify rationally, which have nothing to do with my thought processes. But these strange patterns turn out to be right, in some odd way: it seems that my inner spirit has reached out and touched the inner spirit of the other. Our relationship transcends itself and becomes a part of something larger. Profound growth and healing and energy are present. I am compelled to believe that I, like many others, have underestimated the importance of this mystical, spiritual dimension."[14]

The client who finds an empathic listener and intuitive interpreter of the horoscope discovers personal gold. After the "me first" decade and codependent overkill of the 1980s, books with such titles as *Seat of the Soul* and *Care of the Soul* have become unlikely bestsellers. Why? Because there is genuine hunger for depth, substance, wisdom, caring, and consciousness in the wastelands of Western civilization. Astrologers need to recognize this phenomenon and expand their technical narrowness with humanistic and spiritual dimensions that go beyond the typical past life frame of references.

Intuition and empathy are twin spirits, guardian angels to bring light to the process of understanding and healing.

---

13. *Clinical Empathy*: David Berger, M.D., 1987, J. Aaronson, Inc.
14. *A Way of Being*: Carl Rogers

Listening with the Heart

The most important thing in music is not in the script.
—Gustav Mahler

There is a wonderful word in German, *Herzensbildung*, which has no equivalent in English. The closest is a literal translation, "the education of the heart," which does not convey its true quality. Herzensbildung implies an opened heart, full of wisdom and compassion. Also implied is that one has to work for it, that it is not a given. Education of the mind and the heart should go hand in hand, especially in the helping professions.

Recently, two opposite indications within the medical helping profession came to my attention. *Newsweek*, June 7, 1993, had an essay on "A Prescription for Healing" wherein the writer, a cancer patient, urges his doctor to consider a patient's emotions as important as the actual pathology. It seems that the writer read an article about his doctor and did not recognize the accompanying photo of him because he, the physician, was smiling. He had never seen his doctor smile. He addresses his doctor: "You were certainly no kindly healer; rather a competent master plumber, assaying a faulty drainage system and prescribing the necessary repairs to it, not me. There was no compassion in your kit. You forgot that each person is a thinking creature of hopes and fears, joys and sorrows. A doctor's ability to reassure a patient can help to activate the body's healing system. Positive emotions, like faith, love, and determination are biochemical realities. It seems to me, Doc, that you overlooked the mind's power to heal." I think that most of us can identify with these feelings from personal experiences. Medical advances are not enough if the heart has not been educated.

Simultaneously, the schedule for a medical conference in December 1993 came to my attention.[15] The topics give witness that there is a reawakening of the intuitive, the compassionate, the connection between mind and heart. Physicians speak on these subjects "Transpersonal Medicine; Spirituality and Medicine;

---

15. Fifth International Conference, The Psychology of Health, Immunity & Disease. Sponsored by The National Institute for Clinical Application of Behavioral Medicine.

Awakening the Healer Within; Art as a Healing Force; The History, Techniques, and Uses of Art in Healing, A Return to the Art of Medicine Emphasizing Experience and Intuition."

Astrology, with its need for respect and recognition, has either gone technical or esoteric. The astro-psychological texts are more or less "heartless." But is not the ultimate purpose of astrology to find connection and application between cosmos and humankind? Humankind needs hope, faith, and determination not just from medicine, but also from astrology. Just as in medicine, astrology must not forget that first and last; it is a way to relieve suffering and create better living conditions. To paraphrase Gustav Mahler: "The most important thing about astrology is not in the horoscope." It is in the heart of the interpreter of the horoscope.

What is the concerned astrologer to do? Broaden the vision into other fields that deal with the human condition. Become more self-aware, insightful. Go into therapy. Read biographies of substantive people. Read history, philosophy, religion. Practice humility. Practice generosity of spirit. Educate the heart. Think beyond your own routinized frame of reference. Freud once complained that much in American civilization showed thoughtless optimism and empty activity. Become aware of your own empty gestures and thoughtlessness on any subject.

There is an exciting new trend in American astrology—the locating and translating of historical astrological texts, from antiquity through the Renaissance. I consider this development symbolic of a larger world view and a harbinger of the age to come. It is reconnecting the present with the wisdom of the past—when art and science were one. The Neo-platonist Renaissance astrologer and philosopher, Marcilio Ficino, considered all matter ensouled, and he interpreted the planetary forces from such a viewpoint. So should we. So should science, again. The Age of Reason needs to be eclipsed by the Age of Awareness.

Not since the Renaissance have there been so many professional astrologers as there are now, at the closing of a millennium, of a great year, the Age of Pisces. Computers, the loss of traditional religious helpfulness, and the need for meaning within an individuated frame of reference have brought astrology once again to the forefront. There is a person-centered approach to astrology now. The emphasis is on understanding the individual consciousness within a universal framework. There is no room for fatalistic proscriptions. Astrology becomes a language for understanding more about the self, the journey, and the process of choices. Astrology offers a deeper, higher, farther look at consciousness on a cosmic scale. It is the scale that so overwhelmingly points toward dimensions of values. It brings into psychological focus what conventional wisdom qualifies as "don't sweat the small stuff."

Yet, the astrologer sees clients all the time who *do* sweat the small stuff, whose vision is not beyond the fear of loss of love, or hope for material advantage. I like to ask clients where they see themselves ten years from now. Very few can imagine how much growth should have happened by then. It is easier to envision the reaching of tangible goals like status, money, or power. It is easier to imagine the fulfillment of ambitions than the advancement of consciousness. The astrologer is viewed as the agent to bring about such advantages by outwitting the universe. To imagine that we can have power or control over universal forces is hubris and stupidity. To work with and learn from the cyclical cosmos is faith in a higher power. God is an astrologer and all the teachings for human growth and consciousness are inherent in the universal model. The Age of Aquarius will do away with religious dogma and bring forth cosmic-spiritual values.

We live at the threshold of immense changes of consciousness. The Piscean mentality of sacrifice and victimization is bursting at all seams. The coming forth of so many abuse victims at this time challenges societal taboos and passivity. The new Holocaust Museum in Washington D.C. is a symbol to the Piscean Age-old dilemma of Judeo-Christian intolerance and ignorance. It is a shrine to the ultimate dark forces of an age. It is hoped that the powers are diffused by bringing forth the shadow of the Age of Pisces to the conscious side of the planet. Only then can there be hope that a New Age will take hold in enough minds to create a flow of consciousness and a flow of activities to leave old shores behind.

We swim right now in the chaotic currents between two ages. The death and rebirth process is full of misguided and misunderstood principles. There are false prophets among the well-meaning who expect ideal conditions from the start, but first, we must exorcise the demons of the last age before we can hope to transgress toward greener pastures. We must mourn the victims of all forms of power. We must own up to our personal and collective shadow as expressed through the Piscean paradigm.

The falling of the Berlin Wall is one symbol of Aquarian expression. The great awakening of democratic principles in never-before free Russia is Aquarian. The age-old serfdom in the former Soviet Union and the South African slave-like conditions are vestiges of the victims of the last 2,000 years. The Piscean cross will be replaced by a new symbol of greater equality and individual effectiveness. Astrology will find greater application because we will travel through space literally and metaphorically, with a much greater sense of collective awe and personal responsibility. We live, indeed, at the great divide between past darkness and a brighter future if we own up to past mistakes.

So, the planet as a whole needs to listen for the signals of the New Age. Leaders whose power is not based on dogma, fear and control, need to be recognized and voted for. Religious institutions, which have throughout history consistently abused free choice, have set back not only individual lives but the progress of humankind generally. They are losing influence dramatically. There is an old prophecy attached to St. Paul-outside-the-Wall in Rome. Centuries ago, the portraits of all the popes in history were painted on the walls, with many empty spaces left for future popes. The prophecy stated that when all the spaces are filled there would be no more popes. That time has come. Perhaps this is one signal, coming from the bosom of a Piscean institution, that the Aquarian Age is running, like a relay, alongside spent Piscean power, for a short stretch of time.

Astrology is traditionally an Aquarian profession. This is a further indication of why there is a rebirth, a renaissance going on, why knowledge is expanded for the first time since another age. It stands to reason that astrological wisdom will be a guiding force for the awakened individual to make informed choices. It also stands to reason that the new practitioner of astrology is an enlightened human being who does not need to exercise personal power and influence.

Just as three astrologers, commonly known as The Three Wise Men, pinpointed and interpreted the arrival of the King of the Piscean Age, so it should not be at all surprising that it is again astrologers, who point to the arrival of the Aquarian Age. The difference may be that, this time around, it is "wise women," and that there is no king—or even queen, for that matter—but a call for individuated consciousness and choice. The planet, as a class, is graduating.

Many of my clients are gay or lesbian, and the sheer number of souls who have chosen this difficult assignment is indicative of a change of consciousness in the fabric of the planet. My personal opinion is that only old souls would choose such a painful path, and that there has to be a deeper purpose to that heroic choice. That AIDS has become the vehicle of intense growth and broad societal awareness is part of the Piscean sacrifice and part of the Aquarian quest for brotherly compassion. One needs only to visit a display of the AIDS Quilt to be deeply affected by the human spirit at its very best. The polarization of the masculine and the feminine is greatly diminished in the homosexual person, bringing forth a more even balance. I believe that the homosexual vibration and consciousness expresses Aquarian principles of equality and freedom of choice. There is no one way to express love. Homosexuality challenges intolerance in the 1990s on a much more subtle level of fear. The irony though, once again, is that ignorance and hate are the instruments to attack people who dare to be genetically different.

We, as a nation and as citizens of the world, need to practice empathy. We need to listen to the differences between us and within ourselves, and apply the Aquarian message of "live and let live" or, "love and let love" to one and all. The time for fundamentalist intolerance and exclusion must give way to an all-inclusive, humanistic attitude and practice. Astrologers need to serve as role models, as well as guides to such principles.

I am coming to the end of this journey about listening, empathy, compassion, and wisdom, as dimensions of astrology. Thoughts on the different words the old Greeks had for love are crossing my mind. We in the healing professions must indeed be intimately aware of the meaning and continuum of *agape, eros, philia.* We must also be aware of what wise men and women of all ages knew and Martin Buber said so succinctly: "The notion that human life includes awareness of oneness with the universe is endemic in most religions in most cultures."

Diana Stone

Diana Stone is actively involved in an astrology and counseling practice in Portland, Oregon, plus ongoing lecturing and writing projects. Her book, *The United States Wheel of Destiny*, was published in 1976. A health crisis in the 1960s precipitated her studies in healing, psychology, and astrology. In the 1970s, she trained as a psychodramatist and did postgraduate studies in Transactional Analysis and Gestalt therapy. A transpersonal crisis in 1980 preceded extensive involvement in shamanic practices, healing rituals and rites of passage.

Diana currently specializes in work with teachers and healers coping with the psychophysiological transformation process. She is also an articulate teacher, translating her personal shamanic journeys into an eclectic model of healing and therapy.

Diana Stone

A Communication Model for Astrologers

 National accents and regional dialects are key concerns in communication and are associated with generally universal stereotypes, varying from country to country. Certainly an English accent invokes an initial reaction different from a Southern drawl, but the system I am giving you does *not* concern itself with this aspect of communication. Nor does it address even the issue of proper use of the language: the astrologer may unwittingly parrot popular redundant phrases such as "gathered together" or "consensus of opinion"; or redundant words such as "irregardless," when "regardless" is sufficient without the *ir* prefix. Rather, the discussion in this chapter begins with the assumption that the astrologer *is* fundamentally competent in the use of the language, and all of this establishes the point that there are many other communication considerations unique to astrology.

This chapter introduces a communication model limited in application to astrologers working with the natal chart. It should in no way be construed to represent a universal model of astrology. Communication is the interchange of ideas and the conveyance of information. Certainly there can be no argument that this goes to the heart and soul of the astrologer's interaction with clients. A model, on the other hand, has rules, structure, and processes which are used to achieve a particular result. The result we are looking for in this system is to *increase awareness and affect positive changes in the lives of clients.* Communication outside the context of a model lacks the predictability, repeatability, and consistency a model affords.

A model is just a tool. It is not a religion, not a philosophy of life, not a belief system; only a tool to conceptualize and implement a list of things that must be present in order to achieve a very specific outcome. It is not predicated on universal law, and sometimes may not even be true when applied outside the boundaries of the model itself. A model is only required to work, that's all. This system is a collection of processes developed over many years of trial and error. I rarely, if ever, encounter a consulting situation that is not best worked through within the model. Something that works 99 percent of the time is justification enough.

The first premise of this model holds that an individual's outer life circumstances in every respect *reflect an inner life pattern.* Detail for detail, the outer situation, whatever it is, mirrors the inner workings of the psyche. Furthermore, the inner pattern comes from experiences of *this* life, can be identified, can be traced to *current* behaviors, and can be brought into conscious awareness, thereby facilitating changes in both behaviors and the life situation.

To repeat: stay clear as to the nature of models. They don't have to be true, they just have to work. Just because our model says that every life circumstance originates from inside ourselves, that doesn't prove that every situation without exception really *does* come from inside. It just means that to achieve the desired results from astrological consultations with clients, *the premise* of this model works better than any other.

Let's test the waters with an example that turns up fairly frequently in astrological practice. Many astrologers believe in reincarnation. They therefore attract many clients who believe in it as well. It is not unusual, then, to have the subject of influences from past lives come up one way or another, either from the client or the astrologer. The model here rests on the absolute that everything in our life proceeds from the psyche; and, furthermore, that the origins are from this life.

Recall that a model does not argue philosophy. Its only reason for being is to increase awareness and induce positive changes in the lives of clients. It follows then that it matters not one whit if there really *are* influences from past lives. In fact, a great body of evidence suggests that there *are* such influences. The model does not even rule out using past-life information if handled properly outside the model structure. True or not, the point is whether the past-life information leads to the desired result, a result that is always worked toward without exception.

Here is an example that involved an astrologer and my friend, Mickey. Mickey took a course in creative visualization and was practicing by manifesting parking places and whatnot. The astrologer told Mickey that this was an abuse of power and probably originated from an abuse of power in a past life. (Incidentally, this is not true of Mickey's life.) However, I know the astrologer to have personal power issues and certain spiritual convictions that came into play here. That exchange was undisciplined, sloppy, judgmental, and a consequence of that astrologer's working without benefit of a system designed to flush out dogmatic pronouncements (without having to justify the truth of them), let alone help the client be more aware and make positive changes.

The astrologer in question would probably be the first one to howl in protest at the idea of astrologers dogmatically "laying their own trip" on clients, but with all the best intentions, that is exactly what happened. It isn't so likely to happen when stubbornly holding to tried and true techniques which exclusively focus on bringing about positive change in the client's life. That includes interactions tainted with the counselor's own issues and beliefs. Cases like these do not fulfill the purpose of the model, even when the astrologer's unverified pronouncements *are* true. Again, the point is not to be right, but rather to be effective.

So, we have the primary premises of the model: outer life circumstances reflect our inner life pattern; effectiveness is our dominant concern, not proving any point one way or another. Now let's consider the individual processes that pull it together. The first step involves *listening*. That certainly is a necessary aspect of communication. In this system, listening has a precise application and one objective, however.

What do I mean by listening? Clients give *us* a great deal of information. They ask any number of questions. What you want to listen for is the story. I define the story as what is *really* happening in the life; or more accurately, what is the real storyline in the particular situation being communicated. This is not as simple as it may sound at first. The story is not what the client wants to happen; it is not what the client necessarily thinks is happening; it is precisely and exactly what actually *is* happening.

It takes a certain turn of the mind to identify these storylines and not get sucked into the client's reality, which is incredibly powerful. It has led many an astrologer on wild goose chases that accomplish nothing much of substance. It takes concentration and imagination to pick up the thread of the real story. This is what it means to stay centered and in control of the consultation. You are doing something, something active rather than passive. You are not just hanging out with your ears, as it were. You track exactly what is happening and know where you are going. You are listening hard for something specific. You are not leaving a void for the client to move in and lead you astray. You are working inside the model.

The client reports that she hates her job and wants to make a career change. The story is *not* the career change. That is what the client *wants*. The story is that the client hates her job. Another client says that her boyfriend won't make a commitment and she wants to get married. What is the story here? Again, the story is not what the client wants. The story is that she is 45 years old and has not brought a commitment into her life. Another client tells about his wife, saying that she is not exciting, hates sex, and seems to be disinterested in his career. Don't be misled here. The story is that the man is isolated in his relationships. Here is a hint. To sort out the storyline, ignore the "other" people in the tale or the circumstances described and focus solely on *what is happening to the client.*

Now hark back to the premise of the model which says that the outer life circumstances are a reflection of inner life patterns. The hated career originates in the inner life. The reluctant boyfriend is an expression of the woman's inner patterns. The bored and distant wife is a player in the man's own inner world.

I hope it is becoming clear just how radically this shifts the vantage point from which the astrologer will work in these cases. The astrologer who unerringly follows this thread of inner and outer life relationships is not going simply to give information, however accurately, but will instead *consistently facilitate awareness and change for clients.*

My client, Eve, is a good example of how differently a case may be handled using this system. Eve asked me to tell her what would be the ideal career for her. Outside this model, a typical next step would be to use whatever vocational indicators the astrologer favors and look for some likely vocational choices. Right there *the astrologer has lost control of the consultation.*

In this case, the client has dictated the direction for the astrologer to go. Avoid this knee-jerk response. The primary criterion of our model says that we aim for awareness and change in the client's life, and unfailingly recognize when we are not working in that direction. Even if the astrologer identifies the woman's ideal career, does that guarantee heightened awareness and positive change for the client? Does it even mean she will manifest this ideal career? No, it does not. That route fails the test of the model.

Working within the model, we proceed quite differently. First, we actively pursue the story. It is not a matter of what the client may perhaps volunteer as information as the consultation proceeds. The astrologer guides the direction of the process and knows when to ask specific questions. In this conversation with Eve, I knew to question her judiciously, rather than automatically to look for the "ideal" career. Instead, I asked Eve what her career was now and if she liked it.

She was herself a career counselor. She said she really enjoyed the counseling aspect of her job but hated the bureaucracy, politics, and red tape involved. Immediately I made a mental note of the storyline. This woman likes her work but hates the context of the job. For now, we'll leave this case study hanging and develop the process of the model another step or two. Then we will circle back to Eve and discuss the other techniques utilized in my consultation time with her.

The storyline is the reality of the client's situation. The story equals reality, and the reality equals a choice. The issue of choices is the next step in understanding this system. Returning once more to the premise that the client's story, or reality, reflects the inner life, the actual dynamics of the inner life patterns are the next consideration. Just where did the patterns in the psyche come from, these inner forces that wield so much power as to create outer life realities, even those we don't like?

The model takes the position that all the patterns of the inner world are created from the client's own choices, both the conscious and unconscious choices. Again, it doesn't make it true because the model says it; it only means that it works. Incidentally, this supposition does rest on solid psychological theory and is born out in psychotherapy. Regardless, for this system to work the astrologer must maintain the position that whatever the situation of the client, *a part of the client has chosen to have things exactly the way they are.* The astrologer must confidently maintain this stance, even in the face of clients' disbelief, and further than that, lead clients to realize for themselves that a particular set of circumstances did, without any doubt, proceed from the client's own choices. That increases awareness and that leads to change. The process stays clean of any prejudices or judgments which may unwittingly scuttle the desired result.

So just what is the nature of choices? We are familiar enough with mundane choices: what to have for dinner, what movie to watch on television, or what house to buy, etc. These may, at times, *be* important choices, but the choices that most often confront the astrologer—and the ones that are most important to work with—are the choices which create outer life realities beyond the awareness of the client. If the client is stuck in a painful situation, it comes from a choice; an unconscious choice. That certainly casts in a different light the agonies in the lives of clients, and it also dictates a radically different approach on the part of the astrologers.

The techniques of this system call for extremely careful handling when communicating with clients around this matter of choice. It must not be used to accuse the client of "wanting" painful situations because of some neurotic need to suffer or get attention. It must not be used to blame the client. Do not say to clients, "Well, you chose this situation, so what are you complaining about?" We do not judge the client, blame the client, or put the client on the defensive. Such behaviors and attitudes toward clients are beyond the pale and inexcusable. Besides, they aren't helpful. The dynamics of choices are, first and foremost, a process for the astrologer to understand so that this model may be used effectively.

Most choices that come to our attention are choices made in early childhood in relation to parents or other parental role models. The choice lays down a pattern. If childhood reality includes a violent, drunken, father then the choices will revolve around how to cope with that reality, and the choices about how to cope with that reality create a pattern. The decision is made, the pattern is set and it plays itself out by manifesting life situations which mirror the reality and the pattern. After that happens, the only way to change the pattern is with some kind of therapy or, as I would like to think, through the intervention of an astrologer using this system.

The drunken father reality can lead to many different choices, but all of them will stem from the reality of the drunken father. Perhaps the child's personality is the sort to conclude that being a drunk gives a person the power to throw his weight around, so the child decides to be a violent drunk. Maybe the drunken father reality is so terrifying to another child that he or she hides under the bed and decides to be invisible. That child will grow up to be constantly fearful, with a set of extremely passive behaviors, and will most probably choose an abusive partner.

Imagination and creativity are necessary to deduce some of the choices which might logically emerge from a given reality. Just keep in mind that choices or decisions as defined in this system lay down patterns within the context of a given set of realities and these patterns are the best choice a particular individual could come up with at the time. Maybe it is a better survival choice than the astrologer would have made under the same circumstances. The point is not whether some one individual coped and survived personal past experiences one way or another; the point is that a situation was created in which an unconscious pattern emerged and now is the only choice available in every future situation, no matter how destructive or inappropriate.

Let's get back to Eve and her question about the ideal career. You will remember that she liked her work but hated the bureaucracy. Now we can look at this from the perspective of what we now know about the model. Remember, Eve's situation is an acting out of the inner drama she chose for herself some time in her past. Somewhere in her inner world is the pattern which dictates that she love part of her work and hate part of her work. Furthermore, we now understand that the pattern would indeed re-establish itself, even in any so-called ideal career. The question then is: why would anybody want to choose this kind of a situation?

Be sure that this question does not shake you loose from the premise of the model. There is a pattern inside *that wants this situation exactly as it is.* It has its own reasons, and they are powerful enough to override any conscious objections or painful consequences. Before moving on with this case, it is time to introduce some astrological considerations into the equation. What a tremendous advantage that is going to turn out to be!

The next step in the model is to find the pattern in the natal horoscope. It will always be there. The only problem is that you may not know enough about astrology to find where the pattern is represented. Obviously, there is insufficient space in this one chapter to include all the patterns associated with various astrological influences. One thing is certain, though, you'll never make the connections if you don't look for them. There is no reason that even beginning students can not learn this model and use it at least as far as their astrological knowledge carries them. In fact, the model is a powerful learning tool and gets a lot more mileage out of the astrology you do know.

Eve's chart (Chart 1) is reproduced here, so let's have a look. When we turn to Eve's chart, it is with the idea in mind that the inner self decided, for reasons as yet unknown, to have two aspects to her work. She likes the counseling work. She is good with people. Where in Eve's chart do we find an astrological signature of this pattern? We need look no further than the Gemini Ascendant with Uranus in close conjunction aspect with it.

Once the astrological indicators are correctly matched to the pattern, what you know about the case makes a quantum leap. Suddenly my mental computer downloaded the details. Where before I was just sniffing around the perimeter, now the picture blasted in with crystal clarity. When I saw Uranus sitting there big as life on the Ascendant, I tasted sweet victory in this case. Of course, this woman hates the bureaucracy! We also know a whole lot more than that: namely, that she is a free spirit, very independent, likes to work alone, need lots of space to express creativity, needs variety, is good at many different things, communicates well, is good working with people, is nontraditional and oriented toward the future, is not interested in material things, is a natural counselor and teacher and, of course, hates red tape, politicking, structure, and the bureaucracy. In a nut shell, it is Uranus in Gemini on the Ascendant.

At this point it is important to stay with the premise of the model. She does not necessarily hate the organizational structure simply because we find Uranus conjunct the Ascendant. If Uranus did not conflict with anything else in her reality, her job story would reflect that exclusively and there would be no problem then. She would simply have a job that totally suits the Uranus in Gemini needs. She would not be complaining to the astrologer about it. So, we have worked through only half of the story. Why and how did the inner self manifest the job situation she hates and where in the chart might we find some clues? That is what remains to be sorted out.

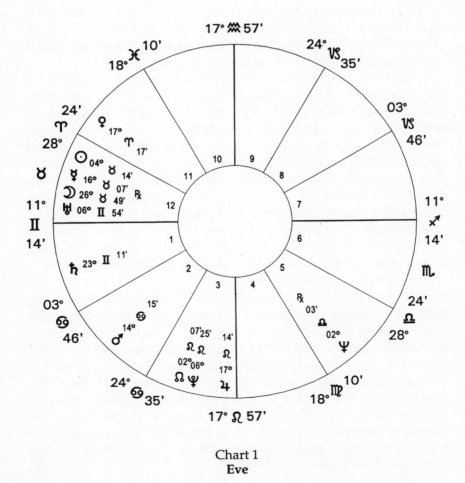

Chart 1
Eve

We have yet to fulfill the goal of the model in this case. So far we have not led the client to awareness. Astrologers are too often guilty of saying things like, "Oh, of course, you hate structure, you have Uranus conjunct the Ascendant!" That doesn't solve anything. It's just a piece of useless information at that point; accurate maybe, but it does not accomplish what we want.

So some inner pattern wants structure, and it doesn't seem to care how she feels about it. It planted it there and it wants it there. Referring to the chart again, the stellium in Taurus seemed a likely place to begin. We can ruminate on some Taurus themes and see where they lead. One of the advantages of this model is that it gives the astrologer the freedom to go ahead and explore some themes in the chart until things begin to fall into place. If one line of questioning leads nowhere, then explore some other avenue. Less experienced astrologers can feel comfortable using this system because it removes our work from an "is this wrong or right?" mode.

Taurus is traditional, conservative, needs stability and financial security. This fits close enough to proceed to the next step. We want to know from what reality those powerful Taurus needs ended up in such an unhappy situation. Once you find the astrological pattern that is unhappy, you have to get busy and track it down. We can begin to ask some really specific questions now that we have the Bull by the tail. Examine the astrological factors involved in Taurus. You will always take your cue about where to begin the dialogue from the particular planets involved in each case. Both the Sun and the Moon are in Taurus. A safe guess is that both of the parents are probably involved. Actually, this is a safe guess in most cases. If in doubt, go after Mom and Dad.

This model demands that you bring much more to this system than astrological knowledge. You must really develop creativity and use your imagination. What question are you going to ask Eve about her parents? *You are going to ask about the identical sphere in the parents' lives* that is now creating a problem for Eve in her life. This is a career problem. So, ask Eve about the work history of both the father and the mother, and their attitudes about their working years. If I can tempt you to use this model, you will be astounded at how much the client is involved in this process. Consider the answer Eve gave to my question. I will be surprised if you don't begin making some solid connections between her history and her present predicament.

Her father wanted to be a priest or a musician. (Pisces must be prominent in his chart.) His mother said that neither of those careers was acceptable so he became a lawyer instead, a bad lawyer. When he was 52 years old, he had a heart attack. After that, he was limited in his capacity to work, so held clerk jobs and the like. "He was never able to follow his heart," she said. Father died when he was 59 years old. Mother was the practical one, so she went to work to support the family, although she had to "give up herself" in the process. That is basically the story as Eve told me. That is enough information to start piecing this whole thing together for the client.

Clients may have some unconscious booby traps but they aren't stupid. Eve was already catching a glimpse of where I was going. The striking relationship in her story between her father's heart attack and his never having followed his heart's desire was not wasted on her. She hadn't put that together before, but just as soon as the words were out of her mouth, she got it.

Now we will lay all the pieces on the table and see what we have. It is from the experiences and attitudes of her parents' work history that Eve learned a certain reality from which she made decisions about how her own career would be. This happened at the unconscious level and will operate from the unconscious all her life unless some appropriate intervention is forthcoming. It is now the astrologer's task to analyze the childhood events to which Eve was exposed, and begin to identify some themes.

We have father who learned that you cannot do what you want. You must have a job that you hate. In fact, you must hate it so much that it kills you. We have mother, on the other hand, who is practical and provides survival and security, but chooses to sell herself out to do it. Ugh! It is a wonder Eve is doing as well as she is! You can see that the astrologer does not have to play guessing games with the horoscope to discover what happened in the person's past. The system I am teaching you gives the astrologer a way to control the consultation skillfully, and guide it unerringly to the appropriate material in a way that the truth is apparent to the astrologer and the client.

How is all this communicated to the client? With the case history in hand, it was easy to explain to Eve that her present job situation comes from a pattern inside herself, a pattern she learned from her parents' reality. It is empowering for people to realize that their situation did not happen capriciously, or because they are stupid or lack good judgment. My clients brighten when I tell them that all things hinged on their early decisions, which means that *they can make new decisions and change their lives.*

After she explained her parents' history, she rapidly put two and two together with me as we went along. In fact, when we discussed the unfortunate symbolism of the father's heart attack, she admitted that she is just a few years younger now than her father was when he died, and she has begun to worry that the same thing might happen to her if she continues with work she hates. The truth is, it well might.

Then I put it to her, "Finding the ideal career isn't really the issue. When you alter the inner life, this alters the course of the outer life. You have some inner work to do first." Interestingly enough, in Eve's case, she came up with a solution before this session was over. She realized that she actually could work part time at the counseling job, part time at a teaching position she was offered, and part time at still a third position. What a wonderful variety for Gemini, and it pays the bills and takes care of her Taurus needs for security and stability as well. We discussed her real needs for some stability, the Taurus pattern, and I pointed out that she should free up the learned reality, and find security in ways she enjoyed. I told her that she could achieve a stable solution in an unstable way.

I needed to deal with one other interaction in this case, a dynamic that one frequently encounters when the unconscious is up to something. Here is what happened. Eve asked me why this pattern did not come along until she was well into her thirties. Oh, Oh! Has this unexpected piece of information ruined everything? Follow this carefully, because here you will see how imperative it is to stick with the philosophy and techniques of the model and use your head.

Whenever you see that question coming; i.e., "If that is the pattern, why didn't it show up before?" don't think this wrecks your entire premise. (Clients love to throw that question at the astrologer.) The first thing to do is find out what the *early* pattern was. Eve had been a free spirit in the early years of her life. She traveled all over the world, she did what she liked, she never worried about getting a job. When she needed work, it was always there for her. She had a great time. This is obviously the Uranus in Gemini out there kicking up its heels.

Thinking this through very carefully in light of the messages from the parents, we know this flies in the face of the inner reality. Why? Because the parents' messages dictate that you can't do what you like and you must sell your soul for security. In fact, you must do what you hate and die from it. Perhaps hoping to cheat the fate ordained by the parents' example, doesn't it stand to reason that many of us simply rebel and do just the opposite?

This is a typical scenario and one which you can expect to encounter regularly. The premise of the model, however, remains the same. Once you know the inner pattern, you count on it to show its hand in the reality of the life one way or another. Uranus in Gemini and the planets in Taurus were never given positive ways of expression. A means is needed to integrate what she likes and does well with her practical, financial demands. The way things stand, it is a catch twenty-two. If she follows her heart, that turns out to be scary free-floating. If she does not follow her heart, she has to be miserable and even die. If she wants security, she must sacrifice herself.

So why not go with the Uranus and run? Why wouldn't that work? It doesn't work because the inner reality and decisions about the way life is have not changed at the unconscious level. Based on the earlier work we did in examining role models and unconscious decisions and realities, the unconscious perceived her free-floating lifestyle as hopelessly divorced from practical needs, stability, and security.

We safely assume that her grasshopper live-for-today philosophy will be eroded at some point by the prepare-for-the future ant mentality. Let's appreciate how very important money and stability must have seemed to a child who saw her mother sacrifice so much for them. One fine day an astrological transit will come along, activate those Taurus planets, and turn her thoughts to the things of which bank accounts, investments, and retirement income are made. Of course, that is exactly what happened.

We might ask, if it was this simple to find a solution for Eve, why she hadn't realized this herself before now? It wasn't simple! It may have taken only 20 minutes for Eve, but it took me 20years of astrological practice to have that conversation. If it looks simple, it is to the experienced practitioner's credit. I hope when you use this model, it looks easy; that means you are really getting good. I would have sold my son into slavery to have this model 20 years ago (just joking, David).

Twenty years ago, I had a vision about how the way I intuited astrology could be practiced. It was elusive and I couldn't translate the vision into any articulated process. In fact, I didn't think about trying to explain it. There certainly was never any intention to create a model. At one point in my work, I just realized that things were really coming together, but just how and what I was doing bedeviled me no end. The whole process was so natural and instinctive by then, it was like trying to figure out how I made my heart beat.

Now let's put things into perspective. This model is remarkably powerful in its proper place. That doesn't mean it is appropriate to every situation. Sometimes a straightforward answer to the client's query is all that is needed. There is not some unresolved, unconscious problem lurking behind every question. You can find out quickly enough and then just move on. The model does not preclude the use of any other favorite astrological tools that work for you.

My experiences teaching this method in all-day seminars have taught me that introducing a variety of case studies is a tremendous help for students. Let's turn, then, to some real life examples to see just how the interplay between this model and the natal horoscope really works.

This next client we will call Keith. He came for a complete natal interpretation. During the course of the consultation, we had the following conversation:

Astrologer: And now I would like to know what is happening in your relationship life right now. How is it going?

Keith: My relationship just ended. I am terribly depressed. My partner just won't be close. But I'm resolved to it.

Astrologer: When you say you are resolved to it, do you mean that your relationships always end this way?

Keith: Yes, I always seem to choose partners who won't be close.

If you want to test yourself, study Keith's chart and write out the strategy you will use according to the model. The first step is to ascertain the story: in other words, the reality of Keith's relationship life. It is *not* what he thinks is happening; namely, that he always chooses partners who won't be close. To determine the reality, *always focus on what the client is doing.* He is avoiding intimate relationships. Once we determine that, we realize that this pattern is a choice, and operating outside Keith's awareness. The next thing to do is to ask questions in order to find out what experience in Keith's past taught him to create a relationship life devoid of intimacy. Here is a hint: transiting Pluto at the time of consultation was at 17° degrees Scorpio. Continue on and see how this situation was handled.

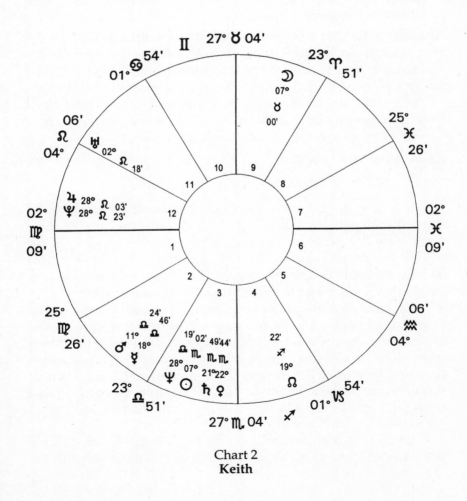

Chart 2
Keith

Astrologer: When you were a little kid, did you grow up fast? Were you responsible, maybe had to care for siblings or get a job very young? Could you say that you never really had a chance to be a kid?

Keith: That is exactly right. I was always the one who had to be responsible, and I have worked since I was ten years old.

Astrologer: What you learned as a kid was to be the parent, the one who does all the giving and takes all the responsibility. How similar is this to your relationships now?

Keith: I take care of everything. My partner wouldn't do anything. I pay the bills, just everything. And now that I think about it, it is always that way.

Astrologer: Keith, I want you to realize that your relationships are coming from internal patterns projected onto external life situations. You learned from early life to be the parent who gives. This sets up a dynamic that polarizes with the irresponsible child in relationships. You are locked into a parent-child relationship with your partners, with you as always the parent. How easy is it for people to do things for you?

Keith: I won't let them. I don't even like to receive gifts for my birthday.

It is obvious from this case that the astrologer needs to be familiar with patterns associated with different planets, including some early life experiences peculiar to each one of them, along with some typical behaviors and life situations that develop later on. You probably realize by now that I was focusing on Saturn in the chart. Why did I go to Saturn first to question Keith?

The astrological system you are familiar with gives clues as to where to begin. The transits are often tremendously useful indicators showing what to zero in on first. Pluto was the direction-pointer in this case. It was transiting Scorpio, a relationship sign, and one in which he has three planets, including Venus. Venus is one of the relationship indicators in a horoscope. This wasn't the first time a Pluto transit over natal Saturn and Venus got a client into my office!

Venus with Saturn natally certainly is a combination that we can easily imagine being devoid of intimacy. Familiarity with the patterns of Saturn led me straight to the key issues to explore; responsibility, parental behaviors, and emotional isolation. Once you have experience with this archetype, you will begin to recognize it despite variations in particular cases.

His chart shows a singleton Moon (alone in a hemisphere) which could lead one to a conclusion that Keith's life was perhaps dominated by intimacy, even the smothering relationships which so often characterize the Moon/Taurus type. However, the current transits in the chart along with Keith's comments led me to look at Saturn, which was the present issue.

This is why I like working in my model so much. I don't have to guess. It also circumvents absolute pronouncements that play the percentages of "hits" against the misses. I don't even have to be right on the first conjecture. No, it is a matter of setting up a communication with the client that smoothly invites him or her to enter a dialogue with the astrologer until the whole picture makes sense. You want to handle the initial contact with your client in a way that does not imply that you know everything there is to know just by looking at the horoscope.

This brings us back to an earlier discussion about how the astrologer's own belief system can unwittingly influence communication with the client. By now the structure of the model and the example case study make this dynamic more understandable. However, there is one philosophy about astrological work itself so absolutely critical, and so universally corrupted, and that has so hamstrung professional practice, it could well sabotage our collective hope for astrology one day to command the status of other professions. It calls for a closer examination.

There is a lot of talk in astrology that the stars do not have a direct cause and effect influence on our lives; that the horoscope is just a map. There seems to be general agreement in the West, at least, that life is not fated, we do have choices, and blaming things on your horoscope is not taking responsibility for your life. Yet, I find it a widespread and commonplace practice among astrologers to read charts and repeatedly communicate absolutes to their clients. "Your Sun and Moon are square. Your parents didn't get along (actual quote)," *ad infinitum,* including more subtly insidious examples.

Aside from the fact that these kinds of statements (even if they are right) don't accomplish anything by way of enlightening the client and facilitating change; there is a direct paradox here. The philosophy is contradicted in practice. If people have free choice, *how can the astrologer possibly know for certain what those choices are?* They could be any one of a hundred things.

I explain to my clients right from the beginning that I don't know what choices they have made in their lives, and that they must understand the limits of prediction in astrology. This avoids a common attitude among lay people that says, "You are the astrologer. You tell me." I don't let my clients get away with that attitude. It's not because I am arrogant. It's my job. I am the one who is supposed to know better than they what astrology can do for them. I'm not about to let their misperceptions undermine it. It is time we astrologers stop trading on the fact that the public generally has no idea of the true scope and power of astrology and are amazed that we get anything right. Their amazement should not be a straitjacket delimiting the benchmark of professional work, but rather our own more accurate perceptions of what astrology is really capable of. Only then will we push the boundaries to the cutting edge of what's possible.

I stay in control of the consultation because I am clear where I stand and have carefully thought through how to communicate it. The relationship with my clients is very good. It is not necessary to bully them. They trust me because they sense that I am confident of what I am doing. When they understand my style, they appreciate the powerful results. Clients are not stupid. They get the idea. The ones who don't can be brought into line if you hold your ground. Understand that I am not saying astrologers never predict anything. You do. I do. There is always the option of working outside the model altogether anytime we want to.

Remember, the model is for natal astrologers whose goal is to increase awareness that facilitates positive changes in their clients' lives. Back to the one example about whether the client's parents got along. Isn't it better to ask the client whether the parents got along or not and be done with it? From the answer, you might pick up the thread of the person's pattern. Otherwise, you send the message that you know things that you really can't know for sure. My late friend and astrology great, Richard Idemon, and I used to have many discussions about the importance of working this way. He taught that the consultation requires a horoscope and a client with whom you dialogue about the actual history. The crucial point in my discussion is the gap between what we say we believe and what we are actually doing without realizing it. This model I give you has safeguards to thwart some gremlins from creeping in.

Earlier I pointed out the obvious limits of space in just one chapter, precluding a comprehensive discussion of all of the patterns associated with all of the planets. I am including only those patterns incidental to the charts I use in the case studies. If you want to learn from your work as you go along, the model is a remarkably effective teacher. You have learned some important lessons about Saturn from Keith's case. You see how the pattern of early responsibility laid down some unconscious decisions and how they manifested in his parental role with partners. It is predictable that something of this nature would happen. All we need are the details so Keith himself understands.

If you can identify a Saturn relationship problem, you should be able to solicit the history from the client along that theme, even though the details vary from case to case. You know what to look for, you know what questions to ask, you are in control of the counseling session. There are only ten planets. Each one presents problems according to its nature. Use your experience to build up a collection of patterns that go with each planet or sign. Each case expands your library of examples, until you recognize only variations on known themes.

Before moving to the next case study, it might be well to keep in mind that, although the histories are written out in detail, there is one spectacular missing piece. Everyone who has worked in the consultation setting, one on one, knows what I am talking about. That is the indescribable energy charge in the air. These words on paper cannot communicate the formidable force that is really determining the outcome as much as anything the counselor may say. Believe me, this electricity between two people forgives a lot of mistakes. If you remember that the client supplies just as much current as the astrologer, it brings technical knowledge and flawless techniques into perspective behind just being a human being who cares.

As for Keith? He was absolutely jolted by the information we shared. I received a letter from Keith a year later telling me about his continuing amazement at our session and how much it helped him work through his relationships. When the dynamics of this system become absolutely predictable to you, it is easy to lose sight of the impact this sort of work has on the client. Most of my clients are stunned by some of the insights that come to them in their sessions. They never heard of anything like this before, and sudden insights are accompanied by some startling energy releases. This is not just an intellectual affair.

The situation requires that you stay attuned to the clients' reactions and not come at things too fast. I have used this system for so long now that sometimes in just the first few minutes I have the whole thing pieced together. At first when my professional work was really falling into place, I was so excited about it, I forgot all about the other person. I threw things at people so fast, they walked out of my office as though they were in shell shock. I learned to be more sensitive, to keep the pace appropriate to the client's comprehension.

The astrological perspective often brings understanding of an entire syndrome for the first time. Sometimes people come to me in conjunction with their therapies and gain fresh insight into the very same issues they have not resolved with their counselors. Simply because we astrologers can sometimes fill in holes left by other therapies doesn't mean we have switched from astrology to psychology. Why shouldn't astrology be just as capable of adding dimensions to understanding as, say, some other psychotherapeutic model often does? This is why I believe I can justifiably disclaim some suggestions that this system is basically a counseling model somehow twisted around to fit astrology. Psychology has its justification for being, and what I do in my work does not cancel out the legitimacy of client's therapies. Albeit astrology offers a different perspective, it is one as legitimate as any other profession's and its separate identity deserves to be acknowledged.

While on this subject, it might be well to make some clearer distinctions about just what we are doing in astrology, if we are not overlapping so far into other fields that we overstep the bounds of our knowledge and the astrological paradigm. I think the boundaries are really very clear. The astrologer is not a counselor in the sense of the psychotherapist who sees people weekly to treat a particular problem. Nor are we lawyers, investment brokers, or doctors who handle specific legal matters, financial decisions, and health problems. The natal astrologer deals only with the analysis aspect of these various situations. I say this not only for the astrologer to be clear about boundaries, but for another reason that involves interaction with clients as well.

When I move through the process with clients that nails down a pattern which is impressive to them, the next question to quickly follow often is, "What can I do about it?" It is easy for people to assume that if you are this good at ferreting out their inner demons, you must also be as good at fixing them. In answer to this question, it is important to remind the client that the astrologer only identifies the pattern, but does not treat it professionally. However, you can go on to say that conscious awareness is often 50 percent of the battle. When people enter therapy, months may be devoted to analyzing the history and piecing together the picture. I think this is where astrology is amazingly effective and can save so much time. Let's not just jump over it. No one can change anything unless first conscious of it.

My clients, in the majority of cases, do not need professional help. I encourage people to work with their issues themselves for a while. I am not disappointed by my confidence in them in many cases. If someone is in over their heads, then professional help is always an option. In other words, keep clients focused on the importance of understanding the workings of the pattern itself.

The tendency is to jump too quickly to the cure. It is tempting to respond when your clients are so incredibly impressed with you that they think you can do anything. Keep in mind, however, that our boundaries are established by clearly understanding what we are doing, not the client's unbridled enthusiasm.

Let's study another real case history and see how the relationship issue in this example was handled. The conversation is altered for simplicity's sake to include some of the astrological factors.

Glen is a long-time client. He's a college professor. He is an alcoholic in recovery several years following a long struggle and many problems. I like Glen. He is personable and good looking with a sense of humor. He is a family man still married to his high school sweetheart. He has three grown children.

Astrologer: There is now a concentration of planets in your Moon sign, Capricorn. Saturn, Uranus, and Neptune are grouped together there. The Moon relates to your family life.

Glen: The reason I came in is to ask you what the relationship picture looks like for now.

Astrologer: Are you talking about the relationship with your wife, or are we talking about someone else?

Uranus and Neptune are conjunct his natal Moon. This along with the look on his face led me to ask the question.

Glen: Well, I have a woman friend I see now and then.

Astrologer: How much of a friend?

Glen: Mostly it is a friendship. Now and then we spend the night together. But she is in my life because she is the excitement. I can't complain about my wife or my life. Everything is really stable. Even my job, at last. But I really need the excitement, not sexual, but she just is exciting and interesting.

We have enough information right there to piece everything together. First, what is the man's story? What is really the issue here? What in the chart reflects the pattern in astrological symbolism? Once we know that, the next step is to question Glen along the lines of the astrological key themes.

Astrologer: I think we will work with the relationship patterns in your chart. You are really telling me that your relationship life is not exciting enough, it is humdrum and boring, even though stable and dependable. That describes very accurately one of the ways the Moon in Capricorn can express itself. Now an astrological cycle has come along and wants to have more excitement. That is primarily Uranus at work. Let's see if there is any liveliness in the chart. There is plenty! Gemini and Sagittarius planets with Mars conjunct the Sun; where is all that fire and excitement disappearing to? If it is not finding expression in your life, you have had some life experiences that were traumatic enough to suppress their expression. Something inside you is saying it is not comfortable with the aliveness and excitement.

Glen: If I don't like it, then why do I want my woman friend in my life so much?

Astrologer: The lack of excitement is your pattern. The liveliness in your chart is projected onto a woman *who acts it out for you*. She can never be a major part of your life because you don't have permission to have that in your life. You have managed to sneak around every now and again, that's all. You are favoring the Moon in Capricorn. The role is to be mother and father in relationships. You take all the responsibility and it tends to cut off the *receiving* end for you. Uranus is very prominent in your chart. It represents the spontaneity and equality relationships that are missing. You have strong needs for friends and lively interests.

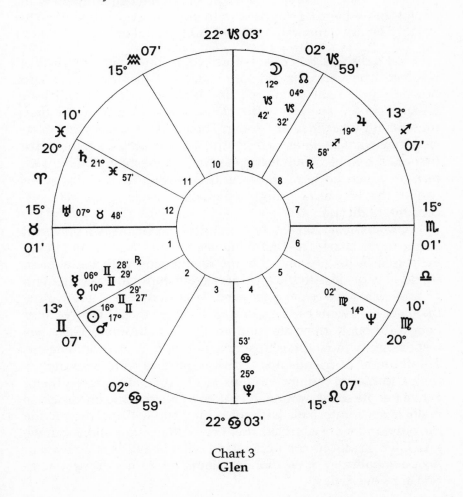

Chart 3
Glen

Glen: I never make any friends. I was totally traumatized in my earlier friendships.

See how the client comes right in with the history! That is because we found the right planet, realized how repressed it is, and just tapped into some basic key themes of Uranus in regard to relationships. Even beginning students know Uranus rules friendship relationships, and here it even rules the 11th!

Glen: In college, I had three close friends. All three of them died. I have been afraid to have any close friends after the last one died. I was real supportive of all of them. I helped them with lots of problems. I stayed with them to the end. I did not go to the last one's funeral. I still feel guilty about it.

Let's discuss this case before we go on to see how it was resolved. The woman friend posed no moral dilemma for me. I do not pass judgment on my clients. I do admit that I will lean toward people staying with relationships, at least until they understand what they are doing. Then they can make any decision they want as far as I am concerned. I wanted Glen to realize first of all that his relationship life was manifesting an inner pattern of which he was unaware. It came out in the history, of course, that he was favoring the parent role as his Moon in Capricorn might dictate.

Uranus, just rising at the Ascendant, is obviously a powerful theme in his chart. The first thing is to realize that it is not being expressed in his life, and that the relationship with the woman friend is very close to the type of relationships we associate with Uranus. *It is a projection of his own unconscious need.* Here we see that later life events can be as traumatizing as those of early childhood, although they are seldom this catastrophic. Glen has responsibility in relationships mixed up with his freedom needs. The thought of friendships probably implies some very heavy things to him at the unconscious level, so he is avoiding them. When people sneak around, it is often a clue that the unconscious really is not comfortable with something and will allow it into the life only under very limited situations. What suggestions can we give Glen so that he can understand what he needs to activate in his personality to draw more excitement into his primary relationships every day?

Astrologer: I would like you to be more aware of the heavy parent role you have taken on. You need to lighten up. There are books and men's groups that might appeal to you. Explore the possibilities. Perhaps you can feel more alive and exciting. Did you ever stop to think your wife may have some of the same feelings about the relationship? She would probably like it if you were more exciting yourself. Why don't you think about these things for a while before you decide about the other woman in your life. I would like to see you in a couple of months and discuss this further.

Glen: I have to admit that I have thought about leaving my wife and pursuing this other relationship. I am so glad I had this conversation with you before I walked into something without thinking.

Astrologer: Just remember that the inner pattern will prevail in all your relationships unless you change it. If you went off with the other woman, it wouldn't be long before you would be in here complaining that *she* is boring. That's how powerful those unconscious influences are.

The next case involves my client, Jane. I have seen Jane through rough times. She comes from a dysfunctional family. Her mother is an alcoholic. Jane had been an alcoholic in recovery about three years at the time of this consultation. She has battled her way through deep depressions, severe health problems, and a continuing problem in finding a career and earning enough money for even basic needs. After a lot of work with therapists and healers and many false starts, Jane settled into a good job in a field in which she was talented and experienced. Here, I thought, my faith in the universe was restored, that there was hope for everyone, and Jane was launched into a whole new life.

The name of this consultation is "Bursting My Bubble." The conversation picks up after Jane told me that her big break had come. The leading company in her field had called her for an interview. This was the dream job.

Astrologer: And so, how did the interview go?

Jane: They want to hire me, but I am not going to take the job. This company uses tons of paper products and none of it is recycled. I am an activist for recycling and other environmen-tal issues. I told them my beliefs about this. I just can't work for a place that does not respect the environment. The man wants to hire me, but he said it just would not work out for me to work there all week and then join picket lines on the weekend in front of the building. And I would!

Why are you looking at me like that, Diana?

Astrologer: Because I am going to KILL YOU, that's why!

Jane: You can't blame me for sticking by my beliefs.

Astrologer: I might. It remains to be seen. You can't blame me, after all the things we have been through, for feeling disappointed that you are missing the golden opportunity of a lifetime. I have watched you live on the edge for so many years, I just hate to see you get back into that. You at least owe me your attention long enough to check out some patterns in your chart.

Now for some comments on this case. What is the pattern? The answer is in her own conversation. This is a pattern that involves her *belief system,* and what in astrology rules belief sys-tems? Jupiter is the answer. But that is not all of the pattern. The belief system is operating in a way that is going to put her in the poor house. The belief system is not aligning with her career and survival and financial needs. What planet rules those things? Sat-urn is the answer. We have a house divided against itself. What is she actually doing. Isn't she giving up an awful lot for her beliefs? Is that really necessary? I am sniffing out the hand of the uncon-scious at work here. So what questions do we ask Jane? Read on and see how the rest of this session was handled.

Astrologer: Jupiter and the 9th House are heavily emphasized in your chart. Jupiter is a focal planet in a kite pattern, and your Sun is in the 9th House. The element earth is weak in the chart by comparison. There is not a good balance between practical matters and idealism. It is so out of balance that I am afraid you are going to pass up an opportunity that you have worked toward for a long time. I want to be sure this is just a simple matter of standing by your beliefs. Now I want you to answer this question: do the words *needless sacrifice* mean any-thing to you?

Jane: Do you know what I went through taking care of my mother? She is *still* a drunk. Do you know how far this has gotten me? I have taken care of people all my life and it never makes the slightest difference. Everything just goes right on as before. My kids even left me to go live with their father. I sometimes think I am invisible. I just have no impact on the world, but I keep trying and trying to make a difference. Look where it has gotten me. I just end up sick and broke.

Astrologer: What appear to you as deep beliefs here are actually unconscious patterns, ones that you learned early. You

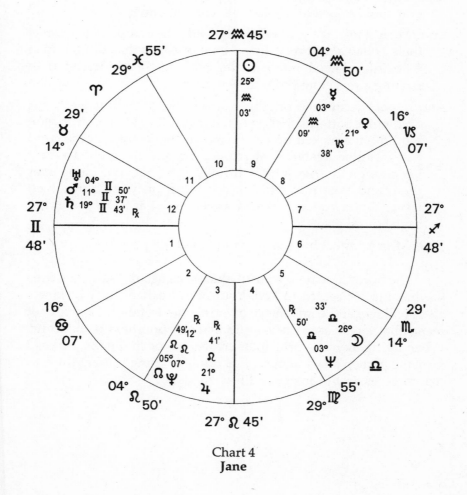

Chart 4
Jane

learned that your role is to make needless sacrifices so that you can end up sick and broke. And you are about to act this out again.

Jane: But I really do believe that we are endangering the planet by cutting down all the trees. That company should recycle.

Astrologer: Tell me how many trees are going to be saved if you don't take that job? Tell me how that is going to change the company?

Jane: It's the principle of the thing.

Astrologer: I am going to pretend I didn't hear that. Tell me how you could take that job and still change things.

Jane: I could take the job and work inside the company to change their policy about recycling. I hate to admit this, but the man who interviewed me said the company was interested in putting a recycling program together.

Astrologer: It isn't the principle of the thing at all. It was your own inner patterns that were talking. If that weren't true, you would have picked up on the man's statement that the company wanted to start a recycling program. He opened a door big enough to drive a truck through. You get your fanny over there and take that job. We can work on your unresolved issues when you are on easy street. So what have you got to say about that?

Jane: I think I must have been a nun in all my past lives.

The horoscope here was invaluable as usual. I saw Jane during her Jupiter return in Leo. Your own further study of Jane's chart will reveal the imbalance of the elements. Jane's life does not mean that every sacrifice people make is pointless or neurotic. When living by one's principles creates havoc in the life, unless I hear the person's last name is Ghandi, I'm going mining for hidden motives. In this instance, I rest my case.

To summarize, the model described in this chapter involves a *process* of

1) active communication with a client to
2) elicit a history
3) from which a storyline is identified that is
4) assumed to represent an inner pattern
5) formed in reaction to an earlier life experience and
6) manifested as a present-life situation,
7) the counterpart of which is identifiable in the horoscope,
8) setting up the interaction whereby the astrologer can work with the client to connect the relationship between the inner and outer life.

The fundamental *premise* of the model rests on the philosophy that the astrological symbols are impersonal archetypes that structure our collective inner worlds. Individual experiences script the dramas that manifest as our personal mythologies and our roles in them. The model is organized around this internal architecture. If this premise forms the basis of the astrologer's communication with clients, I have discovered it to be the effective and powerful utilization of the astrological system which we have always intuited was possible.

Donna Cunningham

Donna Cunningham has a master's degree in social work from Columbia University, and over 25 years of counseling experience in health care facilities, psychiatric clinics, and in alcoholism. She began her astrological practice in 1969 and has been certified as a professional by Professional Astrologers, Inc. and the American Federation of Astrologers. She has written hundreds of articles and ten well-received books, including *An Astrological Guide to Self-Awareness* and *Healing Pluto Problems.*

Convinced that training in counseling skills is the key to acceptance of astrology as a profession, Donna pioneered in developing a professional-level curriculum which she has taught in seminars around the world. She also conducts a private mentorship program by phone and mail, which helps advanced students and newly-professional astrologers make the transition into doing astrological consultations. Her studio-recorded training tapes cover such topics as conducting effective readings, counseling clients in crisis, working with children's charts, and communication skills. Her newest work, *The Consulting Astrologer's Guidebook* (Samuel Weiser), distills the experience of her dual background in astrology and psychotherapy. Donna lives in Port Townsend, Washington.

Donna Cunningham

Solving Problems: Key Questions to Ask Yourself and Your Client

 While some clients come for readings for self-knowledge or out of curiosity, in today's economy they have become rare. The majority come because of some problem they are wrestling with. They may feel overwhelmed or defeated by the major issue or issues in their lives, and they are looking outside themselves for answers.

We do them no favor when we couch our answers primarily in astrological terms—"The problem is Saturn, ma'am." Bombarding clients with jargon creates the impression that they can blame the planets for their difficulties. It even lets their families off the hook for a while. "It's not my husband's fault after all, it was Pluto all the time!" However, it leads to no real solutions, no improvement, only to fatalism.

When someone is used to looking within for the source of difficulties, a chart reading can be an important problem-solving tool. We can lead clients to explore their major issues through the insights the chart provides. In doing this, we can give them a more detached perspective and motivate them to take action to resolve the difficulties they face. In order for the session to provide a matrix for resolving issues, we need to hone our skills in identifying and working through problems. One productive problem-solving process consists of helping clients examine four key questions:

1) What is the problem?
2) What is your contribution to the problem?
3) What are your options?
4) Where can you turn for help?

In this chapter, we will learn how to help clients sort out these considerations. First, however, there are some questions to ask about the questions you ask.

Asking, Not Telling—The Need for Dialogue

Many astrologers are more accustomed to telling than to asking—to monologue rather than dialogue. An extreme example was an astrologer who gave a demonstration reading at a conference I attended. As he assured us he did in his private sessions, he conducted a one-hour, rapid-fire tap dance around the volunteer client's horoscope. Only at the end did he indicate that he would now accept a question or two from her. This was not astrological counseling, it was a performance. In no sense could it be considered problem-solving. Few of you would exclude the client in that fashion. However, a great many consultations are closer to a monologue than a dialogue. This style often arises out of a lack of understanding of the importance of asking the right questions and listening attentively to the answers.

One hurdle to getting the information needed for successful problem solving is the belief that we shouldn't have to ask any questions. We often buy into the public's belief that we should know everything from the chart. Yet, we have as much right to ask questions as any other professional. People wouldn't expect a doctor to know all about their illness if given only their lab results. They wouldn't demand that a lawyer draw up a mutually agreeable divorce settlement with no more than their financial statement.

When clients believe you have a crystal ball that will reveal the minutiae of their existence, you can gently or humorously disabuse them of that notion. When they fold their arms and challenge you to tell them all about themselves, it is rather simple to dazzle them with some of what the chart shows. Once they are convinced that you are bona fide, explain that they'll get more useful information if this is a conversation rather than a lecture.

Certainly, natal aspects and transits or progressions give you a wealth of useful information about clients and the conflicts they are experiencing. However, specific details of the situation and the evolutionary level of expression of aspects are not revealed. In a counseling session—and a chart reading certainly is a counseling session—we need details in order to be more helpful. Ask questions like these:

1) What, exactly, do you mean by that?

2) Could you give me an example?

3) Can you say more about that?

4) How often does that happen?

5) Is it worse sometimes than others?

6) What seems to make it better?

Those of you with some counseling background may see this list as elementary, but it may be helpful to those who haven't had the opportunity to study counseling formally. Since astrology lacks the institution of apprenticeship, one place where interviewing skills are honed, start by listening to the questions you ask clients. Note which ones are productive, and compare them to the ones that are unproductive. Ask yourself:

1) Are your questions open-ended, or do they only result in yes/no answers? (Open questions stimulate discussion.)

2) Are they leading questions, subtly guiding clients to give the answers you want or feel comfortable with?

3) Are your questions relevant to the client's issues or are you off on a tangent that is more interesting to you?

4) Are you convinced that your preconceived answers hold the solutions to the client's problems?

5) Do you believe you have the right to ask clients for details, or do you think the chart holds all answers?

6) Have you made the client comfortable with asking you questions about anything the chart shows?

Now I'm asking some leading questions of my own! However, self-questioning and self-awareness are crucial for astrologers. Without the capacity to step back and observe ourselves, we can easily impose our own values, judgments, and preconceptions onto clients' situations. The solution that arises would then be colored by our own experiences, rather than necessarily being the best one for them.

This is a good place to mention that, although I will pose dozens of questions in the following sections, they aren't meant to be used word for word. Rather, they are lines of questioning to pursue, with sensitivity to the personality of the individual you are addressing. Key Question #2, in particular (page 113), would almost never be spoken literally. Unless you were working with a truth-talking Sagittarius or a truly detached Aquarius, "What is your contribution to the problem?" might be too straight-shooting.

In dealing with a difficult relationship, for example, I'd probably say something like, "You know, we'd all like to believe that we're blameless in these conflicts. We're just innocent saints, and the other person is the villain. But the truth is, it takes two to tango, and sometimes we do things that contribute to the problem without really being aware of it. I wonder if we could take a look at your part in this."

Having defused the person's natural defensiveness, a productive discussion can ensue. The charts and composite can then be a reference point for discovering attitudes and traits the client brings to the relationship that contribute to the conflict.

Key Question #1: What Is The Problem?
Establishing Communication with the Client

In order to answer this, the foundation question, we must first assess whether we are listening, rather than doing a monologue, and whether the client is really opening up. Communication is rarer than we recognize. Most social conversation is designed to keep intimacy at bay, rather than to reveal what is under the surface. Even when people go for help, they generally conceal more than they reveal. In part, they do this because they want to look good and not be judged.

Another reason that people communicate little useful information is because they haven't the slightest idea how to convey what is bothering them. If they had a clear picture of the problem, they'd be halfway to solving it. Your first job is to clarify the issues.

Listen to the following opening of a chart session:

Astrologer: What do you want to discuss in this reading? What's going on for you now?

Client: Well, I'm worried about my marriage.

Astrologer: What seems to be the trouble?

Client: My husband and I aren't getting along.

Astrologer: That's not surprising, given that Uranus is crossing your Descendant. It will finish in about six months, so you should see some change by then.

Do you see that no meaningful information was communicated in this set of exchanges? The client's statements are vague—typically so. When she says that she and her husband aren't getting along, we don't know whether she means they are exchanging raised eyebrows and sighs or whether he has put her in the hospital twice with broken bones. By accepting a vague statement, you lose crucial information about the seriousness of the conflict and the ways it is being expressed.

The string of jargon from the astrologer at the end of the exchange also provides no information that can help the client—it only raises her anxiety level. The astrologer has moved too quickly into interpretation, perhaps due to anxiety about dealing with upsetting material. A more helpful track would have been, "What sorts of difficulties are the two of you experiencing?"

Granted, many clients feel reticent to talk about such private concerns. There may be shame or embarrassment when the fights are serious or when their sex life or finances are involved. In ordinary conversation, we are uncomfortable about prying into other's secrets, so we allow vague allusions and euphemisms to pass unchallenged.

As professionals, we must learn to put our own discomfort aside and also help clients to be comfortable. Sometimes merely acknowledging that they may be finding it hard to discuss such personal matters helps, as does reassurance that the session is confidential. If you live in a small town and work out of your home, the confusion over whether this is a social conversation or a professional consultation is intensified. You need to work harder to set a professional tone.

Chief Complaint versus Core Problem

A red herring on the trail of answering Question #1 is that clients will often *give symptoms rather than the real problem*. They may say they are depressed, when really the trouble is that their marriage is ending. They may express hopelessness about the future and lack of a will to live, when the true issue is unprocessed grief over the death of a loved one. They may complain of chronic fatigue, when the real problem is a life-style of relentless workaholism which has depleted body and soul.

In medicine, the presenting symptom is called the chief complaint. We would never want to minimize the symptom—the workaholic truly feels depleted, and the bereaved individual may really not want to go on living. However, if we accept such statements at face value and only address the symptom—if we never look to the core of the issue—then our recommendations and results will be also superficial. That's like putting bandages on tumors.

For instance, when presented with the complaint of chronic fatigue, you might be tempted to reply, "You're tired? Well, why not set aside a week or two to rest? You deserve it." All true, but anyone, including Mom, could tell the workaholic to take time off. Chronic fatigue sufferers, however, are often driven individuals who need a complete life-style overhaul in order to recover.

By analyzing the birth chart and transits, you can demonstrate the underlying attitudes, work patterns, and long range consequences of this life style. There is something about a reading—maybe the detachment it provides, maybe the divine dimension—which often enables clients to hear consequences and take them seriously. Further, astrological analysis can provide valuable information about the source of the attitudes and behaviors creating the workaholism. Finally, it can help in vocational planning, finding a way out of the pattern.

A number of people with chronic fatigue who have come for readings have had difficult outer planet transits to the 6th House. An outer planet transit to the 6th House can represent health difficulties when the person is unable or unwilling to change damaging work habits. Such once-in-a-lifetime transits, however, can also show new vocational directions, often a shift into a work that has more to do with the needs of the collective.

What Issue is the Problem Designed to Solve?

The question above almost merits being listed as a fifth key question. One of the teachings of *est* was, "Your problem is just a solution to another problem." That is to say, often the symptom, as distressing as it might be, *serves a valid purpose in the psyche.* Some dysfunctional traits are actually highly functional ones, once you untangle their true intent. They protect or excuse the sufferer from things that are even less pleasurable or more frightening.

You see this dynamic in some of the knotty, chronic financial problems people raise. When you analyze the situation carefully, you may find that lack of money is a way people often get out of things they don't want to do or are afraid to tackle. "I can't afford it," or, "I'd love to do that, but I just don't have the money," are excuses others are too polite to question.

There are, of course, people who have money troubles due to hardship, poor health, heavy family responsibilities, lack of marketable skills, or economic reversals beyond their control. There are others who value their art, their cause, or their spiritual path more than money and who willingly sacrifice toward these aims.

I'm not referring to these folks here, but instead to those who have what might be called a money neurosis. They often have good potential, good health, and minimal family responsibilities. Yet, they never establish financial security and may even be economically dependent over the long haul. They appear to suffer greatly over their poverty, on a conscious level. Unconsciously, failure serves an important purpose, *so success would be threatening.*

You see this pattern often in birth charts with a strong 8th House or with outer planets in the 2nd. Looking closely, you often find some very murky motives behind the person's seeming hopelessness and helplessness. With Pluto in the 2nd, for instance, financial dependency may be a means to manipulate and control a partner or family members. Given this seeming helplessness, they then feel obliged to support the native or not to expect much in the way of give and take. Alternately, there may be a revenge motif, wherein the person fails in order to spite the parents, mate, or other potent figures.

People who need to control or extract vengeance through money don't readily relinquish this pattern. Nor will they necessarily thank you for blowing their cover. You may, in fact, heartily regret it! Do not enter unless invited. The client may invite you in, however, at a point where a critical transit or progression has brought the situation to a head and given a shove in the direction of change.

This is one of several reasons it is important to focus on clients' expressed concerns, rather than by jumping in with all the problems you detect. You may regard a particular life-style or pattern of behavior as unhealthy. If it is not a problem to the client, it is not your business, and your judgements will be resented. Suppose you see difficult Moon aspects in a man's chart and conclude that he has serious, unresolved issues with his mother. Unless you can demonstrate that these issues are related to the concerns he is raising, leave it alone. If, however, he is asking about conflicts in his relationship with his wife, then those aspects are relevant and can be productively addressed.

The tendency for the symptom to be an unconscious effort to resolve another, deeper issue is particularly true of chronic physical ailments—generally seen in the 1st or 12th House, rather than the 6th. (As suggested earlier, illnesses connected with the 6th may be related to life-work crises.) I am often impressed with how the body says *no* for us when we can not. Friends, partners, relatives, coworkers, and society as a whole will sympathize if you're too ill to carry out a particular function, but may judge you if you just say no. Thus, those who are uncomfortable with self-assertiveness may develop psychosomatic symptoms or flareups of physical ailments when they can't refuse an intolerable demand.

People with important Virgo and Pisces placements are especially prone to sacrificing the body in this way. One woman with Mars conjunct Neptune in Virgo in the 1st House contracted genital herpes. By conscientiously attending to such Virgo concerns as incessant cleanliness and a strict dietary regimen, she was able to keep outbreaks to a minimum. It was almost guaranteed, however, that if she started going out with someone, and the relationship was on the verge of becoming intimate, she would have a painful and protracted outbreak.

In the consultation, I helped her to see that her body was protecting her from intimate contact which some part of her found anxiety-producing. True to form, with Mars and Neptune in the 1st House, sexuality brought up fear of boundary invasion. It also evoked anger toward men, related to her alcoholic father. She was able to see that healing her wounding in these areas, especially the after-effects of her father's alcoholism, was crucial to changing this health and relationship pattern.

I also suspected, as reconfirmed by additional elements in the chart, that she might have been sexually abused, and that early violation might be one psychological factor in the outbreaks. However, I dropped the inquiry after gentle probing brought a flurry of alarm on the client's part.

DC: I also wonder, given this chart aspect, whether there weren't some unfortunate early experiences with sexuality.

Client, agitated: Well, um, maybe. Do you think Chinese herbs would help me heal the herpes?

It was enough that she had agreed to go into healing work to deal with her father issues. Any sexual abuse would be likely to surface and to be more appropriately dealt with in ongoing counseling, where the bond with the healer or therapist would provide a safe space to do the work. There was no need to press her to confront it in our session—that would be an additional violation.

When a chronic health problem or other limiting condition is addressed, ask yourself what purpose the problem may be serving. Suppose a young mother with several small children comes to you with a complaint of severe menstrual cramps and PMS, starting after the birth of the first child. She has the Moon in Aries squared by Mars in Cancer. If ever there were a signature of PMS, that is one! However, it doesn't solve anything to simply give the astrological interpretation. She could then conclude that her PMS is just something to live through until menopause—which she projects will probably be hellish, too!

What underlying issues does this square suggest that might not only clarify the pain and its purpose but also lead to some solutions? Conflict between the lunar and martian functions are seen three ways here: the Moon is in Mars' sign, Mars is in the Moon's sign, and the Moon and Mars are square. Obviously, some anger about nurturing and about the feminine roles of wife and mother can be suspected.

In getting more details, you may find that her one week a month in bed with cramps is her only time off from the demands of her family. She even gets a little nurturing herself during that time from her husband and female relatives. The physical suffering is a high price to pay, but it does serve a purpose. If you took the symptom away, what would you replace it with?

Unless another means of getting time away from the role she finds so frustrating is found, there appears to be little incentive for the body to heal itself. Discussing the symptom in terms of the underlying issues and exploring other possibilities can be the fulcrum for a change in lifestyle. Perhaps this is a woman who would be happier working and having a live-in *au pair* to handle the housework and grittier aspects of child care. You'd want to explore the possibilities for this type of arrangement or others which would relieve her of the lunar roles she is finding so intolerable.

As you can see, the presenting symptom often plays a complex role in the unconscious. Thus, your first task may be to redefine the problem. Use your knowledge of the chart to uncover the deeper issues the symptoms represent. Such issues have generally been unresolved because they are difficult, ones which may require a radical change in lifestyle or behavior, and because change is hard for most of us.

Discovering the connection between the painful symptom and deeper life issues is often an important revelation to the person in front of you. Usually neither the symptom nor the underlying issue is outside the person's awareness. However, the realization that the unaddressed issue is one cause of the symptom that is causing so much suffering can be a turning point. The reading becomes a cleansing moment which galvanizes the motivation to face and heal the underlying issues. You then need to refocus the problem-solving efforts to explore solutions for those issues.

Key Question # 2:
What Is Your Contribution to the Problem?

Few of us like to face our own contribution to our toughest problems. Thus, this second line of questioning needs to be pursued with compassion, so that the client doesn't feel judged or patronized. Self-awareness is a constant responsibility for the consulting astrologer. Here, we need to be aware of any attitudes within ourselves of blaming the client for the problem. Blaming the victim is a common human trait, and helping professionals are far from immune to the practice. Work to become aware of when you are doing it, because it is humiliating for the client, as well as counterproductive in the search for solutions.

Before you succumb to the temptation of correcting a client, summon to consciousness one of your own self-defeating patterns. Remember one of the times you felt thoroughly defeated by it. Then, you are coming from a place of empathy and peership—"I've been there too"—rather than from arrogance. Engage in this part of the problem-solving process with your receptive planets (the Moon, Venus, and Neptune), rather than the conquering ones (the Sun, Mars, and Jupiter.) Later, it may be appropriate to suggest solutions based on coping skills you have developed in the course of living. However, the first order of business is to be able to identify, if not with the exact problem, at least with the experience of feeling defeated.

If the question of the client's contribution to the situation is handled well, it can be a source of rich insight as well as leading to a direction for change. When done gently, the astrologer can call people on their behavior in a way no one in the situation can.

If we do it lovingly, we can tell people things their best friends wouldn't, given the detachment the horoscope provides. For instance, one aggressive New Age practitioner, an Aquarius/ Aries combination with some knowledge of astrology, was able to see that her pushiness could be turning business away when I demonstrated it through the chart. Humor can also be a source of self-confrontation for the client. However, make it heart-centered humor, laughing with rather than at the person.

The Red Herring of Blame

Another red herring on the path to fuller understanding is placing the blame outside oneself. Where someone else is involved, clients often present a litany of complaints about how the other party has been abusive, exploitive, insensitive, or deceptive. The grievance may have gone on for years, while the long-suffering client has bent over backwards to make Mom, spouse, child, or boss happy. It is easy for helping professionals, astrologers included, to make the mistake of viewing the sainted client as the victim and the other party as the bad guy. Fortunately, as a young social worker, I was able to meet enough of the so-called villains first hand to know that clients are rarely as blameless or the abuse as unprovoked as their stories would have you believe.

We should not allow clients to remain stuck in blaming others or the planets for their problems. Blaming can be a comforting—and exceedingly human—response, but it is only a temporary solution. The trouble is that blaming is a passive response and leads to the conclusion that nothing can be done. When the fault is apparently outside yourself—it's the boss, your mate, or Neptune—then you are powerless to alter the situation. You can't be expected to do anything about it, but you also stew ineffectively.

That same anger can be channeled usefully into change. After all, Mars is anger, but it is also action. Generally, anger is a useful signal that some action is required. Anger is uncomfortable, but can serve as motivation to change. Blame undercuts motivation and diverts anger into the more passive response of frustration. We disempower clients when our language or implied belief in the power of the planets allows them to blame their horoscopes. While momentarily gratifying, blaming the stars, the people in their lives—or even themselves—is no solution.

Four Ways Clients May Contribute to the Problem

Faced with the question of how they might be contributing, clients often genuinely don't have a clue. They may give such saintly-sounding answers as, "Oh, I guess it's my fault for being so good to him," or, "I'm just too easy-going." Such responses are face-saving, but not productive of solutions.

The chart, however, is a rich source of clues to the part clients play in the situation. Remember that they are likely to be on their best behavior with you, so that you'll have a good opinion of them. You will be more able to tell what they are actually contributing by analyzing the houses and planets involved. We are different at work than at home or with relatives than with love interests, and the chart reflects those differences. Here is where astrology has a major advantage over other counseling modalities. The traditional counselor may take months to penetrate the mask of good behavior.

As the chart can illuminate, there are four major ways people contribute to chronic conditions that limit their lives and happiness: attitudes, projections, perpetrations, and choices. Questions to help you sort out these factors are:

1) What attitudes and beliefs underly and contribute to the dysfunction?

2) In what ways does the client project these attitudes and beliefs onto the outer world, recreating the problem pattern?

3) What perpetrations are involved—i.e., how does the client's behavior evoke problematic interactions?

4) What mistaken choices is the client making that result in these unwanted consequences?

In this series, one question usually leads to the next in an orderly progression. For example, by discovering the underlying attitudes, it is easier to see how outer reality is perceived according to core beliefs. Those core beliefs attract experiences which recreate the beliefs, according to the principles of metaphysics. Let's explore how these factors can contribute to the problem and how changing them can lead to healthier solutions.

Very often, the problem is not so much in the situation as in our attitudes toward it. One older couple in a retirement community may be delighted to be among peers and appreciative of the conveniences the setting provides. Another couple in the very same development may be miserable, feeling isolated from family and society, and resentful of this confirmation that they are growing old. One vice president may feel fortunate and grateful for the same job that leaves another vice president in the corporation feeling dead-ended. In both cases, the situation is the same or similar, *but the emotional experience is totally different.*

The second couple and the second vice president regard their situation as a problem. Their *attitudes* are making them miserable. Furthermore, those attitudes go on to create further misery, as people act out their frustrations or negative beliefs on others in their living or work situations. An attitude adjustment can sometimes be all that is needed to make a major difference in the comfort level for all concerned.

As an outsider with some perceived authority, you can be a cosmic chiropractor, providing the needed attitude adjustment. One method is the technique called reframing in Neurolinguistic Programming (familiarly called NLP). In reframing, you shake up the client's perceptions of reality by giving an entirely different view of the same situation. If done effectively, it produces a deep change in the client's perceptions, behavior, and comfort level. The highly readable material in all of the books about NLP can enhance your counseling skills. I would especially recommend *Reframing,* by Richard Bandler and John Grinder. (Real People Press, Moave, UT: 1982.)

To give an example of reframing, I once did a reading for a New Age healer, an inveterate rescuer with a pattern of befriending troubled people and becoming drained by their needs. She had Pluto in the 11th squared by Venus in Taurus in the 7th. She enumerated her husband's good qualities and felt very sure of his love. However, she complained bitterly that he never seemed interested in the insights, wisdom, and healing tools her clients and friends valued so much.

DC: You're a very lucky woman, to have a husband like him.

Client: HUH? What do you mean?

DC: Well, your friends and your clients want you around for what you do for them. You have to be wise, you have to be strong, you have to be caring. You have to be the healer all the time. But he doesn't need you to do any of that for him. He just loves you for who you are.

Client: (Silent, stunned.) I never thought of it that way! You're right, I *am* lucky.

In the person with a strong Pluto, an attitude of contempt often plays a powerful role in the areas of life governed by Pluto's house and aspects. Where present, this mordantly superior attitude arises from the existential isolation Plutonians feel, but also creates further isolation. The contempt may or may not be openly expressed, but even when it is unspoken, the targets of this attitude feel it keenly and resent it. Their natural reaction to being treated this way is to shun the Plutonian or to strike back, thereby creating still more alienation and mistrust.

For instance, I've worked with many clients with Pluto in the 10th—the closer to the Midheaven, the stronger the pattern. They often come in when something is transiting that natal position, outraged at what the powers that may be at work are doing to them. They fear that current politics on the job may result in them being scapegoated or getting fired. They want to know if they should accept an offer of a new job or stay where they are.

I sometimes shock them by replying, "It doesn't matter." After they finish spluttering, I explain that the basic issue is their relationships with authority figures, and if that doesn't change, the new job will wind up just like the current one. They will take the same attitudes and behaviors with them to the next job, alienate the new boss, and wind up creating the same nightmare all over again.

I ask them if they do or don't have a basic contempt toward their bosses. They can confess to the fact that they do, but justify it with as many examples as I can bear to hear of how incredibly stupid and incompetent their superiors are. We track it back and generally discover that incompetent supervisors have been their sad lot in life for as long as they can remember.

At that point, I might tell them that even if Albert Einstein himself were their boss, they would create the same pattern on the job. Their innate contempt for authority figures would be felt, would make old Albert decide to watch them very closely because of the attitude problem, and would ultimately wind up causing them to get scapegoated, betrayed, or fired. Plutonians generally don't operate in denial, so they are often able to concede the point and even to find it wryly funny. They are then open to looking at where it all began, in the twisted power relationships with their earliest authority figures, Mom and Dad.

Attitudes also create actions. Our belief systems guide our behavior. If we believe that people won't accept us, we act in ways that create a lack of acceptance. If we believe we will fail at a job interview, that lack of confidence makes us come across as less desirable candidates than interviewees who believe they will succeed. If we are suspicious and mistrustful of others, those constant suspicions can ultimately make the others so resentful that they betray us. If we believe that we will inevitably have to shoulder most of the responsibility for the family or the workload on the job, sure enough, we wind up having to shoulder most of it. These are metaphysical principles, but there is nothing intangible about the ways we make things work out just the way we believe they will. There are specific, concrete behaviors that make our beliefs a reality, and you can help clients examine what they are.

More destructive actions that arise out of attitudes and beliefs are called perpetrations. Often they are cases of doing unto others *before* they do unto you. Those who have studied Chiron often say that where Chiron is in the chart, we have suffered a wounding. Sheila Belanger's further insight is that, where we are wounded, we unconsciously wound others, through the shadow side of the Chiron sign. With Chiron in water signs, she often finds that the wounding is of the boundaries, especially the emotional ones. These people, in turn, may cause harm by not respecting other's boundaries. This is a productive insight about Chiron, but might be said of the effects of other hard outer planet aspects as well.

A final way people contribute to their own problems is in the mistaken choices they make. One gay client had Venus in Aries in the 1st House squaring Mars in Cancer in the 4th. He could be the Don Juan, compulsively chasing men he met in impersonal situations. Once he met someone, his Mars in Cancer made him want a stay-at-home, fully monogamous relationship. Unfortunately, the men he met this way were there strictly for the chase and did not want a commitment. He became increasingly embittered about men and love, as well as more and more reclusive. When we analyzed the aspect, he could see that his choices were the problem and that he was unlikely to meet anyone in bars who was as much of a homebody as he was. He needed to find another way to meet men and also needed to select possible partners through the Cancerian side of himself rather than the Arian.

Taking clients through an examination of the various ways they contribute to their own difficulties can be helpful. By examining how their own beliefs, attitudes, actions and choices contribute to their persistent difficulties, they stop feeling so powerless and instead feel empowered to change. When done in a non-judgmental way, this process can be a great service.

Key Question #3: What Are Your Options? The Consequences of Lack of Choice

Many clients who are enmeshed in difficult situations don't even know they *have* options. They see the situation as set in stone and haven't even considered other ways of handling it. Their thinking has become rigid, being a conglomerate of values and operating principles they learned from their parents and other influential elders, from the church, or from the way things were done 20 to 40 years ago. (You see this rigidity especially in the fixed signs or earth signs.)

When those who are in painful and overwhelming circumstances believe there are no options, their frustration and depression make life seem very bleak. With no sense of having a choice, resentment and bitterness can poison their attitudes toward those involved, toward life, and even toward God.

For instance, those with strong 6th House placements are often deeply involved in work as a gratification in its own right. Should the work become stale and unrewarding, especially if the person feels trapped in it due to other responsibilities, the frustration can result in health problems. Thus, with a 6th House transit or a transit to 6th House planets, ask how the client is *feeling* about the job. If it is stagnant or otherwise repugnant, you can make an important contribution by a detailed exploration of the client's options for changing jobs or careers. The Llewellyn anthology,

How to Use Vocational Astrology for Success in the Workplace, can help you counsel those who need vocational planning. (Tyl, Noel, editor, Llewellyn's New World Astrology Series, Llewellyn Publications, 1992.)

Likewise, under Uranus transits to key natal positions, a surge of desire for freedom and newness creates frustration over feeling stuck. People can wind up making explosive changes, whether through their own drastic actions or because they magnetize catalytic events from outside, such as accidents. With Pluto or Neptune transits, they may implode rather than explode when they feel so trapped in a hopeless life path that they seek a way out through self-destructive actions.

As you can see, exploring the question, "What are your options?" is more than an intellectual exercise. It can literally be life-saving, if the problem is chronic enough or gruelling enough. When you show clients a way out of despair, you make an important contribution to their lives.

Naturally, the majority of clients are not going to present you with such disparate situations. Life hasn't dealt everyone such a bad hand of cards. Still, even those who have been blessed get stuck sometimes and need a fresh perspective. Under outer planet transits to key points, they may even undergo a dark night of the soul, in which they feel trapped.

Generating New Approaches and Solutions

A chart reading at such times can be an opportunity to consider alternatives. Being outside the situation, the astrologer can see with fresh eyes and can suggest additional courses of action. Encourage clients to brainstorm, using their wildest imagination. There are any number of approaches to a given task. People become set in their ways and often don't even dream of other possibilities. A creative leap can occur in the reading, leaving clients with zest to tackle those limitations.

Suppose you have a session with a young mother who feels trapped at home. She wants more money and more outlets for her capabilities. Refer to the 2nd House for overlooked skills and resources that can enable her to make money on the side. Perhaps she has Mercury in the 2nd, which suggests a wide variety of ways to earn extra cash. This is a resourceful individual who has many talents related to either words or hands or both, and who can easily pick up new skills as well. Explore what those skills might be and how to pursue them part-time or free-lance. If she needs child care in order to pursue her chosen sideline (or, more likely, sidelines), perhaps she can organize a group of mothers in her neighborhood to exchange babysitting services.

Creative people often come to astrologers, and a chief complaint is that they don't have time to pursue their talents. People with Neptune in the 2nd, 6th, or 10th are especially likely candidates. They seethe with frustration at the necessity for earning a living, feeling it keeps them from pursuing their divine gifts. Often an attitude shift is the first order of business.

A common erroneous attitude is that not having a job will increase one's creative output. One writer felt hampered by working full time, leaving only the weekends to write. When he was finally able to switch to a three-day-a-week job, he found that he only produced the same amount of words per week as he used to on the weekend. He wasted the rest of the time daydreaming, staring at the computer screen, watching mindless television programs, and beating up on himself for not writing.

Committed writers, painters, and other artists who must work or who have family responsibilities manage to make time for their talents. They may get up at 5:30 A.M. for a quiet, uninterrupted hour or two of work, or may set the alarm for 2:00 A.M., work for two hours, and then go back to sleep. Mothers may make agreements with their children's devoted grandparents—or their best friends—to babysit so they can gain one cherished afternoon a week to pursue their gift. Time that hard won is rarely wasted. Time spent washing dishes or in commuting is also time to muse on the next painting, poem, or photograph to be developed.

Sometimes, simply questioning a particular mode of operation stimulates the client's thinking. You can help by asking questions like the following:

1) Why is it done that way?

2) Is there another way to do it?

3) Can the task be broken down into manageable pieces?

4) Can you do less—or more—of it?

5) What would happen if it were postponed?

6) What would happen if it weren't done at all?

7) Does your (boss, group, family) really need and want you to do it?

8) Can others take on that responsibility?

9) Can someone else take on part of the job?

10) Can you organize your time differently?

11) Can you set some new priorities?

Inquiries like these can shock and even annoy clients who are locked into rigid thinking. Where they have assigned moral judgments to fulfilling what they see as their duty, they may not be able to contemplate other ways of operating. If the questioning is done kindly rather than with a superior (read Jupiterian) attitude, it can be a benign shakeup. The client may leave saying, "You've given me a lot to think about."

Having uncovered a variety of options, it is not up to us to recommend one course of action over another. We cannot know the totality of the picture and what is best for everyone involved. Neither are we there to approve or disapprove of clients' choices. That would be to impose our own values, which are no more than a set of personal prejudices.

Looking at the Consequences of Various Options

The process of considering options includes thinking through possible consequences. Ask questions like these:

1) Which of these options do you favor?

2) What would be involved in implementing that option?

3) Do you have the skills/resources you need to do that?

4) How would that choice affect others close to you?

5) What would be the best possible outcome of that choice?

6) What could go wrong? How could you prevent it?

7) What would be the long-term result of that choice?

8) What impact would it have on your other priorities?

9) Do any other options have more favorable results?

Allow clients to do their own thinking, but mention any major effects they miss. Sometimes it is obvious that the option the client is favoring is unwise. The fire signs are especially prone to impulsive decisions, without thought for repercussions. It then becomes part of our job to point out aftermaths of an unwise choice.

One working class double Aries was having a severe family crisis. When asked to consider solutions, she replied that she was thinking about killing the brother who was causing the trouble. It became apparent that she was quite serious—she had the means, motive, and opportunity. She knew enough astrology, in a naive and superstitious way, that her chart could be used as a deterrent. I pointed out the long, difficult 9th and 12th house transits coming up, which suggested she would go to jail for a very long time if she went through with her decision.

Seldom do I invoke the authority of the planets in this way, but it seemed to straighten her up. Invoking my personal authority would have been cause for hotheaded rebelliousness, but the detachment the chart lent was helpful. Few of our clients seriously consider murder as a viable solution. However, they can be blind to the aftermaths of less drastic decisions.

Key Question #4: Where Can You Turn for Help?

When it appears that the client can not resolve the issue without help, the first line of inquiry would be about supports in the client's immediate environment: partner, family, friends or perhaps church. The chart will, of course, give some clues to relationships in those areas. You would look at what might be called the support houses: 3rd for siblings or other relatives, 11th for friends, and 7th for partnership. You would also look for Jupiter's position in the natal chart and by transit, as well as transiting and natal trines and sextiles. The chart can give you hints about these areas, but as to the ability or willingness of actual people involved to be helpful, you would have to ask the client. Given a chronic pattern, you would also want to find out the history of past efforts to solve the problem.

Much of the time, clients have no idea where to turn for help—they turned, after all, to you for that. Thus, part of being a good astrological counselor is becoming familiar with community resources. None of us can meet all the needs clients bring us, even when we have training in therapy. When we have no idea what kinds of help there are, both we and our clients can go away from the chart reading feeling overwhelmed. When we can suggest effective sources of healing, we are more convinced the client can get out of the problem, and we convey that to the client in an empowering way.

Today, there are a large number of modes of therapy, healing, and self-help. The effective astrological consultant becomes familiar with various healing methods. Can you answer the following questions?

1) What kinds of therapy and healing are available here?

2) How, exactly, does the method work?

3) What kinds of people or issues does it help most?

4) What is involved in terms of pain, time, cost, and gain?

5) Who, in the community does it well?

Often the best way to learn the answers to such questions is by first-hand experience. Find out who is out there through the newspapers, New Age papers, yellow pages, or by asking around. When you ask clients where they've gone for help in the past, their experiences can also be valuable clues as to what is available and what actually happens to people who use these services.

It would be good to meet the practitioners and, wherever possible, to have sessions. (Just because they sound nice and know the jargon over the phone doesn't mean they are capable.) Some are happy to do trades, with the side benefit that each of you now knows what the other does, in order to make referrals. Each of you also gets another opportunity for more self-knowledge and healing.

In addition to the healers and therapists in your area, it is useful to have a working knowledge of government and private social agencies that meet the needs of people with serious financial, social, or medical difficulties. Suppose your client has an aging parent who is becoming infirm and forgetful? Where is homemaker help available, and who pays for it? Suppose a couple comes to you when they haven't been able to have a child, and you don't see pregnancy in the chart. Do you know where they might look into adoption?

Where would you get information like this? Many communities have directories of local social service agencies, giving key personnel and describing their services. Check the library for such a directory. Look in the yellow pages for possibilities. Keep a clipping file of articles published in the local paper. Once you begin to see information of this sort as part of your job description, you'll be surprised at the news features, television documentaries, and word of mouth information that you quickly accumulate.

Is keeping a resource file rather far afield from the way you envisioned practicing astrology? Working with live clients isn't all T-squares and asteroids, it is experiencing the realities of clients' situations in an empathic way. It means looking for both insights and solutions for the problems that have them stumped. Astrology isn't the solution to the clients' problems, even though it's a source of deep insight. One of the limitations of both psychotherapy and astrology is that insight alone rarely solves the problem.

Knowing the resources that can support your clients in working through the wealth of new insights gained from the chart reading can be considered a professional responsibility. If you can suggest resources that help clients grow, you are doing a finer form of service. Clients who are helped in this way are far more likely to come back and to refer others than clients who leave the session without a clue as to where to turn. Therefore, knowing local resources is not just good practice, it is good business!

Karen M. Hamaker-Zondag

As a Jungian analyst should be, Karen Hamaker-Zondag was led to astrology, to the link between astrology and Jungian psychology, through a series of dreams. These dreams and her intense study of psychology inspired the first volumes in her output of 11 books on all facets of astrology. These books have been translated from Dutch into English, Spanish, Portuguese, German, French, and Hebrew.

Karen has two degrees from the University in Amsterdam, Holland.

In 1980, Karen opened an astrology school with a four-year professional curriculum, named Stichting Achernar. She has well over 120 pupils in the program! In 1987, she found another school, Stichting Odrerir, for the teaching of Jungian psychology, presently with 90 pupils. Additionally, Karen produces a quarterly astrological journal, *Symbolon*, with high-level educational articles for the Dutch astrology community.

Karen is a popular lecturer throughout many countries, including the United States (UAC). She, her husband, and two children live in Amsterdam.

Karen M. Hamaker-Zondag

When the Client Avoids the Issue

 You've prepared the client's chart very well and now you're busy explaining it in comprehensive terms, but the client doesn't react as you expected or hoped: he or she seems to talk around the "hot" subject and to avoid the important issues. You are looking for a different opening to explain things in another way, but again you realize the message doesn't get through. What can you do?

We tend to put the blame for blockages or shyness on the client, or even worse: on denial, and, of course, very often there are denying or shy clients. Nonetheless, during a consultation, there is much more happening than we are conscious of: the client's subtle and unconscious processes, and, as well, the way in which we solve the problem and deal with the client's avoidance. This can have an enormous influence on the course of the session. A consultation is an alchemical process, as it were, during which both the client and the astrologer play a certain role and change in their own way.

- If a client shows avoidance behavior, we have to look at the situation from two sides:

  a. What exactly does the client do and how does he react, and:

  b. What exactly is "the issue," according to the astrologer, and why?

Answering the last question, astrologers like to justify their point of view with astrological reasoning: "Just look, how many conflicting aspects Pluto is making here!" or the like. But, in a deeper sense, that's not really the point. The question behind this remark is, why does the astrologer find it so important? Why does the astrologer make an issue of this and not, for example, the apparently beautiful trines Venus is making? Let's face it, the laziness coming out of those aspects might just as well be a problem in the client's life. So the choice the astrologer makes from among several possible "sore spots" is as important as any avoidance behavior of the client. Have ten different astrologers do your chart and you will get ten different interpretations. Of course, there will be a lot of similarities, but the accents and the questions that will actually be put on the table will differ considerably from one astrologer to the other. That is why the question "What to do when the client avoids the issue?" can only be answered satisfactorily *if we closely examine the astrologer as well as the client.*

The Astrologer and the Anorexic Patient.

Chart 1 belongs to a female astrologer, who has been practicing for many years. (The time of birth stems from the official birth register, while she claims being born seven and one-half minutes earlier.) She has a very individual look on life and strongly promotes the development of human spirituality. Wherever possible, she tries to stimulate a healthy lifestyle in people, and she has always given a lot of lectures and courses. Her experiences, ideas, and points of view have led her to an outlook on life that she strongly believes in and that is almost religious for her. She is convinced that she is helping people and not doing any harm. Because she has so much confidence in being right, she has for many years not been questioning her opinions and ideas at all.

Chart 2 (page 131) belongs to a patient with anorexia who died of her illness. The astrologer (chart 1) interpreted Saturn in the 12th as karma manifesting in the stomach and Neptune in the 4th as a degeneration-process in the ancestral line. The astrologer regarded the "diet" of the anorexic woman as some kind of fasting, which would induce a strong inner cleansing. This in turn would, in her point of view, dramatically speed up the release of old karma. When transiting Saturn conjuncted her Moon and then squared her Sun, the anorexic woman, who was already thin as a stick, got skin rashes, diarrhea and heart problems. According to the astrologer, all the old dirt, including that of the ancestors, was now being thrown out. "Everything drove her toward redemption," the astrologer wrote. The woman died at 29 years of age.

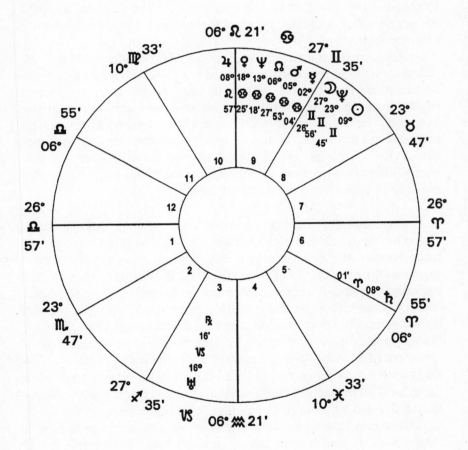

Chart 1
Astrologer
May 31, 1908, 3:39:04 P.M. GMT
Huizen, Netherlands
52N18 5E14
Placidus Houses

Just suppose the anorexic patient had not seen herself somehow in the interpretation of the astrologer, and had protested against it. The astrologer, having no bad intentions, would have been convinced that the young woman was talking around the problem, evading the issue. She would probably have done her utmost to convince the woman "for her own good." Note that the astrologer's Jupiter conjuncts her MC: a strong position, which is very helpful in getting across your own point of view. The disadvantage of this position is that you tend to close your ears to others once you have chosen your conviction: being right can become too important.

Also, in the astrologer's chart, we find a Moon-Pluto conjunction. If these two components of the psyche have been developed in an unbalanced way, one may easily tend to project negative images onto femininity or females, sometimes to the extreme. The anorexic woman's own Moon squares Pluto, so she provides a kind of projection screen for the astrologer's conjunction. If the astrologer is not completely aware of all facets of this Moon-Pluto conjunction, every client with a Moon-Pluto contact is liable to be a victim of her projection.

• An astrologer, like every human being, always looks through his or her own colored glasses. Despite all good intentions, you'll have to face the mirror eventually. The psychological process responsible for this is called projection: that which lives in our unconscious and which we have not yet recognized or accepted as part of ourselves, will be projected onto others. In other words, if we pretend to be all mildness and understanding, the opposing stance of harshness and suspicion has been suppressed. If one is unaware of possibly being harsh or mistrusting in certain situations, one easily tends to see these attitudes in others, to project them, and in projecting those unconscious attributes onto others, they will be exaggerated. The person who happens to be the "projection screen" seems to show those attributes in an obvious and strong way. In reality, this person usually has only a small bit of those qualities someone projects. The painful part for every well-meaning human, and thus also for the honest astrologer, is that one really is not aware of what is going on, and, of course with best intentions, one runs the risk of seeing totally wrong characteristics in people.

• Reading a chart is no exception to this. If, as an astrologer, you haven't worked through the position of power you have with your client—which is a reality, let's face it—and if you refuse to acknowledge this part of your relationship, you will tend, without realizing it, *to project serious power struggles onto the planet Pluto.* Certainly it can work that way, but, in essence, Pluto is different than that. Now, if you get a client with a dominant Pluto in his or her chart, you may not even realize how suspicious you tend to be,

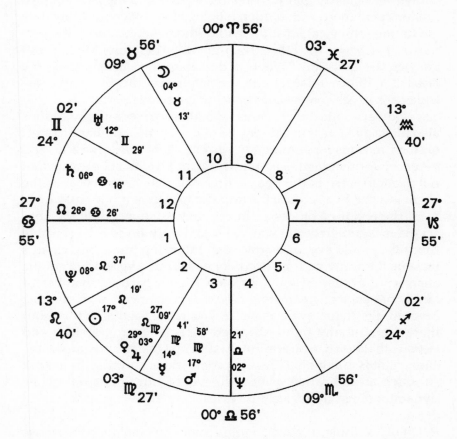

Chart 2
Anorexia
Aug. 10, 1944, 4:30 A.M. DST
Amsterdam, Netherlands
52N22   4E54
Placidus Houses

because you feel the client might be some kind of power-junkie. Unknowingly, *you project your own problem* (your attitude toward power) onto one of the chart's factors and then leave the problem with the client. Again, all this happens in the full conviction that you're doing your work as honestly and well as possible.

• Guggenbühl has written about this trap, which is waiting for all of us, in his book, *Power in the Helping Professions.* His research shows very clearly that the dreams of people in the helping professions deal more with hidden longings for power, the more they try to push things against the will of their clients, under the pretense of it being for "their own good." Therefore, we can not answer the question "What to do when the client avoids the issue?" without relating this question specifically to the astrologer's psyche (especially to the unconscious part).

However, the unconscious with all its drives and projections also plays a big part in the psyche of our clients and has an effect on their reasons for coming to you. The client may give any kind of reason for making the appointment, but we must be aware that not in every case is this the real reason. This is not because the client is a liar, but because the impulse to ask for advice may have been the result of processes in the unconscious, while the conscious is completely unaware of it and only finds it "a sensible thing to go and see an astrologer." Inquiring about my client's reasons for applying for a horoscope reading, I very often get the answer: "I'm just curious" or "My friend/partner/member of family has such an interesting tape with a character analysis on it. I would like to have one as well." When they arrive, it turns out there are so many tightly focused aspects in progressions and transits that you can be absolutely sure that inside and around the client a lot is going on. After all, progressions and transits are not so much an indication of outside events, but rather reflect the dynamics of psychological processes.

• For example, if an Aquarian comes to consult you, whose motive is "Astrology puts things into such logical order, and I would like to have that experience" and if, on top of that, transiting Pluto is squaring his Sun at the same time, you can say one thing for sure: there is a lot of inner agitation. Pluto symbolizes the inner mechanism of bringing shadow-aspects and rejected issues to the surface. Squaring the Sun, it can easily undermine one's sense of identity, possibly in form of a crisis. In a positive sense, this is an aspect of rebirth with new insights about one's self; in the negative sense, it signifies a time full of confrontations with one's being and with the outside world.

• When so much is going on within a person, there is automatically a greater sensitivity for matters of the psyche. Astrology is one of those matters. As a result, this Aquarian, if you will, becomes more intrigued with his own horoscope. In all honesty, the client can say "I simply thought it would be nice and I was very curious," but the *real* reason behind this is the need for new orientation in times of inner trouble. The astrologer can play an important part in becoming aware of those inner processes, providing some insights on how best to deal with them. *If then the client denies these issues,* the astrologer confronts the challenge of how to make things clear.

• The same applies to occasions where clients do come up with a specific question. In most cases, the question is related to a problem, so it appears that the client is well aware of the real motive for seeking an astrological appointment, but it isn't always so. Of course, the specific question may be the right one, but often, there is *another* question behind the one that has been asked. Here, the unconscious again plays an important part. If, for example, someone asks you "Can you see whether I will find another job?" and you see that transiting Uranus is crossing this person's MC, then there is a good chance of some deeper process going on. Although, as a *visible* manifestation of Uranus transiting the MC, you may change your employment or even get fired, the *real* question Uranus is confronting you with is "Just how far can you express your individuality in the work you've been doing up to now? Don't you need to dig into new inner resources? Isn't it time to try something completely different? Do you dare to walk on unknown paths?" All of *these* questions express Uranian themes: individuality, originality, and renewal.

There is a good chance of the client asking the wrong question, because for the psyche it is not important whether he or she will find work again. What matters to the psyche is whether the client starts looking for some type of work that really suits his or her character. If the client, for whatever reason, is afraid of renewal, this could turn into a difficult confrontation, so denial of the underlying issue occurs as a self-protection.

In relating to the client, during which the unconscious of both people involved plays a part, the astrologer has several instruments at his disposal to find out what is going on inside the client and how the client will tend to deal with it. We can organize our instruments into two categories: the technical ones, which use the tools of astrology, and the psychological ones, i.e., those having to do with counselling techniques.

The technical instruments are: 1) The birth chart, 2) Progressions, transits, solar return and other prognostic techniques; and 3) The consultation chart.

The psychological instruments I will refer to here are indirect signals, and alertness for defense mechanisms in the client.

The Birth Chart.

Every horoscope is a reflection of the situation in the heavens at that particular moment, of course: it expresses a time-quality. From the chart you can not conclude whether it belongs to a human being, an animal, or an object. The time-quality expresses a potential on each level: a whole scale of possible manifestations lies enwrapped in that one moment. If referring to a human being, the person who owns that particular chart can still develop in many different directions. There is a fixed pattern of planets, houses, and aspects, but how they are articulated in life can't be derived from the horoscope itself. In the eyes of the outside world, you could very well live completely different lives with one and the same chart. Only the astrologer can tell that a different form of manifestation is indeed another possible manifestation of that one horoscope.

Chart 3, "Drunk Client," illustrates this. It belongs to a woman with an enormous accent on the theme Pisces/Neptune/12th House. Sun, Moon, Mercury, and Venus are in Pisces in the 12th. On top of that, Sun, Moon, and Venus square the ruler of the 12th (Uranus), while Neptune is opposing the Ascendant, squaring the MC, and in a quincunx to the Moon. The woman had asked for a complete character-analysis and further stated that she didn't have any real reason for wanting this. When she came in, she smelled of alcohol and in the pockets of her coat and clothing she apparently carried cans of beer and small bottles of other alcoholic beverages. She interrupted the consultation at regular intervals to go to the bathroom and, it was quite obvious, to consume the necessary dosage of alcohol. Not once during the whole session did I get the impression that *any* of my words got through to her!

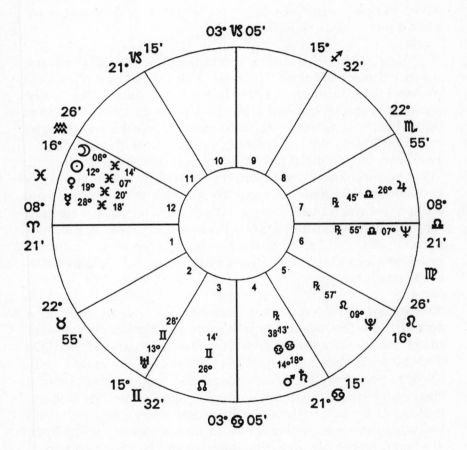

Chart 3
Drunk Client
Mar. 3, 1946, 8:12 A.M. GMT
Amsterdam, Netherlands
52N22 4E54
Placidus Houses

• I always record my sessions on a tape cassette and, since I find it impossible to have a decent conversation with a drunken or even tipsy client, I decided to ignore her drunkenness and just interpret her chart, hoping she might listen to the tape with a clear head later on. Although I naturally mentioned the danger of addiction that can accompany such a focus of Pisces/Neptune/12th House factors, I also pointed out all the positive possibilities to her. She didn't have to end up in the gutter; with the same chart, one could also help people on the shadow-side of life to find their way back into society.

• Now, with such a chart it is very tempting to sigh: there is so much influence of Pisces/Neptune/12th House, that it's almost impossible for this person not to become an alcoholic. It could be a classic example, but still, these horoscope factors *can* point in other directions as well; you don't know beforehand whether you are dealing with a gifted artist or musician, or with an addict. So you have to be careful not to jump to conclusions about it all. What you think it might be could very well be one of your own projections, which has nothing to do with the actual person. Although I wasn't very happy with this consultation, I realized that an alcoholic is often fighting very hard to get out of his problems. That's why I tried to shed some light on all the different manifestations that could express this theme, including especially the positive ones.

• Years later, a happy and warmhearted woman came for a consultation. She wanted to talk about her horoscope, but over the phone she wouldn't tell me why. Coming in, she smiled: "Do you still remember me?" and added "I was the woman, who once came to you drunk . . ." The change was unbelievable! I had a clear-minded and blooming woman in front of me. She told me that she had ended up in a alcoholic coma, during which she had had a near-death experience. From within a glowing white light, she had seen her life up to that moment and had realized what a mess she had made of it. The white light had allowed her to return and she had chosen to do so. Coming out of her coma she was determined never to touch a drop of alcohol again, and to start committing herself to work for her fellow humans. And that is what she is doing to this day.

• In the eyes of the world, my client had turned into a completely different person. As we have seen, the positive part of the Pisces/Neptune/12th House theme is committing yourself to others, working for the Third World, Amnesty International, and the like. *This woman had found another form of expressing the same horoscope.* In her new life-situation, she had listened to the old tapes and had now come to ask a few more questions and to thank me for not letting myself be blinded by her negative traits (which had been overly evident). She was grateful that I had pointed out the positive possibilities, even if all had seemed hopeless at that point.

• This was one of the biggest transformations I have ever witnessed in a client and it has taught me much. I am deeply aware *that a horoscope only shows a potential and never reflects the actual choices the client has made.* From the chart, you can derive a pattern of needs and the structure of personality, but you can't tell to what extent the client has filled in these patterns and which form he has given them. In this regard, as strange as it may sound, the birthchart does not give enough evidence to find out why the client comes to see you. It does provide an excellent framework, though, inside of which other techniques may be of more assistance.

Progressions, Transits, Solar Returns, and Other Prognostic Techniques

The movements of the Ascendant, MC, and the planets through the chart can show you which energies are playing a role in an actual life situation. They often give a good indication of the client's reasons for seeing you. There is only one problem, namely that again you can't tell what the client has done with these planets (i.e., the psychological factors) in the past. This can be difficult, especially if the person in question only comes to see you once or only recently has joined the circle of your clientele. Of course, if someone has been seeing you for some 20 years, you are able to estimate the odds much better. It does make a world of difference, whether someone accepts personal responsibility when, for example, a transit or progression of Saturn is working. So with a transit of Saturn through the 8th House, it is possible to develop depressed feelings if one has always made oneself dependent on the outside world. However, provided that one stands on one's own two legs, the same Saturn transit can present an opportunity to sort out one's feelings and problems and to face the confrontation with oneself. If a new client comes to see you, you simply don't know whether this person swallows vast amounts of Valium or is ready to face himself, but, regardless of how the person deals with it, you do know that his/her psyche indicates that now is the time to clear up old pains, and that's what you can refer to.

The Consultation Chart

I like to make a horoscope for the moment when a client rings my doorbell. That is the actual moment of entrance into the consultation, and, although people may be early or late for their appointment, astrologically speaking they are on time. The chart drawn for the moment of their entrance directly reflects their actual situation and future developments. Therefore it is a valuable aid, which can be combined with the natal chart and the other techniques of prognosis. Concrete questions can be answered rather directly. The chart shows any turbulent areas, and often it is possible to point out which recent events are connected with current problems of that person. The consultation chart is interpreted according to the rules of horary astrology, while the natal chart and the progressions have to be read according to the rules of characterological astrology. There are vast differences between the rules of both systems and the astrologer using the consultation chart has to watch out not to confuse them. [Please see Christian Borup's special focus on this technique in this volume.—Ed.]

A Summary of the Technical Aids: A natal chart reflects someone's potential. Still, it doesn't offer the astrologer any evidence regarding the level of the client and the choices made. Progressions and transits offer a fair indication of current psychological processes and the client's underlying questions. These are also connected with situations and events in the outside world and, thus, the astrologer can help the client to make a connection between inner and outer happenings. The consultation chart itself signifies the most actual situation, and, though it still doesn't comment on the developmental level of the client, it does show current problems and near future developments. If the client denies certain issues, the astrologer can, through the use of this combination of technical aids, at least point out that the charts (natal, progressed, and consultation chart) denote one or more sore spots important in the current situation. In many cases, the client will recognize and accept this, either during the consultation or shortly afterwards.

The astrologer, however, must always be careful not to push the client into any one particular direction (remember the anorexic woman) and to leave enough space for other manifestations of the same planets. This is quite a dilemma for astrologers, because things will not always move on in the anticipated manner. Life holds innumerable possible variations, which make it so much more colorful, but in concrete terms it is unpredictable. Another dilemma is that clients also like to believe what their astrologer tells them and then start just to follow the prediction. This way, they actually avoid the hot spots again.

The technical aids offer us the possibilities, but they also have their limitations. Therefore, we will also have to resort to psychological tools in dealing with an avoiding client.

Psychological Instruments

Indirect Signals

The unconscious never lies. It gives itself away in all kinds of small details, such as gestures, looks, sighing, sweating and the like. Often the client is not aware of this, as these thing happen involuntarily. If you learn to note and interpret these kinds of signals, you will receive abundant information regarding the current psychological situation of the client. For example, study Chart 4, shown on the next page.

This is an older woman, born in 1918, who was in therapy with me. She was determined to face any confrontation with herself and worked hard to free herself from all the negative emotions her past had brought to her. With Mars on the Ascendant in Sagittarius she could come across as very vigorous and assertive, but only as far as others were concerned. Standing up and asking for things for herself, let alone allowing herself to be helped, was absolutely taboo for her. The starting point for her attitude was that she didn't want to bother others, so she never talked about her problems. Astrologers know well how overruling Mars on the Ascendant in Sagittarius can be, and that it is a planetary position, which makes it rather easy to say "I." But this lady would not do it.

Right at the beginning of the therapy program, I noticed that this woman would speak with a particularly soft voice whenever she had to make choices for herself, to work through a problem. She, herself, was not aware of this at all. At home, she wrote

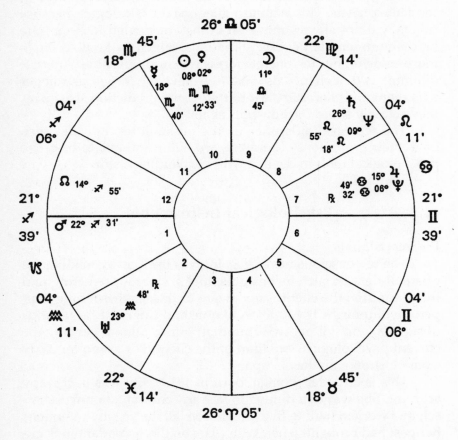

Chart 4

Nov. 1, 1918, 10:13 A.M. GMT
Rheden, Netherlands
52N01 6E02
Placidus Houses

down her experiences to clarify her reactions, how she worked things through. In this writing exercise, she finally expressed her hitherto suppressed anger toward some people from her past. When reading parts of her writings to me, *she immediately spoke softly again*, almost without intonation.

For me, this was an obvious symptom of her Sagittarian Mars on the Ascendant *not* being able to express itself properly. When I asked her why she spoke so softly (she also made her body small on these occasions), she reacted with surprise and said that she wasn't aware of this at all. She then realized that, at this point, some old fears were playing out within her; fears which, after thorough analysis, turned out to be connected with Saturn in the 8th House.

In the therapy, we then worked on this fear issue first. The difficulties around her Sagittarian Mars on the Ascendant vanished in time totally naturally.

• During a consultation or astrotherapy, a psychologically well-trained astrologer will be quite sure of the exact location of the client's sore spots. The horoscope denotes the possibilities, while the client himself indicates through indirect signals, which of them have actually turned into problems. Even further: watching for this type of signal, I often encountered problems in areas where one wouldn't suspect them at all: in aspects and in planetary positions usually looked upon as "friendly." So for me, the whole horoscope is wide-open: everything can turn into a problem, but, as well, everything can also be presented in a creative, positive way.

• A classic way a client rejects what you offer is when the client crosses his or her arms (sometimes the legs as well) and maybe turns (half) away from you. Even if he keeps listening politely, he has already indicated with his arms the creation of a certain distance. He may also drum his fingers nervously or wiggle his feet, or display some other kind of nervous behavior. Watch out though: this only applies if the signals start *simultaneously with the discussion of a certain subject*. If the client acts like this from the very beginning of the session, it may be one of his natural traits or he may just be very tense about the consultation. In this case you have to watch for significant changes from that norm. Increased intensity in the activities is one thing to look for, but so are sudden stuttering, spilling coffee, sweating, or cringing. The expression of the eyes can change significantly all of a sudden, as well.

• There are very quiet clients who hardly move. In these people, you have to watch for very small details, like the raising of an eyebrow, rubbing a finger, etc.This type of client can stay very well-meaning, while you go on explaining something. They can listen calmly, throw in an occasional comment, ask questions, etc., but something in their attitude shows you that there is a difference between their verbal expression and their unconscious. When I see/feel such a reaction, I try to check how I can best make use of it at a certain point. If a client sees you for therapy during a certain length of time, you can mention this kind of thing at the appropriate moment, but you also have clients who will see you only once, because they "just thought it would be nice to have their chart done." Then you're caught in the dilemma of noticing a (possibly important) blockage, which might, if recognized and accepted, unleash a lot of emotions, and not have the opportunity to counsel the client in dealing with it all and working it through, since this pointedly was only going to be a single session.

• I believe there are no fixed rules for this situation. One client can face the confrontation with the unconscious attitude much better than another client. There are even those who vigorously deny their attitude, like "But I didn't cross my arms at all!" In a single session, the foremost rule is to avoid an exchange of "You did! No, I didn't!" Neither party profits from that.

Alertness for Defense Mechanisms in the Client

Some clients can manifest certain defense mechanisms that create (for the client) lots of difficulties. A well-proven method to avoid having to think about themself is to put the astrologer on a pedestal. By almost equalling you to God or the universe (after all, you're reading it all from the stars!) your words become law, which will be faithfully obeyed. *The horoscope becomes their excuse:* how could they help it? They praise you to the skies; in their eyes, you are the best astrologer of all, and mistakes or misinterpretations on your part are immediately forgotten, since they would taint the lofty image. Often, these clients are very nice, eager, and well-meaning, but the very moment you, as an astrologer, walk into this (unconscious) trap, you are doomed. You won't be able any longer to draw the client's attention to his own role in life and to his own responsibilities. Before you know it, you start leading their life, they follow your words, and you become their central point of reference. Of course, it is nice to hear a client say that you're very good, but do watch out! Before you realize it, you might start thinking the same thing and the process of inflation starts to work!

Many of us know of a therapist, professional helper, or astrologer, who started out most promisingly, but after a few years became bigger than life and with whom a sensible conversation became impossible. This is partly the result of the idolatry of our clients: for them it is a defense; for the astrologer, it is a dangerous pitfall.

The technique of "creating an atmosphere" works along the same lines. Your client provides so much warmth and coziness that it becomes difficult to tell him of nasty things or problems. It is impossible to imagine that such a person might carry any aggressions at all! If, on top of that, this someone has Mars in Pisces in the 12th house, well, who would even dream of boiling fury? Beware: Mars is there! Only, in Pisces and in the 12th, it will be expressed in a very subtle way. In a negative sense, this position could make a person's whole neighborhood sigh under the weight of the aggressive stance of "Let me help you or I'll shoot you!" As an astrologer in a single session, you needn't necessarily become aware of this, especially when everything is going so nicely. So you don't go around looking for symptoms of defense in the form of a nicely built atmosphere, either.

Another manifestation of client defensiveness is when the client agrees with you on all the points you make and then adds that he/she has been working on this problem for years and has learned so much. Full of understanding, they look at you, nod approvingly (you have hit the nail on the head), *but what you had just mentioned was valid about ten years ago.* In the meantime, they have grown *so much* that it doesn't apply anymore! True, there are clients with whom this is indeed the case. They have fought a hard battle and have grown much more mature, but those clients won't use this kind of defense mechanism. Through their deeper insight, they understand that their personality is able to express the negative traits of a planetary position just as well as the positive ones. They know that very often, for instance if one is tired, one may not exactly show one's happiest face.

The client who keeps insisting that he has matters under control can impose some difficulty on the well-meaning astrologer, especially if the consultation (combined with a certain amount of non-verbal communication) suggests that the problem is *still* bigger than life. Pointing this out to the client may sometimes help, but it may just as well cause some turbulence. You might find yourself confronted with a whole load of projections, stating that you are a bad or very subjective astrologer, etc. (That is why I never get involved in discussing complaints about other astrologers. The client's disapproval might be related to this kind of mechanism on his part!) There is no golden rule, only the warning not to let things escalate into a power struggle.

Chart 5 belongs to a man with Sun conjunct Mercury and Jupiter, all three in Leo and on the MC, in combination with a Libra Ascendant and Moon in Pisces. Upon entering the room, he was already talking at length about his modesty and his talent to listen, while not letting me finish one single sentence or letting me speak at all! It didn't matter whether I raised my voice or simply continued speaking: he just kept on talking, mostly about his modesty and his attention for others. He had only come for a personality analysis out of curiosity, so this was to be a single session.

Finally, I gave in and let him talk. When I could manage to squeeze in a word, I said what I had to say in very rudimentary form, since I knew I would have only a few seconds to make my point. As usual, everything was recorded on a tape. Listening to the recordings at home, he may have heard how open he is to the words of others and how extremely modest he is, not in my words, but in his own, and three hours of them to boot! Had he come for therapy, I might have had better tools at my disposal, but I would have had to distribute them over a certain length of time.

There are also clients who don't give you the chance to fully discuss a certain issue, because they repeatedly have to go to the bathroom. Just as the two of you are working your way through some important matter, there is another interruption and you will have to invest more time and energy to return to the same point. Often, it is a real physical urge, which possibly expresses a whole complex, that wishes to avoid any confrontation at all. I have had clients whose career went downhill through this mechanism, simply because they had to go to the lavatory every fifteen minutes. Of course, this is impossible during business meetings, in the car, while giving a lecture or in other, similar situations. If a client shows these symptoms of avoidance, I usually advise them to work out the underlying problems in psychotherapy. In cases like

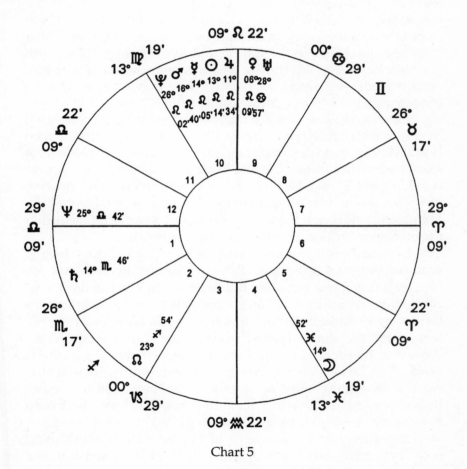

Chart 5

Aug. 6, 1955, 12:33 P.M. GMT
Rheden, Netherlands
52N01 6E02
Placidus Houses

that, I try to use the consultation as an opening toward a confrontation with this kind of escapism.

• A consultation is never a one-way street. The client reacts, you start to converse, to analyze certain subjects deeply; so every consultation becomes a unique event. However well you may have prepared, *the client's contribution makes it all a surprise.* All those client's responses have taught me a lot, especially about the wide range of possible expressions for one single factor in the horoscope! A hidden danger is looming, even in this: the client can show an initially adequate reaction to the choice of issues you offer him; he relates to the subject, but reacts to everything with anecdotes and true life stories, which take up so much time that certain points just won't be touched. This may well be what he (unconsciously) had in mind: *avoiding issues!*

Listen to the anecdotes themselves. They are often connected by a common underlying theme. One client, for example, who was full of inferiority complexes, came up with a whole load of stories featuring himself as the hero; and, if the story's course wouldn't allow that, he'd state that others could never deceive him, because he was always up to what they wanted from him. "I'm looking through them," he mentioned several times during the course of various anecdotes in one single session.

In such a case, you know that the horoscope factors dealing with identity and self-esteem, like the Sun or the 10th and 5th House, just to name three, are not functioning in a balanced way. While the client is busy stealing your time by telling all these little stories with the intention of keeping you from touching his sore spots, the stories themselves indicate exactly where those spots are! As soon as you get the picture, confront the problem head on. A lot of emotion may be released, but that is what the client is struggling with. You can never tell beforehand whether he will recognize and accept the problem, but at least you have a fair chance. A follow-up through therapy might be necessary.

Experience and knowledge of human nature are of great help, of course, and become some kind of sixth sense in the astrologer as to the best way to deal with any particular client. However, these processes can not be taught. Only your own experience of looking, learning, falling, and getting up again can give you the knowledge you need.

Your own way of dealing with a client who tries to escape the hot issue will differ considerably from one session to the other. In the case of a single session, you can't tell what the client is going to do with the results, so you'll have to be quite careful. If the session is part of a series of therapy meetings, you have a lot more time and techniques at your disposal and, above all, you have the opportunity for follow-up, which allows you to intervene when the client appears to actually confront the question, but doesn't know how to deal with it at first.

The Teaching Approach

For the client, the circle of the horoscope may appear to be abracadabra and pure magic. Although it is quite obvious that you do not mean to bore the client with a lot of technical terms, I have realized several times that the client stays in this state of bewilderment, if he knows that there is "something" in the horoscope. It's a protected position: "What I don't know won't hurt me." This sense of magic (and the accompanying projections) can easily be erased in many cases simply by showing the circle to the client and by briefly explaining the pieces of the puzzle to him.

With a client who avoids important questions, you can simply point out the horoscope patterns that refer to them. It is as if the constellation turns into tangible reality. The same applies to progressions, transits, and the consultation chart. You can visibly prove the evidence of what you are talking about in the circle itself. With a number of really difficult clients, I have simply reversed the style of the consultation: instead of bothering them with any technical terms, I turned the session into a kind of lecture, teaching them what a horoscope is and how certain patterns can work out, all of it using their own chart and their own progressions. The "lecture shape" created a sort of *positive distance:* on the one hand, the client is thrilled and doesn't get the feeling of being threatened or having to deny, but on the other, he or she is conscious of the fact that you are talking about him/her. The teaching approach may give the client a chance to realize that the problem obviously does exist. In my own practice, it has repeatedly helped me to discuss issues which were initially avoided.

The teaching approach does provide its own problems as well: one of them is that it installs a lot of power in the astrologer, which may tempt him to fence the client in, all under the cloak of the astrological system's objectivity. So we still have to be careful, although it is obvious that we can use astrological technique itself to deal with an avoiding client.

The Use of Therapeutic Instruments in a Single Session

Body language and other indirect signals from the client can be used to bring up the subject in question in a non-astrological way. Sometimes it may be necessary to put the chart aside completely and to talk with the client as one human being to another about the emotions coming free. In many cases, the confrontation with their indirect signals will release a lot in the client. Although denial and defense may prevail, I have often experienced that this approach *can* create an opening and make the client think hard.

Be aware that the whole of the unconscious can go into red alert if you touch a tender spot in someone's psyche, and that the attitude of the client can go through dramatic changes during the course of one session. Even if the client still denies, for example, by using common defenses like "But a lot of people have that" or "I've always been like that"; still the fact that you have touched a sensitive area may cause a lot of inner turbulence. This tumult can create openness, but in any case it will sharpen the senses in the direction of the problem.

The inner tornado you have unleashed can't be pacified easily. It will cost the client a lot of energy to put the lid back on the pot and to go on avoiding the question after the consultation. In many cases the confrontation will show some after-effects, activate dream-life, or make the client more emotional. If a client appears to have a breakthrough in a single session, then you mustn't let him end up in a vacuum afterward. You may offer the possibility of a follow-up or send him on to a therapist. Sometimes it is sufficient for him to phone you a couple of weeks later and exchange a few thoughts before he carries on on his own.

A List of Questions

Instead of explaining horoscope factors to a client who circles around a particular subject, you may choose to put some specific questions about those factors in front of him or her. By aiming well and repeatedly changing from one facet of the issue to another, the client may be led to discover *in his or her own answers* what exactly the point is, for if you discuss a real difficulty, the answers to your subsequent questions will indicate the exact location of the sore spot. This method is especially suitable for astrologers who are therapists as well or who possess a lot of psychological knowledge, for, above all, it is important not to make the client feel as if the questions are pushing him or her too far in a certain direction.

How you formulate your inquiry depends on the kind of person sitting in front of you. Sometimes you may simply sense that the client has reached an important crossroads, and change to a more pressing form of asking (by using a certain choice of words, but also through intonation or your expression). On other occasions, it might be best just to give some quiet hints.

Dreams and Other Externalizations

If you are working with the client for a longer period of time or if he or she is seeing you for therapy as well, there is a whole range of therapeutic means to help the client find their own way into the problematic area in the chart or in its progressions. Dreams, fantasy, experiential astrology, drawing, painting, or hypnosis are very valuable tools. After the client has used them to work through a number of smaller problems, a more important issue will all of a sudden cease to bring up his defenses and can be faced without resistance.

The Astrologer's Poise

A very subtle point, which nonetheless plays quite a part in working with clients, is the question of whether you, as the astrologer, *accept yourself*. It does sound crazy, but still, if you, as an astrologer, can accept that life knows light and darkness, that in spite of all your astrological knowledge you are still liable to make a mess of things, to have relationship problems, to suffer from pain, to make the wrong decisions, in short, to remain a human being, then you will develop a center of peace inside yourself and you will be able to build up an inner equilibrium. Light and darkness will have both found their respective places in your soul. This kind of self-acceptance will improve your ability to accept the client unconditionally. If you radiate it and communicate it indirectly, the client will respond unconsciously. The feeling of being accepted and the sense of security this will instill in him may often prove sufficient to open him up to the issues you wish to discuss.

A consultation will always be a unique experience. It is an alchemical process between astrologer and client. Next to good will and conscious motives, a vast and difficult-to-explore area plays a big part in this: the unconscious of both client and astrologer. This turns every consultation into an intricate pattern of relations between all kinds of dynamic factors. Inside this pattern, you may hit upon a client whose views obviously differ from yours.

Therefore, the question of what to do if, in your opinion, the client is avoiding the issue, can not be resolved simply by a handful of recipes. Insight into the processes involved may provide you with a much more effective resourcefulness in dealing with it. In this chapter I could have been easy on myself and just worked out a few success stories, but such cases can never be representative, because each client is different. That's why I chose the more difficult and more confrontational way. I am convinced that only if we astrologers dare to get involved in the process, to watch our own emotions and to question ourselves—since after all, we are the ones who say what it is all about—will we have a chance to break through the resistance and defenses of our clients.

We can bring up subjects as honestly as possible and respond humanely to the reactions of the client. This can happen very politely, but sometimes it has to take place more intrusively. Each new situation will teach us which way is the best. Whether the client gets the message or not will largely depend on her- or himself. There are those who only listen to what they want to hear! But it is really nice to be called up years later by a former client. The message: "I listened to the old tapes again. Only now I understand, what you were talking about back then, and now I can work with it."

So it *did* have an effect after all, even if you, the astrologer, have not been a witness of the proceedings. When the time is ripe, understanding will emerge; and, after all, it *was* you who brought up the subject years ago, in a calm and controlled way, completely conscious of the risk that you might be wrong, even though you get your knowledge "from the stars."

Bibliography

Guggenbühl-Craig, A. *Power in the Helping Professions.* Zürich, 1978.

Guggenbühl-Craig, A. *Eros on Crutches: Reflections on Psychopathy and Amorality.* Irving, 1980.

Jung, C. G. *Collected Works* 1–20. Routledge & Kegan Paul.

Susie Cox

Susie Cox has been the staff astrologer at Canyon Ranch Health Resort in Tucson, Arizona since 1981, and during her entire career has interpreted over 22,000 charts. She publishes the *International Directory of Astrologers,* a world-wide listing of individual astrologers, astrological organizations and businesses from 56 countries. Susie is listed in Marquis' *Who's Who in the West.*

Born on June 17, 1949 at 9:40 P.M. MST in Tucson, Arizona, Susie began the study of astrology as a child of seven and has been a professional astrologer since 1971. Carl Payne Tobey was her mentor for many years.

Susie has owned a metaphysical bookstore and published two astrological periodicals, *The Aquarian Almanac* and *The Astrology Newsletter.* She lectures at and produces entertainment for international conferences, and produces astrological videos. She studies astronomy at the University of Arizona and teaches workshops on experiential astronomy and astrodrama in Europe and the United States.

Susie Cox

Bottom-Line
Astrology

Bottom-Line Astrology presents a simple formula that provides a structure for interpreting a client's chart. It doesn't matter which house system you use, or even which Zodiac you use. This style of interpretation works with any system and can be used with transits, progressions, synastry, composites, or whichever technique in astrology you choose.

In my 25 years as a professional astrologer, I have learned some tricks to make the interpretation process more systematic. For the last 13 years, I have been the staff astrologer for Canyon Ranch Health Resort in Tucson, Arizona. This world-class resort offers a wide range of health and life-enhancement modalities, with astrology as one of the services. At the ranch, astrology may be scheduled between a facial and an aerobics class. My sessions usually last an hour and 15 minutes.

Approximately 90 percent of my clients have never had their chart done before. In fact, most barely know their Sun sign. Curiosity is the main reason that people come to me to have their chart done. Almost every person needs the absolute basics explained to them. My experience indicates that many clients would appreciate astrology made simple and easy. No one says it has to be complicated. Even though I see a 40 percent return of my clients at the Ranch, many I will only see once, so I feel I should make the interpretation complete and understandable.

The first process in making astrology easier to understand is to simplify. I use the main planets: Sun, Moon, Mercury, Venus, Mars, Jupiter, Saturn, Uranus, Neptune, and Pluto. I leave out all the extra points like the moon's Nodes, vertex, east point, part of fortune, asteroids, midpoints, and the hypothetical planets. I suggest you save these for your own research. These points are more interesting to astrologers than to clients. Most clients won't understand them, and they will add to the client's confusion.

Another area in which to simplify is the aspects. I only use the major aspects: conjunctions, squares, trines and oppositions. Clients usually don't relate to semi-squares or biquintiles, for example. In addition, for all the aspects, I use a tight 6-degree orb. I suggest you only aspect the planets and not the Ascendant, Midheaven, or other points. Using tight orbs and only aspecting the planets are very important parts of simplifying. If there are too many lines in the chart, the client immediately gets intimidated. Many are afraid of the numbers and geometry; additional aspects only complicate the picture.

Save astrological jargon for talking with other astrologers. Interpret charts to your clients in non-astrological terms. I introduce the planets once, and then interpret in clear words that the client can understand. For example, "Your Sun is in the sign of Gemini in the 5th house, which means your energetic purpose in life is directed toward creativity." Until the client learns to speak astrology, it is a foreign language to them. Astrologers are bilingual. We can read the symbols and then interpret what they mean into words. Our clients have hired us as interpreters to translate this ancient symbolic language to them. If they do not understand, we have not done our job as translators. The art of interpretation is not easy; the key is experience. The more charts you do, the smoother you become. Be patient with yourself. With approximately 22,000 charts under my belt, I realize that the holistic picture of the chart only came into view at about the 5,000 mark.

Astrologers know all the individual pieces of the chart, but how do we put them together in a coherent fashion that the client can understand? It is crucial to synthesize the chart. I have asked many people who have had their chart done, "What did your chart say?" They said, "Well, I have my Sun in Aries and my Moon in Pisces." But what does it mean? "Well, it means that my Sun is in Aries and my Moon is in Pisces." Surely there is more to the horoscope than all the individual pieces. What is the bottom line to the chart? What does it really mean? What is your client here to accomplish in life? The chart tells a story and the astrologer is the storyteller.

It is our job as astrologers to bring all these pieces together and communicate the story to our clients so that they understand it. By the time you understand Bottom-Line Astrology, you will be able to sum up your client's chart in one simple sentence.

The astrology chart defines our purpose in life. It points out very clearly our lifetime challenges and our talents, our karma, and our destiny. The chart provides priceless information with clues to our mission in life. That is, if we understand what it means.

How to Interpret

I use two main styles of chart interpretation. With new clients, I use what I call, "3 Times Around the Wheel." When clients return, I use the "Holistic Picture." These two systems address all my client's needs.

Three Times Around the Wheel

All new clients get a complete, basic interpretation, regardless of their level of astrological knowledge. I start with a short introduction, explaining the over-all concept of astrology. Then I explain their Sun, Moon, and Rising Sign/planet. I orient the client to the chart with a bit of astronomy showing the horizon and the Ascendant. Now the client realizes that we are actually talking about the planets in the sky at their time and location of birth. Do not assume that the new client understands the basics. Even if this information is familiar to them, it never hurts for them to hear it again.

With the introduction finished, I start the first time around the wheel. This is when I explain the planets, the signs, and the houses, using simple sentences. The second time around, I synthesize the chart, using the aspects, which can be done in one sentence. Of course, it takes most of the session to reach this point. The 3rd time around, I add on transits, progressions, solar arcs, or whichever predictive tool I choose. With this package, the client has a complete overview of their life.

The Holistic Picture

When a client returns for a second session, my emphasis switches to the holistic picture of the chart.

Now that the client is beginning to learn the language of astrology, more dialogue can take place. I synthesize the chart at the beginning of the interpretation, using simple sentences. Then we discuss their areas of interest. This could be a more in-depth look at a part of their natal chart, or a situation in their life. The sessions are always completed with a look at the current transits or progressions. Astrology is a tool for timing, and my clients always look forward to knowing the power dates in their near future.

When I can work with a client over a period of time, I feel the "third time's a charm." It takes a while for people to process this information and see how it connects with their daily lives.

Many of my clients have come to me for 10 years or more, and by now some of them are very good at using astrology for their own life. I've taught them the language of astrology and now we can actually speak using the jargon. Ultimately it makes it easier for me, because now we are both involved in the decision making of their life.

Forming a Sentence

The basis of speaking any language is forming a sentence. Astrology is no different. What is the structure of a sentence? A sentence is composed mainly of nouns, verbs, adjectives, and adverbs. Of course there are more minor parts, but these four will be the basis of our astrological sentence structure.

When interpreting a chart, most of the sentences are fairly simple. For example, "Sun is in Taurus in the 10th House." Translated this would mean, "Your life purpose is to be secure in your occupation." A more complex sentence would interpret an aspect, such as, "Your Aries Sun is squaring your Cancer Moon." Let's analyze this sentence. "Aries" is an adjective explaining the Sun, which is a noun. "Cancer" is an adjective explaining the Moon, which is also a noun. The sentence has action with "is squaring," which is the verb. Now replace the astrological words with key-words, and form a new, non-astrological sentence: "Your Aries Sun is squaring your Cancer Moon" can be translated to "Your aggressive nature is in conflict with your sensitive emotions." Another possible sentence could be, "Your impulsive ego is threatening your sentimental mood."

Here is another sentence to translate, "Your Mercury in Gemini trines your Jupiter in Libra." One translation might be, "Your intelligent communication skills enhance your social opportunities," or "Your witty mind brings to life your charming sense of humor."

Start with a sentence that explains the planet in its sign and in its house, then create a sentence that translates just one aspect between two planets. Then, advance to translating aspect config-urations, such as T-squares and Grand Trines. Later, more com-plex sentences can be formed by adding on the houses. Eventually, a sentence will form that translates the holistic mean-ing or essence of the chart.

Make up several sentences describing each aspect. Brain-storm with your client. They will be able to invent much better sentences than the astrologer, since it is their life. These sentences are strung together, using keywords. Many astrologers talk around an issue and never quite get to the point. Keywords force us to get to the point, because it is only one word and had better be the most descriptive.

Each client is unique, and the keywords must be adapted to that individual. For example, Venus in a person who just got mar-ried will be related to their love life, while Venus in an artist's chart might be related to their talent or career. Each chart is total-ly different and has a personal story of its very own. Be careful not to use pat answers when you interpret.

Make a list of your own keywords. Try them out first on your own horoscope and other horoscopes you know well. Write down the analytical sentences. Edit them. Make the keywords work together.

The following samples are just suggestions. Notice that the keywords for the planets are all nouns, the keywords for the signs are adjectives and the keywords or phrases for the aspects are verbs. These are the vocabulary words that will be used to form sentences.

Keywords: Planets

☉ — SUN: Inner essence, nature, individual, ego, consciousness, purpose, center, light, creativity, spirit, life, vitality, nucleus, being, intention, will power, and Apollo.

☽ — MOON: Emotions, unconscious, soul, reflection, fertility, mother, memories, feelings, moods, sensitivity, and Isis.

☿ — MERCURY: Communication, intelligence, thoughts, reason, logic, ideas, speech, observation, conscious mind, the winged messenger, and Hermes.

♀ — VENUS: Love, femininity, beauty, art, harmony, romance, refinement, the senses, gentleness, sensuality, and Aphrodite.

♂ — MARS: Energy, force, action, stress, anger, masculinity, sexual drive, and the warrior.

♃ — JUPITER: Confidence, abundance, aspirations, generosity, autonomy, indulgence, excess, opportunity, humanity, success, philosophy, Santa Claus, Zeus, and a sense of humor.

♄ — SATURN: Responsibility, structure, restriction, ability, duty, authority, stamina, determination, accomplishment, limitations, patience, reality, karma, discipline, maturity, caution, boundaries, ambition, Father Time, and Kronos.

♅ — URANUS: Surprise, freedom, chaos, independence, change, eccentricity, originality, release, intuition, electricity, the humanitarian, and the rebel.

♆ — NEPTUNE: Spirituality, visionary, psyche, dreamer, wisdom, addictions, drugs and alcohol, co-dependence, meditation, fantasy, illusion, rose-colored glasses, devotion, guilt, escape, Poseidon, angels, God, and Goddess.

♇ — PLUTO: Power, transmutation, evolution, death and rebirth, control, purification, elimination, regeneration, the Phoenix, Shiva, and Hades.

Keywords: Signs

♈ — ARIES: Energetic, fiery, aggressive, courageous, assertive, angry, self-centered, impulsive, brave and dynamic. *IMAGES:* The ram, the pioneer, the athlete, the warrior, Leonardo da Vinci, J. P. Morgan, and Harry Houdini.

♉ — TAURUS: Stable, earthy, sensual, dependable, stubborn, persevering, conservative, material, needs security, determined, strong, sophisticated, loyal, luxurious, and practical. *IMAGES:* The bull, Minos, the builder, Queen Elizabeth II, Harry Truman, and Fred Astaire.

♊ — GEMINI: Enthusiastic, airy, versatile, nervous, independent, intelligent, talkative, flirtatious, quick, positive, unstable, restless, curious, child-like, and clever. *IMAGES:* The twins, butterfly, teacher, communicator, Bob Dylan, Marilyn Monroe, and Frank Lloyd Wright.

♋ — CANCER: Nurturing, watery, protective, emotional, family-oriented, moody, sensitive, sentimental, and affectionate. *IMAGES:* The crab, mother, Helen Keller, Nelson Rockefeller, and the Duke of Windsor.

♌ — LEO: Proud, fiery, generous, entertaining, flashy, powerful, arrogant, grandiose, egocentric, dramatic, dictatorial, and noble. *IMAGES:* The lion, king, president, leader, celebrity, Napoleon, Henry Ford, and Mae West.

♍ — VIRGO: Earth mother, meticulous, linear, critical, analytical, productive, efficient, shy, caring, dedicated, vulnerable, problem-solving, computer-like, and intelligent. *IMAGES:* Mother Nature, virgin, Spock, the craftsman, Lauren Bacall, Lyndon B. Johnson, and Peter Sellers.

♎ — LIBRA: Artistic, airy, social, beautiful, graceful, charming, indecisive, submissive, slick, diplomatic, refined, sympathetic, and romantic. *IMAGES:* The scales, marriage, lovebirds, diplomat, artist, Julie Andrews, Truman Capote, and John Lennon.

♏ — SCORPIO: Private, watery, deep, decisive, questioning, curious, jealous, sexual, manipulative, intense, psychic, healing, passionate, and powerful. *IMAGES:* The scorpion, the phoenix bird, the serpent, the inspector, a volcano, Grace Kelly, Pablo Picasso, and Billy Graham.

♐ —SAGITTARIUS: Independent, fiery, philosophic, futuristic, demanding, undaunting, impatient, cultural, expansive, and straightforward. *IMAGES:* The centaur, professor, counselor, traveler, Mary Martin, William F. Buckley, Jr., and Mark Twain.

♑ —CAPRICORN: Cautious, earthbound, unyielding, ambitious, authoritative, tenacious, responsible, and accomplished. *IMAGES:* The goat, businessman, lawyer, politician, Mao Tse-tung, Martin Luther King, and Marlene Dietrich.

♒ — AQUARIUS: Rebellious, airy, open-minded, revolutionary, scattered, unpredictable, cause-oriented, aloof, fanatic, impractical, and humanitarian. *IMAGES:* The water bearer, scientist, inventor, computer programmer, Galileo, Mozart, and Abraham Lincoln.

♓ —PISCES: Empathetic, watery, extremely sensitive, abandoned, fearful, inspired, whimsical, fanciful, spiritual, spacey, creative, gentle, confused, and kind. *IMAGES:* The fishes, Christ, psychic healer, minister, visionary, drug addict, poet, Michelangelo, Elizabeth Taylor, and Albert Einstein.

Keywords: Houses

1st HOUSE: Personality, character, personal image, appearance, and the self.

2nd HOUSE: Personal finance, possessions, material values, and the ability to make money.

3rd HOUSE: Communications, thoughts and ideas, short trips, and mental attitude.

4TH HOUSE: Early home life, heritage, and the foundation of security.

5th HOUSE: Creative self expression, games, flirting, love affairs, children, and business speculation.

6th HOUSE: Health and healing, personal habits and hygiene, service to others, and cooperation with co-workers.

7th HOUSE: Marriage, partnerships, and committed relationships.

8th HOUSE: Other people's money, inheritances, lawsuits, investments, powerful associates, and sex.

9th HOUSE: Religion, philosophy, long journeys, higher education, and searching for the meaning in life.

10th HOUSE: Public image, occupation, reputation, and status.

11th HOUSE: Goals in life, friends, and group associations.

12th HOUSE: Hidden wisdom, meditation, psychological outlook, and hypnotherapy.

Aspects: Red Lines and Blue Lines

Aspects can be very confusing for clients, so I color code them on the charts. Red lines show hard aspects like squares and oppositions. Blue lines show soft aspects like trines. Remember, we have simplified the aspects by only using conjunctions, squares, trines, and oppositions. By only using the major aspects and tight orbs, the planetary patterns are very obvious and easy to see.

The red lines define our lifetime challenges or our Karma. The blue lines define our talents or our destiny. Most clients don't care about the specific angle between two planets. *They just want to know if they are red or blue!* Clients will lovingly refer to their blue lines as their "gifts." They also learn their red lines symbolize their challenges and, therefore, personal growth. It is important not to interpret the red lines in a negative and fatalistic way. The clients know very well what their challenges are when they see the red lines. *They* are the experts on their lives. Definitely let them help you interpret their chart. It will be much more pertinent and meaningful if they are involved.

After all the planets have been introduced during the first time around the wheel, it is now time to synthesize the chart using the aspects. I interpret the red lines first, using the major configuration, and then go on to the other single red lines. If the chart contains a Grand Cross or a T-square, start with that. I then interpret the blue lines, starting with the major configuration, such as a Grand trine, and then go onto the single trines. The

ASPECTS

RED LINES: HARD ASPECTS:	BLUE LINES: SOFT ASPECTS
In conflict with	is compatible with
challenged by	is empowered by
in contrast to	likes to work with
fights	enjoys
disagrees with	is in harmony with
is compounded by	strengthens
is threatened by	is in agreement with
needs to make friends with	likes
doesn't like	works well with
needs to balance	is motivated by
can't understand	intensifies
contradicts	energizes
inhibits	invigorates
is contrary to	places emphasis on
weakens	is fond of
not to be held down by	vitalizes
clashes with	brings to life
differs with	stimulates
compromises	
argues with	

aspects in many charts do not form a major configuration, but have scattered red and blue lines all over the chart. These types of charts are not as easy to synthesize, but it *is* possible.

The same technique is used to interpret all the aspects, whether red or blue. Just plug in the keywords to make a sentence. The only difference is that the keywords for the red lines show conflict, while the keywords for the blue lines show harmony.

After you have made up a sentence for each of the red lines, *combine them all into one sentence.* This is the client's sentence that describes personal lifetime challenges or Karma. Create several sentences with the help of your client.

Now that both of you are satisfied with your red sentence, go to the blue lines. Create a sentence for each of the blue lines, then *combine them all into one sentence.* This is the sentence that describes the client's talents, gifts, and destiny. Make these sentences as simple, positive, and straightforward as possible. Now is the time to be precise and choose the most appropriate words to create these sentences. If clients forget much that occurred during the session, at least they will have their "sentence."

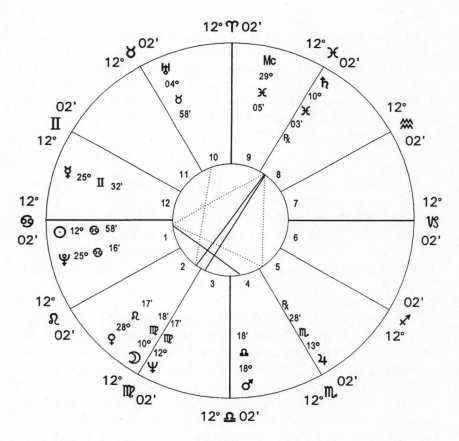

Chart 1
Dalai Lama
July 6, 1935, 5:00 A.M. RS5
Taktser, Tibet
29N40   91E09
Equal House

Putting it All Together

Now you have created two sentences, one for the red lines and one for the blue lines. It is time to combine them into one sentence that sums up the entire chart. This is the bottom line to the chart. I usually put the red sentence as the first clause, and then end it with the blue sentence. Here are some examples of actual charts and a brief interpretation. I use the Equal House system.

Chart 1

Client background: This chart belongs to the Dalai Lama of Tibet, whose birth information is public knowledge. His Holiness is the political and religious leader of the Tibetan people, currently in exile from his native country and living in India. He lectures all over the world about compassion and patience in the face of adversity. He is well respected as a kind, yet very savvy, player in the international political scene.

Interpretation

Sun, Moon, and Rising Sign: This chart has both the Sun and Rising Sign in Cancer with the Moon in Virgo: *He has a gentle, nurturing spirit with emotional dedication to service.*

Solid (Red) Lines: Moon and Neptune in Virgo oppose Saturn in Pisces: *His challenge is to confront restrictions from others with spiritual compassion and patience.* Sun in Cancer square Mars in Libra: *His calm inner essence is in conflict with the aggression he receives from others.*

Dotted (Blue) Lines: Grand Trine with Saturn in Pisces trine Sun in Cancer trine Jupiter in Scorpio: *His destiny is to use spiritual patience combined with his gentle nature enhanced by his ability to heal humanity.* Uranus in Taurus trine the Moon in Virgo: *His persevering desire to promote change works well with his dedicated soul.*

The Bottom Line: The Dalai Lama's karma is to react to limitations and violence from his adversaries with compassion, and, in doing so, he will accomplish his destiny of helping to heal the world.

Chart 2

Client background: This is a high-powered businessman who buys and sells companies and is very successful occupation-

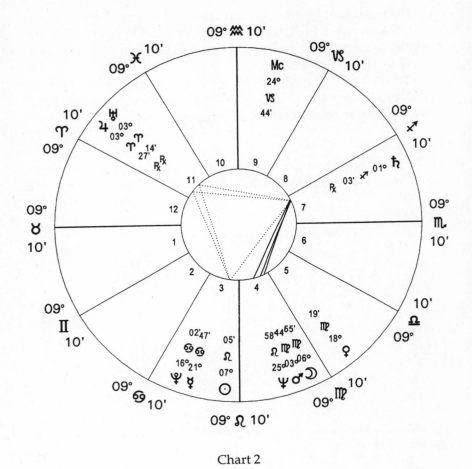

Chart 2

ally. His mother was extremely critical of him during his child-hood. His wife is also critical. He struggles with low self esteem and nervousness.

Interpretation

Sun, Moon, and Rising Sign: His Sun is in Leo, and his Moon is in Virgo with Taurus Rising: *This is a powerful individual, with shy emotions and a strong exterior.*

Solid (Red) Lines: Neptune in Leo and Mars-Moon conjunct in Virgo square Saturn in Sagittarius: *His vulnerable emotions and ability to act are threatened by demanding authority figures.*

Dotted (Blue) Lines: A Grand Trine with Sun in Leo trine Saturn in Sagittarius trine Uranus-Jupiter conjunct in Aries: *His inner strength, combined with endless stamina, will help him achieve autonomy and freedom courageously.*

The Bottom Line: His challenge is to stay emotionally strong in his convictions when confronted by the women in his life, so he can achieve personal liberty and independence.

Chart 3

Client background: This woman started a very successful computer business with her husband. Later they got a

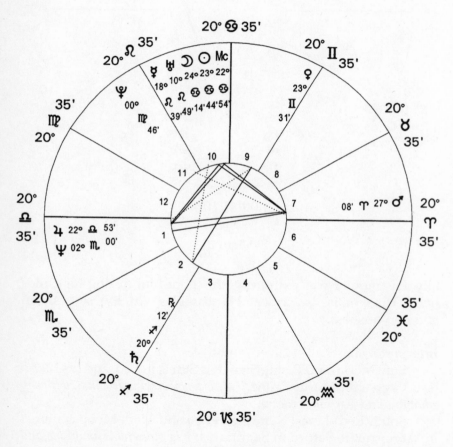

Chart 3

divorce; she sold her portion of the business and became independently wealthy. She now finances non-profit, humanitarian projects.

Interpretation

Sun, Moon, and Rising Sign: Both her Sun and Moon are in Cancer with orientation to Libra Rising: *Her inner and outer selves are nurturing with a diplomatic personality.*

Solid (Red) Lines: T-square of Sun-Moon in Cancer squared by both Mars in Aries and by Jupiter in Libra conjunct Neptune in Scorpio: *Her family business and the stress with her husband is in conflict with her personal dreams and aspirations.* Venus in Gemini

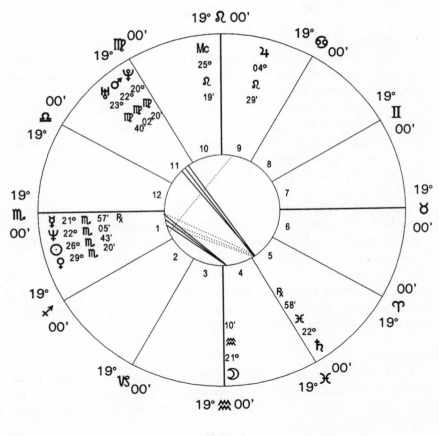

Chart 4

oppose Saturn in Sagittarius: *Her unstable love life weakens her ability to help humanity.*

Dotted (Blue) Lines: Saturn in Sagittarius trine Mercury in Leo: *Her business philosophy is strengthened by her leadership in the communications field. Jupiter in Libra trine Venus in Gemini. Her generosity with people is motivated by unconditional love.* Pluto in Virgo trine Mars in Aries: *Her efficient strength complements her assertive energy.*

The Bottom Line: In resolving personal conflicts, she will free herself to serve humanity and achieve peace of mind.

Chart 4

Client background: This woman is very capable and has several degrees, including one in psychology. Yet she has trouble deciding on one occupation and jumps from career to career.

Interpretation

Sun, Moon, and Rising Sign: She has both her Sun and Rising Sign in Scorpio with her Moon in Aquarius: *She has a very deep and questioning spirit and need to free her soul.*

Solid (Red) Lines: Pluto-Mars-Uranus conjunct in Virgo oppose Saturn in Pisces: *Her challenge is to analyze her power, drive, and opportunities in life and not be held down by fearful caution.* Moon in Aquarius square Mercury-Neptune-Sun all conjunct in Scorpio: *Her scattered emotions are confusing her personal, mental, and intuitive search for herself.*

Dotted (Blue) Lines: Saturn in Pisces trine Mercury-Neptune-Sun all conjunct in Scorpio: *Through inspired determination she will succeed in her personal quest for discovery.* Jupiter in Leo trine Venus in Scorpio: *Her proud confidence helps her understand and love herself.*

The Bottom Line: Her karma is to dig deeply into her inner nature and decide on her mission in life. When she does, her destiny is to realize her strength and power.

Chart #5

Client background: This woman is a dedicated mother who also wants to accomplish something in the world. She needs to realize her potential but feels guilty when she thinks about leaving her family alone.

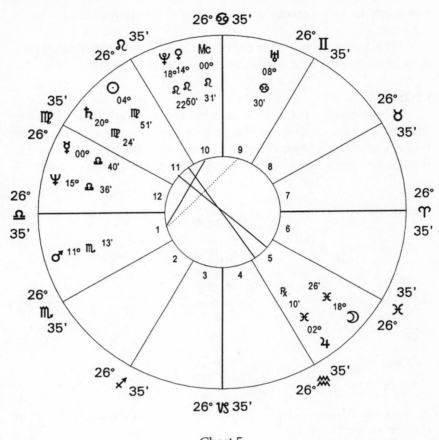

Chart 5

Interpretation

Sun, Moon and Rising: Sun in Virgo, Moon in Pisces and Libra Rising: *She is a caring individual with very sensitive emotions and a focus on relationships.*

Solid (Red) Lines: Sun in Virgo oppose Jupiter in Pisces: *Her serving nature is compounded by a fear of indulgence.* Saturn in Virgo oppose Moon in Pisces: *Her goal for productive accomplishments needs to be balanced with her devotion as a mother.* Mars in Scorpio square Venus in Leo: *Her intense drive clashes with her family pride.*

Dotted (Blue) Lines: Mars in Scorpio trine Uranus in Cancer: *She needs to take decisive action that is compatible with her family activities.*

The Bottom Line: Her challenge is to discover fulfilling projects in the world that don't interfere with her family.

Chart 6

Client background: This man is a financial advisor who does fund raising for environmental projects. He is spiritually motivated and tends to get emotionally involved with his business. He has the tendency to take on several ventures at the same time.

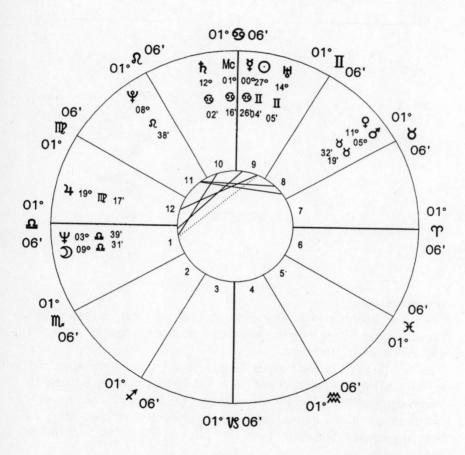

Chart 6

Interpretation

Sun, Moon and Rising: Sun in Gemini, both the Moon and Rising in Libra: *His nature is very witty and intelligent, and he has a charming and sensitive personality.*

Solid (Red) Lines: Moon in Libra square Saturn in Cancer: *His emotional sensitivity is needed in his business affairs.* Jupiter in Virgo squares Uranus in Gemini: *His success in accomplishing a project is compromised by too many activities.* Pluto in Leo square Venus and Mars conjunct in Taurus: *His powerful effect on humanity is dependent upon the use of other people's money, sometimes creating stress.*

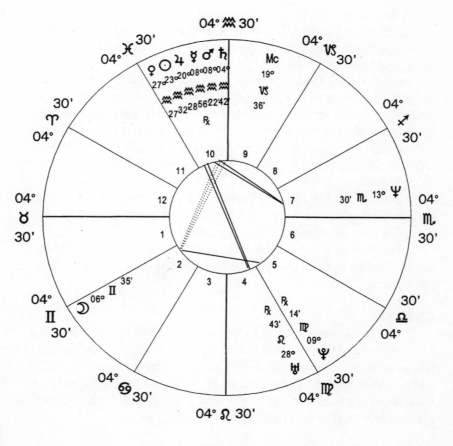

Chart 7

Dotted (Blue) Lines: Moon in Libra trine Uranus in Gemini: *His social awareness is empowered by his spiritual knowledge.*

The Bottom Line: His Karma is to focus his energy so he can accomplish his spiritual plan to help the environment and have fun while he is doing it.

Chart #7

Client background: This is one of the 1962 "Aquarian Kids" that had a stellium of planets in Aquarius. She had a very stormy upbringing with her parents and has never gotten married, even though she has lived with a man for many years. Her occupation is as a clinical psychologist.

Interpretation

Sun in Aquarius, Moon in Gemini and Taurus Rising: *Her inner essence is independent, with a need for understanding her emotions, and she is very capable.*

Solid (Red) Lines:Uranus in Leo opposed Sun-Venus conjunct in Aquarius: *A fiery, unstable upbringing needs to be balanced by freeing herself through open-minded techniques in her career.* Neptune in Scorpio square Mars-Mercury conjunct in Aquarius: *Psychological questioning will change her mental attitude about life.* Moon in Gemini square Pluto in Virgo: *Verbalizing her emotions is inhibited by rigid controls.*

Dotted (Blue) Lines: Moon in Gemini trine Saturn, Mars-Mercury conjunct in Aquarius: *Her talent is the ability to talk to people about their emotions and help release old mind-sets.*

The Bottom Line: Her Karma is to use her experiences in her early life to help people understand and change patterns in their lives.

Chart #8

Client background: This woman is one of the last true cowgirls. She was born and raised on a large, working cattle ranch in the southwest. Her entire family is very strong and physical. For years she was a stunt woman in Hollywood until she got badly injured in a stunt accident. She was rehabilitated, and is now a successful artist and sculptor of the human form.

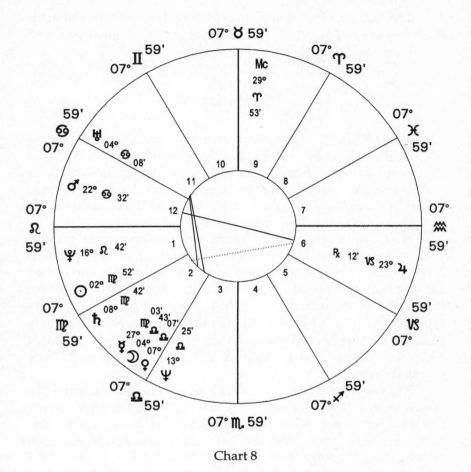

Chart 8

Interpretation

Sun, Moon and Rising: She is Virgo, Moon in Libra with a Leo Rising: *Her nature is shy, with sensitive emotions, yet she has a strong outer image.*

Solid (Red) Lines: Jupiter in Capricorn oppose Mars in Cancer: *Her strong physical body is challenged by dangerous situations.* Uranus in Cancer square Moon-Venus conjunct in Libra: *Her eccentric activity is in contrast to her creative and emotional refinement.*

Dotted (Blue) Lines: Mercury in Virgo trine Jupiter in Capricorn: *Her intelligent mind, working with her ambitious determination, has created a safe and successful career.*

The Bottom Line: Her karma is living dangerously and hurting her body, and her destiny is to develop her artistic talents and to portray the human form with beauty.

Summary

These examples show how to interpret a chart in simple, meaningful terms. It takes practice, but your clients will benefit from this clear picture of themselves. The more they understand their purpose in life through astrology, the more astrology will become a part of their daily life. There are a few additional suggestions that I have for your client interactions:

Astrology is a service industry. You are serving the need of your client, so *cater* to your audience. Approach them on their level. If they need specifics, present a more technical view. If they are spiritual, talk about God, keyed to concerns within the chart. If people are visually oriented, introduce the planets as archetypes. Be creative. One of my clients was born on a farm, and we pictured each of her planets as an animal. Her Sun is in Leo with a Moon in Taurus. She imagined a lion with a tortoise on its back giving directions!

It is very important to tape each session for your client. Otherwise your words of wisdom are lost forever. Dedicated clients listen to their tapes over and over again. The initial tape for my clients is a study guide. Included with their chart and tape is a list of suggested reading. Most of my clients actually buy the books and study their chart. Many come back with pages of notes they have taken. Plus, the tape can be easily transcribed and highlighted for future study.

It is time for astrologers to empower their clients with the knowledge of astrology, instead of keeping all this information to themselves, and giving clients snippets when "we" feel they are ready. If the astrologer keeps all the knowledge, it is a co-dependent relationship because the client must ask the all-knowing astrologer for everything. Granted, not all clients want to do their own transits, but many will and could do so easily with our help. The more available we make astrology to the world, the busier we will be in our practice.

As an astrologer, you need to know what astrology can and can not provide. Astrology is a diagnostic tool. It explains our life patterns, but it does not say how to resolve them specifically. Deep-seated problems should be handled by psychologists, therapists, or certified counselors. As Rob Hand says, "Astrologers are the seers, and therapists are the healers." Know your boundaries. Therefore, it is important to have a handy list of qualified professionals to whom you can refer your clients.

The astrological interpretation is a sacred event. We are holding our client's very soul in our hands. Any one word that we say may change this person's life forever. Please take this honor and responsibility to heart.

Jeff Jawer

Jeff Jawer holds a B.A. in Astrology from the University of Massachusetts at Amherst, and has been a professional astrologer since 1973. He is one of the pioneers in experiential astrology, and is well known for his work with astrodrama in the United States, Canada, Brazil, and in Europe.

Jeff holds professional certification from the City of Atlanta's Board of Astrology Examiners (which he has served as chairman) and the American Federation of Astrologers. He is one of the founders of AFAN and served on its Steering Committee for four years. He also helped establish UAC and served as its president for six years.

Jeff has written scores of articles which have been published in astrology publications throughout the world, including Llewellyn's *How to Personalize the Outer Planets, Intimate Relationships,* and *Spiritual, Metaphysical & New Trends in Astrology.* He is a lecturer and workshop leader, and has appeared three times at the prestigious World Congress of Astrology in Switzerland.

Jeff spent two years in France associated with the Network for Humanistic Astrology. He met his wife Danick there, and the two of them lead experiential astrology workshops together in the United States and Europe. Jeff, Danick, and their two Leo daughters live in Atlanta, Georgia.

Jeff Jawer

Telling Stories to Make Your Point

 The role of the astrologer is to help the client. This is a sacred trust, a position of honor as intermediary between heaven and earth. It requires confidence and humility, the ability to speak well and remain silent, to ask questions and to provide answers. We need the wisdom of Jupiter, the objectivity of Mercury, the love of Venus, the compassion of the Moon, the courage of the Sun, and the discretion of Saturn. Our job is to turn cycles and symbols into meaningful information for our clients. This requires successful communication.

Communication is the act of connecting with another person. It takes place in many ways, and on many levels. Lovers can communicate through a gentle touch, a knowing look in the eyes or with special words of endearment. Scientists may communicate through formulas and statistics, businesspeople with profit and loss statements, and artists with their paints and brushes. Astrologers, naturally, use astrology for communication. We begin with the birth chart and go on from there. We can add transits, progressions, solar arcs, midpoints, and harmonics. We can also talk about archetypes, the inner child, karma, faith, the oedipal complex, or anything else we choose to add. "You make your own reality," "it's your father projection which stands in the way of successful relationships," "serve or suffer," "be your own best friend." The choices we have are endless. There are no rules about what we can and can not say in an astrological consultation. We can be Buddhist astrologers, Christian astrologers, neo-pagan astrologers, born-again Jewish, Hindu, Sufi, or agnostic astrologers. We can even consult with our clients without mentioning astrological terms.

All that counts is whether or not we help our clients. How and what we communicate to them will determine our likelihood of success. But communication is not just about the words that we speak. It is also about the pauses, voice tone, body language, and everything else that is present during the counseling session. "Communication takes place on all levels, particularly in the patient's unconscious," according to the famed hypnotherapist, Milton Erickson. This means that we need to connect to the unconscious part of our clients if we want to be effective counselors. Without awareness of this level of communication we not only miss opportunities to help, but we may inadvertently damage the client's capacities for growth.

One of the most common ways to do this is to place excessive importance on being right. Clearly, an astrologer must be reasonably accurate in interpretation to gain the trust and confidence of clients. However, being right is not always being most helpful. For example, you tell someone with Pluto in the 7th House that he or she is likely to attract manipulative partners. The client confirms this as true. Where do we go from here? Is the client to assume that she is destined to only have relationships with manipulative partners? Must that be true in the future? What do you think, Mr. or Ms. Astrologer? Because if your analysis stops at this point your client would be better off without you. Perhaps you've dashed whatever hopes your client has for relationships which are not coercive in nature. You are accurate, *but the client suffers.*

It takes a good deal of ego to put oneself in the position of being a counselor, even more so for astrologers who do not have the support of cultural institutions like universities and professional organizations. But we have heaven on our side, literally and figuratively, when we employ the names of the gods and goddesses (the planets) in our consultations. By using these ancient archetypes we can connect with the client at the soul level, which enables us to have a powerful impact. Still, the astrologer lives the paradox of having access to powerful sources of information, while being relegated to the margins of contemporary society. This slippery position can leave the astrologer more vulnerable than he or she may imagine.

To counteract this vulnerability, we take ourselves seriously. Sometimes, perhaps, too seriously, invoking the rigid, shadow side of Saturn. Yet we are under considerable pressure to provide the client with right answers in a single session. No psychotherapist would work under such restrictive conditions, but we astrologers are professional information machines. You put in a question and out comes an answer. Or you put in birth data and out come a hundred answers about love, family, health, sex, and everything else under the Sun (to say nothing of the Moon, planets, asteroids, and nodes). For 3,000 years we have been paid to have answers, so we take ourselves seriously. The present-day price for wrong answers may be losing a client. In the past the price may have been losing our heads. Fortunately, time and astrology have changed.

A counseling astrologer is a communicator. All our wisdom and insight will be of little value unless it is received by the clients with whom we want to share it. An astrology reading is often a recitation of interpretations based on the leading texts of the day, and the astrologer's personal experiences and values. Readings are not objective; they are intense one-to-one experiences in which *the manner of transmission is as important as the message itself.* As Marshall McLuhan said, "The medium is the message." Television, regardless of its content, transmits a particular energy which is different from film, radio, books, or magazines. Applying this to the astrological counseling session, we can say that the medium of transmission, the astrologer, is more important than the words she or he says. Clearly, if an astrologer is a hopeful person, the client is likely to receive a hopeful message. A fearful astrologer will conduct the consultation around the subject of fear. Though we may believe that we are objective sources of information, the words we choose, our voice, body language, and inflection all give a meta-message, *which is really what the client receives.*

If the medium is the message, the astrologer can be a very serious message like *The New York Times*, gossipy like *People* magazine, inspirational like *The Daily Word*, analytical like a Jungian text, mythological like Joseph Campbell, or folksy like a down-home grandpa. The style will be retained by the client on the unconscious level, and will be the effect we have on the client. What may be most important then is not what we say, *but how we say it.* It occurs to me this message-communication bond with the client may account for successful readings done with incorrect birth times.

An astrologer may change styles throughout his career and will focus on different issues and approaches according to his current processes. Haven't you had your spiritual "give it up to God" phase as well as your practical "check the interest rates" cycle? In any case, the astrologer transmits these concerns to the client, regardless of the actual contents of the natal chart. What else do we have to give but ourselves, what else can we teach except who we are. If this is true, then the way to be of most service to a client is to include all of yourself, to range from high to low, to include sin and salvation, seriousness and humor, humility and pride. The astrologer is not just a talker of words, *but the embodiment of astrology itself,* an agent of cosmic forces. To do this we need to be all of the planets and all of the signs, to be able to play in the fields of the cosmos with the open spirit of the child, so that we can continually discover who we are becoming, rather than defending who we already are.

The purpose of this article is to explore ways in which the astrologer can regain the spirit of discovery and the joy of playing with the horoscope. This frees the astrologer from the onerous demand to be all-knowing, and offers the client a model for creativity. You can try these ideas with your own chart, with family and friends, or in a teaching setting. You may then be able to integrate some of these principles in more serious counseling sessions.

I propose that you consider reading the birthchart as you would a fairy tale. The horoscope becomes not a cosmic Rohrschach, but a cosmic comic book. Approaching the birth chart as a piece of fiction, rather than a factual document, permits the astrologer to be much more creative. If you are not seeking the right answers or trying to fix the problems of the client, a shift occurs in your relationship. The astrologer is freed to imagine and play, to evoke life-enhancing qualities *which are healing in and of themselves.* The traditional image of the astrologer is somewhat

Saturnian. Perhaps we need the freedom to make things up, to tell stories and play to release the Jupiter in us. Remember that we teach who we are. What is *your* message? What feeling would you like people to leave with after you've met with them?

Creativity for the Astrologer

Telling stories with the horoscope expands an astrologer's creativity. It helps us to leave the box of left-brain analysis, and move into the imagistic realm of the right-brain. Most astrologers have played creatively with the symbols. Astro-Dice, three dice of 12 sides each for the planets and nodes, signs, and houses, are a great means to stimulate this sort of play. Someone asks a question and throws the dice. For example, what kind of person would I be most happy with? The dice are thrown and Uranus in Cancer in the 6th House comes up. What are some of your answers? An extra-terrestrial working mother? An idealistic health care provider? A radical feminist service worker? A nervous fat person with indigestion? An electrician in a day-care center? An illegal alien house cleaner? A robotic nurse?

It's a bit like putting together one from column A, one from column B, and one from column C. You can do this with lists of keywords for planets, signs, and houses. Normally when we learn to read a chart, we synthesize the different elements, we search meaning by finding links, but when we play, we don't have to find meaningful links. We are free to put together the most nonsensical ideas and to have fun. The value of this is that we can discover things. Life is not as well organized and predictable as most astrology texts would have us believe. Contradictions run rampant, mixed messages mingle freely, paradox prowls the corridors. In fact, it is paradox which can open the brain and expand our consciousness. It is used in Zen, Gurdjieff, and the movement work of Moshe Feldenkrais, as well as by mystical teachers throughout the ages. By taking us to a seemingly nonsensical place, we are led to discover truths which ordinary logic can never reveal.

We can open up our thinking by deconstructing astrology as we know it, the logical process of describing what's real, and reconstructing it to include new ideas and images. In this way, we expand our astrological vocabulary, we move beyond what is known, and are able to evolve and grow as astrologers. This permits us to offer more ideas to our clients, but even more important, it offers us new ideas about ourselves. Without this evolutionary process we and our work remain stagnant. Can you imagine if astrology did not change? Saturn in Taurus in the 6th might mean that the client would be an enslaved pyramid worker. This absurd notion, though, is only an exaggeration of what happens with all astrologers: we find our pat phrases, our basic concepts, and we repeat them to our clients until something changes us and our work.

Imagination is an essential tool for successful astrological practice. You can not know all the possibilities in someone's life. You have to guess, to make it up, to invent new scenarios to hope to expand yourself to the level of your clients' potentials. Think again about the essential philosophy behind your counseling. If you believe, as I do, that growth is possible, that life is to be discovered, rather than endured, you must be willing to discover yourself. If you are what you teach, you must be willing to rediscover yourself on a regular basis. Here's one way to do this: take a new look at your chart and try to interpret every element in it differently than you have in the past. If the Sun in Capricorn in the 10th house represents your father as the autocratic head of the household, what other ways could you read this. You can stretch your imagination and stretch the symbols without doing damage to their essential meanings.

Symbolic truth is the truth of possibility. It is not about finding the right answer or interpretation; it is exploring possible interpretations and meanings beyond those already known. What are the shades and colors of Capricorn that you can describe? Authoritarian, yes, but also the martyr, the savior, the spiritual servant. Can you make up a story about the Sun in your chart that could show it as hero, victim, witness, partner, etc.?

The willingness to be wrong, to make mistakes, is vital in any creative process. The desire to express and discover during the process needs to be greater than one's fear of criticism. Virgo follows Leo, which suggests that perfection *follows* expression. The child needs the self-confidence to explore the world of his own creation before he needs to refine that expression in some culturally understood form. Notice how children play. They make up their own version of reality which, ideally, is for them and not for some critical public. If the criticism comes too early, creativity is stifled. As astrologers, we are aware of the status we hold in society, a status which puts us, too often, on the defensive. We need to prove to our clients that what we do is valid, that it works. This need to be right stifles creativity. It can also inhibit the discovery process that takes place in a successful counseling session. We always have the option to ask clients if our observations are correct or not, and to offer us whatever feedback they choose to share. If we listen, we can incorporate these responses into the counseling session.

When we are open and flexible, we can turn so-called mistakes into useful material for the client. For example, if you say to a client, "I see that you have the Moon in Capricorn opposing your Saturn. I imagine that your relationship with your mother was rather difficult. Perhaps you didn't feel safe with her or free to show your emotions." The client might say, "No, my mother was very supportive. I trust her quite a bit." This can lead to further dialogue about this relationship. Perhaps mother really was trustworthy. You could explore this by asking questions about what the client could and could not share with mother. Finally, we might discover that the symbolism of the Moon *in this case* operated on a very high level, that the client really *was* happy with his mother. Or the client could discover that this safety and security were contained within a limited context, that the client felt safe as long as he behaved like an adult, for example.

So-called wrong interpretations may lead to the truth just as easily as correct ones may. In fact, correct interpretations can close off dialogue; they are so self-evident that they close the door to further exploration of the issues. Of course, this needn't be the case; the key is flexibility on the part of the astrologer.

Discovery works when we are willing to play. Take a look at your 5th House. It will tell you a good deal about how you play. Pure play has no goal other than pleasure. Creativity and discovery occur as byproducts of this undemanding situation. Many of us, though, have been inhibited in our play as children and in our self-expression as adults. Goal-oriented symbols such as Saturn or Capricorn in the 5th House infer that play must produce concrete results. This often leads to inhibition of spontaneity, although it can also bring a high level of expertise in a particular arena of expression.

One of the best ways to discover is to make things up. Creativity, fantasy, and imagination are encouraged by a willingness to produce responses which are not based on known outcomes or facts, but which come from within (or above). A way I safely do this with clients is *to tell them* that I'm guessing. This way they understand that I'm not trying to provide a definitive answer, but am interested in exploring possibilities which may help the client in her or his discovery process. Another way to frame this is to say, "Imagine if . . ." For someone with the Moon in Cancer square Uranus you could say, "Imagine if you've just hurt yourself and your mother is comforting you by holding you in her arms and suddenly the telephone rings. She drops you to go and answer the telephone." Then ask for feedback. This might certainly awaken some ideas about the meaning of Uranus and the Moon.

Another value in the use of stories and images is that of indirectness. When we describe a situation which is not precisely that which the person experienced, we may be better able to connect with the person's unconscious. The famed hypnotherapist Milton Erickson was a master at making up stories to deal with his patients' problems. However, his stories often seemed to have nothing to do with the stated problem. Encoded in the story, and in his way of telling it, was a message for the unconscious. This indirectness bypassed the conscious aspect of resistance and allowed the information to touch his patients at the deeper unconscious level. Erickson understood that communication takes place on all levels, but that the most powerful impact could be made when connecting with the unconscious. If you are interested in helping people change and grow, this connection may be the most important.

A birth chart is a multi-level source of information. Creative work with the horoscope allows the astrologer to touch more of these levels. How many different interpretations do you have for Venus in Leo? What does she look like? How does she sound? Walk? What are the kinds of events that one can associate with Venus in Leo? What are the psychological needs and experiences of such a person? What are the spiritual lessons to be learned? Every planet placement can (and should) be examined in this way, at least as part of an astrologer's training.

The field of experiential astrology or astrodrama is based on these principles. Its purpose is to open the astrologer to direct experience of astrological principles as a means of learning more about astrology and personal self-discovery. There is a level of meaning which goes beyond words. For example, try to find the meaning of Pluto without using words. Where is it in your body, what color and shape does it have? If Pluto could speak, what would his voice be like. These exercises provide a more direct experience of astrological symbolism than those found through words alone. As astrologers, we talk a great deal; in the process we may overlook other means of experiencing and understanding. For further exploration into experiential astrology I recommend my articles on Astrodrama in *Spiritual, Metaphysical & New Trends in Modern Astrology* and "Living the Drama of the Horoscope" in *Astrology Now*, Number 22 (both from Llewellyn) as well as *Astrology Alive!* by Barbara Schermer (The Aquarian Press, 1989).

Telling Stories with Client Examples

Fundamental to the notion of telling stories with a horoscope is the belief that individuals have choices in life. In fact one of the purposes of the technique is to broaden the choices that are offered in the natal chart. This brings up the question of how we use astrological language. We can interpret a symbol in many ways and on many levels, but Mars is Mars and Venus is Venus, i.e., that each has its own core-meaning. Understanding these core-meanings gives you the solid foundation to explore the symbols without losing their essences.

I have in front of me the chart of a man who has Venus conjunct Pluto in Virgo in the 12th House square Mars in Gemini in the 9th. There is a great deal of material here with which we can work. The facts of the case are that this is someone who desperately wants an intimate relationship. He is homosexual and does not live in a community in which it is comfortable to express this openly. He is also a student of astrology. Venus conjunct Pluto can indicate forbidden love, of course. It combines the principles of pleasure and comfort with those of desire and intensity. This combination is very often associated with those for whom love and manipulation are closely linked. So we are left with hunger and desire for love, but possible distrust of being loved. The 12th

House can be called "the closet" of the horoscope, as it often deals with aspects of self which are hidden. This adds to the complexity of relationships by re-emphasizing that love exists outside ordinary reality.

Mars in Gemini square Venus and Pluto indicates that overt pursuit and sexual energy push hidden desires to the surface. Whenever Mars is square Venus, social and sexual issues may be emphasized. The tension between what one wants (Venus) and how one goes about getting it (Mars) can be evident. For the client in question, it adds fuel to love's fire. Venus and Pluto by themselves in the 12th House might allow relationship issues to be skirted or buried, but the dynamic square from busy Mars in Gemini keeps the issue on the front burner.

Being aware of astrology and having had his disappointments in relationships, this man is left with a somewhat negative image of Venus in his chart. Frankly, this is a complex pattern, one that doesn't easily produce harmonious relationships, but as with all charts it has its meaning and purpose. In fact, when we become who we truly are, the impediments fall away, and we have access to all the love of Venus, comfort of the Moon, warmth of the Sun, dynamism of Mars, etc. This is true for any placement in any chart. The way out is to be ourselves, but to be that self at a conscious level which allows choices and, finally, freedom.

So what is the story? Better yet, what are the stories of Venus conjunct Pluto in Virgo in the 12th House square Mars in Gemini in the 9th? Let's start with Venus: she could be a Virgin (in Virgo) who is held captive by a dragon (Pluto), or by a jealous partner. She could be in a convent (12th House), held against her will (Pluto) as punishment for her excessive sexual desires or because of the fear created by her great beauty. Mars is the traveling knight who spies her through the convent gate. He could be bringing news of a faraway place (Gemini, 9th House) which frees her from her confinement. He could be a lighthearted jokester who tricks the dragon (mother superior, jealous husband) into allowing her to escape. Does she want to escape? Has she given up hope, does she feel too guilty about her sexuality? Mars cajoles her, seduces her. She can hold firm and remain outside the world, or join him in its uncertainty. The rules of the convent are clear (Virgo), but the ways of the world (Gemini) are varied and unpredictable. Let's stop here.

What have we found? We've discovered that the uncertainty of the world can threaten the perfection of the cloistered life. There may be security in the world of unfulfillment, a perverse comfort in being on the outside looking in. We must deal with the paradox that what brings us pain can also comfort us. The unconscious desires familiarity, even familiar pain against the unknown possibilities of pleasure. Individuals can act out multiple facets of any planetary complex. So here we have the victim of unfulfilled love, but we may also have the pride of the Virgin (perfectionist) who holds herself apart from the world of ordinary, less pure relationships. The individual can act out each of the planets in a variety of ways and switch roles among them. This Venus may be willing to make great sacrifices for love, and then change roles with Pluto and become demanding and dominating. Venus with Pluto in Virgo can be tremendously loyal and committed, even with little expectation of return, then switch to Mars in Gemini and start flirting with someone else.

What I have done here is to break down the first series of images and begun to interpret them. You may or may not want to do this with your clients. It can be useful to simply present some versions of a story and ask the client for feedback. You might ask which stories, which roles are the most appealing and why. Any inquiry can help lead the client into further exploration of his motives and feelings around the subject. "No, I don't feel like a prisoner," he might say. This can affirm his capacity to act in the face of limitations. It could also be his denial. Effective counseling requires intuition, experience, or the grace of God to take the next step. There are no hard and fast rules about what will be most helpful. If you truly trust yourself and have an open heart you are most likely to be helpful. There are innumerable other sources of information on counseling to which you can refer for further information.

By creating a story in a fictional setting, the client is also freed to imagine, create, and discover. *Defenses drop when we are making up stories* which are not designed to be literal descriptions of the person's circumstances. For the metaphysically oriented, there is also the possibility that such fantasies could be seen as true in a past life. There is no way of proving this, nor is it necessary. It's an "as if" situation that attempts to create frameworks in which the person can piece together his or her identity.

We can go off into another direction with our Venus-Pluto friend and create a different story. Venus in Virgo is loved for serving. Her position in the 12th House shows her devotion to the sick, the poor, the dispossessed. The conjunction with Pluto adds danger, pressure, the presence of death. Is she Mother Teresa among the lepers of India? It could certainly symbolize a life in which relationships are met through service to those less fortunate. Is Mars coming from the 9th symbolizing one's desire to escape? Is he the mental confusion that comes from opposing ideas (Gemini in the 9th), or fresh ideas for dealing with intractable problems (Pluto in the 12th)?

A possible interpretation here is not that love is shameful or should be hidden, but that personal pleasure must be renunciated. Here, Venus is not connected to a fault, but to virtue. In either case, it is possible that personal intimacy is difficult to come by. It's clear that we can go further with this: is this Venus a woman in a harem, a prostitute, someone disfigured and institutionalized? The possibilities are as many as your imagination and understanding of astrological symbolism will allow. This particular pattern I have chosen is complex and usually difficult to live with, so the challenge now is to tell some stories that have happy endings.

Venus in Virgo, the virtuous princess, held special powers (Pluto). She had the ability to attract any person her heart desired. In loving them, they were transformed (Pluto) and healed of all their wounds and maladies. Her divine love (12th House) not only healed others, but enabled her to accumulate wealth (Pluto was the god of wealth), which she used to improve the material conditions (Virgo) of those around her. She created a magical retreat (12th House) to which people could come for healing of the body and soul. Even though living in a remote place (12th House), people came from far and wide (Mars in the 9th) to see her. They brought stories of their worlds (Gemini) which were shared openly with her. Even though she rarely left her magical retreat it was as if the whole world was open to her. Word traveled far (Mars in Gemini in the 9th) and led others to learn her skills and bring healing to their own communities.

The key element here is that Pluto with Venus is about a love that transforms. Love is not about continuing the ordinary forms of relationship, but in breaking new ground, going deeper toward the essence of relationship. The pain and disappointment that this person might suffer in love is a kind of rehearsal for that love which is both physical (Virgo is, after all, an Earth sign) and divine. The jealousy, mistrust, and backstabbing that could be experienced are the means of seeing all angles (12th House) of relationship so that they become complete in every way. Love and relationship are skills (Virgo) which are learned through purging (Pluto) old patterns.

Mars can function as a distraction from the commitment to relationships, or as a means of standing outside and seeing them objectively. Typically, Mars in Gemini may exhibit behavior which looks detached and belies the intensity of feelings of Venus and Pluto. We can better understand by re-examining the meaning of the word Virgo. Originally the word "virgin" did not mean non-sexual. A virgin was an unmarried or free woman. Perhaps it was too much for men to accept that a woman could be independent and sexual, thus the reinterpretation. This suggests that this person not have a life without sex, but one in which an element of *independence* is maintained within relationships. This may appear paradoxical compared to the intensity of Pluto. However, one can be fully committed to another person while maintaining his or her own identity. This is, actually, the only way to have a fully realized relationship.

Another facet of the sign Virgo is its perfectionism. Taken to its negative extremes, everything is seen as less than ideal or adequate. Criticism of others and of self can create distance and isolation. However, a dynamic approach to the sign Virgo is to see it as "perfecting," not necessarily perfect. The difference is that one can be in a process of improving and refining, moving toward a more perfect state, but one does not have to be perfect now. Measurement of self then is done to see progress and aid its continuation. Excess criticism, though, inhibits progress as it diminishes one's sense of worth.

The examples given thus far were not exhaustive. It would be possible to make up many other different stories for Venus, Pluto and Mars for the combination with which we worked. We could tell humorous stories, tragic ones, modern ones, and ancient ones. If you are working with elements within your own chart, try as many different possibilities as you can. Your mood and situation play an important role in where your imagination takes you. You can use whatever you come across as inspiration.

Imagine that you want to deepen your understanding of your Moon-Saturn square to move beyond its present limitations. You can imagine the Moon as a person, perhaps someone famous, someone who is an inspiration to you. Saturn could be another person, or Saturn could be a set of conditions that inhibit our lunar heroine.

You can reverse this process by plugging inspirational people into your chart. When you find yourself inspired by someone, ask yourself what planet in *your* chart best represents this person. What if you just can't see yourself as courageous as this person. Approach your Mars or Sun and explore what either would need to have this level of courage. If your Mars in Pisces in the 6th doesn't seem strong enough to put you where you want to be, inquire as to what it would take to put him there. Your Mars in Pisces, even the puniest, skinniest, most scaredy-cat Mars, provides a link with archetypal Mars. The archetypal Mars has all the initiative possible. Your birth chart Mars shows you the way to get there. By traveling your own path in your way you can make the connection with the cosmos and make the cosmos work for you. This is the purpose of astrology, not just to predict the future or to analyze oneself, but to connect with the greater whole, the Sun, Moon, and planets, the heavens above.

For the next step, let's go on and tell a story about an *entire* natal chart. This is a method that has been used in workshop settings to stimulate astrological interpretation and open the creativity of the participants. It is often the case that some element in the story is a precise description of part of the person's life. This, however, is not the goal. We don't seek facts, we seek truth. The difference is that truth is about meaning, about essence, while facts sometimes reflect the surface, but hide the inner workings. The suspension of the astrologer's age-old need to be right is liberating. It is a vital part of every astrologer's education. It also allows the magic of intuition to flow more easily. Besides, it's fun.

It is not necessary to be serious when dealing with serious matters. Fun allows us to move beyond certain limits because it is relaxing. When we are not pressured to be right, we can play like children again. After the child leads us to the truth, the adult can go about the business of explaining what it could mean. The game, as I like to call it, has very few rules—in fact, almost none. I'll offer here some guidelines which may help you to do this in a group.

(When I presented this material at the 1993 World Congress of Astrology in Lucerne, Switzerland, the editor of this book was present. Being a good Capricorn, he said that he hadn't "played" before and didn't know the rules. I said there weren't any.)

The game will be played as an adventure, a quest. The protagonist can be any planet. In this example we'll begin with the Sun. The protagonist or hero will define his goal, and then journey around the birth chart. If you want to explore emotions more directly, you could make the Moon the protagonist, or use Venus if your search is for the meaning of love. You can take the hero around the chart in either direction. You can even change direc-

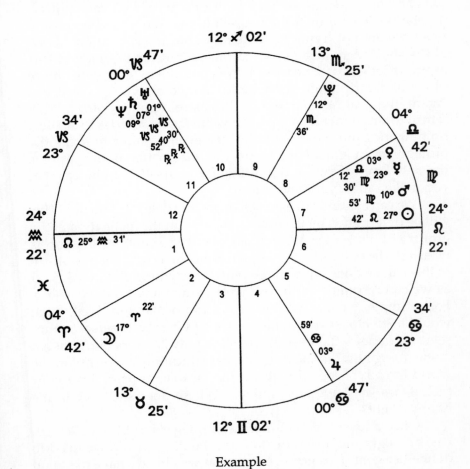

Example

tion in the middle of the quest (the retrograde version of the game). You do not have to follow the houses in order, although this seems most logical and simple for the present. It is even possible to use dice or something similar to advance the protagonist, but, this is our first game together and the first time I've written a description of it, so I'll keep it as straightforward as possible.

To personify the planets, we begin by describing our hero. He's the Sun in Leo in the 7th House. Working with a group, I ask them questions and select the response I like best. You can have the group vote or discuss the options if you like. Of course, if you do this for yourself, such democratic procedures are not necessary. "What gender is our hero, male or female?" We can arbitrarily choose female in this case. While the Sun is archetypically male, we are not trying to be literal in our interpretation. "How old is she?" Any answer is acceptable, but for the sake of this example let's say 22 years old. We continue by asking for more physical description: height, build, hair color, type of voice, etc. Again, the goal here is not to fulfill astrological typology. We'll return to the symbolism later. All we're trying to do is to create a framework from which to build. It's even possible to make the protagonist an animal or a spirit. The imagination of the group is the only limit. If you're doing this for yourself, the choices that you make can be very revealing.

We can continue in as much or as little detail as you like. This will be determined by the time available and the inclination of the group and its leader. We can ask about the clothing the Sun is wearing, the color of her eyes, whether she is smiling or not. All of this can be done without reference to anything else in the chart as we can reconnect with the symbolism at any time we desire. For example, we can ask the profession of the Sun. Well, what would a 7th House Sun in Leo do for a living? Salesperson, counselor for famous clients—oh, but she's only 22 years old. So what is she doing now? Is she finishing her education? Is she out in the world already? Does she live in the far-distant past? Take your pick. Does she have any siblings? Where does she live? Is she happy or not?

Once a foundation of ideas and images has been collected, we can begin the quest, the journey. First, however, we need to define her goal. This grows from what we already have made up and the placement of the Sun in the birth chart. For this 7th

House Sun in Leo, we can say that the goal is to meet the ideal partner. That sounds pretty reasonable, but let's go in another direction just to explore. We could say that this 22-year old is a princess (Leo) whose task it is to meet the king of an enemy nation and to make him an ally. Leo and the Sun symbolize the king; turning an enemy (opposite) into any ally can be a 7th House matter. Before we take that first step, however, there are a few other items to consider.

What is really being described is the journey *to* one's self. In this case it is the Sun's journey, but we could do the same with any other planet. We are going to take the Sun from its position in the birth chart and move it to each house and planet until it comes back to where it began. It is possible, though, to terminate at any point. It is permissible to meet obstacles that can not be overcome. Obviously, to put this in a counseling context would necessitate finding some kind of successful resolution. (Note: There are therapies in which it is appropriate to leave the client with his dilemma so that he must resolve it on his own. However, we are going to approach this in the problem-solving tradition of astrology and make sure our hero does make it home.)

A variant on the game is to consider planets in harmonious aspect with the hero as helpers. Planets in hard aspect would be considered greater challenges. For this version, though, we'll take a straightforward approach and meet each planet as we come to it, considering it as offering both rewards and challenges.

Moving counterclockwise in the order of the houses, the first planet the Sun encounters is Mars in Virgo. We can ask who is this Mars? We can be as detailed as we want to be, but it makes sense to be less detailed than we were with the Sun. Since it's very early in the story, we could say that he is a toolmaker the Sun visits to prepare for her journey. With every encounter with a planet, I like to consider these questions: What does it offer? What does it demand?

Imagine that the group has decided that Mars is making a sword with which the Sun can protect herself. It is very finely made and can discriminate (Virgo) between friend and foe (two faces of the 7th House), and cut without wounding. What does Mars in Virgo ask of the Sun in Leo? To be humble, to be careful, to take time out to help those less fortunate than she? What can you add to this? Mars offers this magical sword in return. There is no anger without just cause, no actions wasted. Mars could ask the Sun to be physically fit and healthy (Virgo), perhaps to renounce marriage for service to the poor. It is possible, as well, to consider what the Sun can give to Mars. Is he sick, weak, stuck in a routine job? The Sun can give him courage, enable him to expand his methods in creative ways. We then agree on what has happened and we go on; that is, unless a bargain can not be struck. This would symbolize that the Sun (or will) would be blocked by the limitations of method (Mars). Can one be noble (Leo) when working in humble ways (Virgo)?

If you want to work more deeply, you can stop at this or any point, and develop the ideas and feelings that have come up in this encounter between the Sun and Mars. The fantasy story can be used or set aside at this point, according to the demands of the situation. Or you can go back and forth between reality and fantasy to develop certain points. We can use the fantasy to ask, "What if Mars was afraid? How could the Sun help him?" or "Is Mars being fair in asking the Sun to give up marriage?" You can even turn this into a role-playing situation by asking one person to play the role of Mars and the other the Sun. Set up the situation and let them improvise their parts. Experiential techniques like this bring astrology down from the realm of the mind and into the heart of the matter.

When the Sun has passed Mars, she is in possession of the magic sword which can cut without wounding. She then meets Mercury, also in Virgo. Who is this Mercury? We could imagine that he is highly analytical. What is his area of special interest? The group can offer up suggestions. When working with an individual, ask him to tell us about Mercury. No expertise in astrology is necessary as you can guide the person by posing the questions in plain English. Who is this Mercury in the 7th House? Is he a lawyer who analyzes contracts (7th House), a psychotherapist, or an advisor to the king? Perhaps he is a scientist. What are his gifts and his limitations? What does he have to offer our hero? We can imagine that he offers the gift of clear thought and the ability to unravel the most puzzling questions. He asks the Sun to be practical (Virgo) and objective (Mercury and the 7th House). Our hero must set aside her will to be able to see clearly. She must give up the need to be important (Sun in Leo) to be able to clearly understand the points of view of others.

What are the weaknesses of this Mercury in Virgo character? Clearly he may be too critical, too involved in deciphering the thoughts of others and unable to express his own. The Sun can offer him the courage to speak his own mind, to overcome his inadequacies, and take risks in self-expression. The Sun and Leo add warmth to the dryness of Mercury in Virgo.

As we come to the next planet, it is necessary to say a word about houses and their cusps. The chart given is calculated in the Koch system. Venus stands at the cusp (or door) of the 8th House. Since there are many different house systems, and birth times are rarely known with absolute precision, I use an orb of about 5 degrees. This means that a planet in the last 5 degrees of the 7th House is on the cusp of the 8th House. It can be interpreted as marking the transition between 7 and 8, the point where contracts (7th House) begin to be consummated (8th House). This is not the time to go further with a discussion of house systems and how to use them, but suffice it to say that a more organic approach to reading charts is to understand the nuance, the shifts from one house to another, and to see them as part of a dynamic system.

As we come to the next house, we can see it as crossing the border into a new country. You could do this when changing signs, but I find that it works best with houses. We can describe the physical landscape indicated by the sign on the cusp of a house. What might be the possibilities with Libra on the cusp of the 8th? Libra symbolizes beauty and harmony, but the 8th is a house of depth and intensity. We could imagine that we are descending into a beautiful valley. We are drawn in by the symmetry of the gentle hills surrounding this valley. The air is soft, the light is gentle. As we come to this place we are met by Venus. Who is she? You understand that you can make up any character that you want. You can elaborate to any degree that you want, but, for simplicity's sake, let's just say that she is a beautiful young woman who speaks in a gentle, even voice. Just describing Venus in Libra in this manner brings to mind that such evenness is often a way to pacify what feels like a dangerous situation. Is that Venus in Libra on the cusp of the 8th House? Is she the calming voice who lures us into the dangerous zone of intimacy and transformation, perhaps even death?

Venus in Libra can offer our hero the capacity to make herself attractive to all who see her. She can offer the gift of diplomacy, the very social skills the Sun needs to fulfill her quest. What dangers does she hold for our hero? Perhaps in developing the skills of seduction she will lose sight of her self and loyalty to her own people. In her desire to appeal to others, she moves out from her center and could become lost. These are some of the pitfalls of Venus in Libra. Her position on the cusp of the 8th House can mean that personal values are lost in relationship to the values of others. Is it also possible that our hero will be seduced by Venus, and forget the rest of her journey?

As we go down into the valley of the 8th House, we find that it gets darker and damper as we come to the end of the sign Libra. We don't see the border between Libra and Scorpio, but the air turns heavy. There's a change in the atmosphere. Does our hero become fearful? Does she long to return to the pleasures of Venus or will she continue? If she goes on, she soon meets Pluto at the end of the 8th House. He stands at the gates of the 9th House. What is required to get him to let us pass? Who is this Pluto? Is he small and dark, tall and fair? What does he want from the Sun, and what will he give in return?

Perhaps he holds the key to knowledge (9th House cusp), the secret to understanding the foreigners (9th again) with whom the Sun must negotiate. Does she have the maturity to deal with his demands? She has acquired the sword of Mars in Virgo, and the intelligence of Mercury in Virgo, which brings her discretion. She is not a bold and careless Leo any more. She has the grace of Venus in Libra as well. Yum, all the more attractive to our hungry Pluto! Perhaps he asks her a question, an impossible riddle of some kind. Sometimes the demands of Pluto are impossible to meet and we refuse to meet them, but Pluto demands his payment: a tribute, perhaps money, to pass through his domain. On the cusp of the 9th House, maybe he's a corrupt priest, a mad shaman, a holy terror whose road to God passes through hell. He asks the Sun to give up her immortality, to descend with him into the underworld after her death. Is she willing to pay such a price to serve her people? We all must pass through change (death) to go to the next level. He may ask her to renounce her old beliefs (9th House) and accept that she knows nothing of the truth. She can enter his world when she empties herself of all old philosophies or religious beliefs. We can imagine that with her pure and noble heart (Leo) she will take on this challenge.

What takes place in this 9th House of Scorpio? It may be a religious conversion, or perhaps she hears that her teacher has died. It can also be about learning about the power behind beliefs, that they must connect with deepest feelings and needs to be useful to us. In any case, the Sun travels on until she comes to the Sagittarius Midheaven. She has come out of the deep valley of Scorpio and finds herself standing on a hilltop, which gives her a view that allows her to see for miles and miles. She feels as if she has come through something, and now is able to continue her quest with new found optimism. The doubts are behind her, and she feels confident that she can fulfill her role as an ambassador for her people. We can elaborate on the important 10th House by examining its ruler Jupiter for more details. With Jupiter in Cancer in the 5th, she may recall the joy of her childhood and the play she had within her family and community. Her generous instincts (Jupiter and the 5th House) allow her to go on after the losses she experienced in Scorpio.

She passes from the high point in Sagittarius into a rocky, mountainous region (Capricorn). The earth is hard and dry; there are no trees, only occasional bushes and shrubs. Upon entering this land (the 11th House), she meets Uranus, Saturn, and Neptune. You can take each of these individually, but it is also possible to interpret them as a group, since they are in conjunction with one another. So she sees *three* people. The first has wild, frizzy hair and jabbers away in an undecipherable tongue (Uranus). The second stands firm and silent; she is very old looking and is the same drab color as the surrounding landscape (Saturn). The third is swathed in billowy cloth that seems to move with her (Neptune). Which one of these is the Sun going to approach? How does she feel about these three different characters? Asking questions like these can lead to a deeper understanding of the Sun's (client's) relationship to Uranus, Saturn, and Neptune. You can make a brief description of these three and ask your client to add more details. This is going to open awareness of these three planets in an indirect way.

How do you see this gang of three? What do they have to offer the Sun in her quest? What do they demand in return? Uranus offers the choice to be free, to stop the quest and go on and live her own life. The Sun comes from the 7th House where she is entangled in relationships, but Uranus in the 11th offers her the ideas of freedom and friendship in which the obligations to others are not so limiting. Uranus also reminds her that she belongs to the universe and not just to her own nation. Does she take this freedom? Are there other gifts that Uranus has for her? The possibility of political reorganization (Capricorn) may show that a treaty with one king is the old way of doing business, and that it is necessary to consider how all the nations can work together.

Saturn demands patience and discipline, but offers wisdom in return. "I will teach you about my experiences in matters of State," he might say. It will take time to share what he knows. Is the Sun in Leo willing to listen to someone else? Perhaps the discrimination she learned from Mars and Mercury in Virgo will serve her well here in Capricorn. She can take the best of the ideas here without taking on the entire Capricorn structure. What does Neptune offer? Vision, imagination, escape? Neptune can almost always offer us the possibility of remembering that we are one spirit. This is not the political notion of Uranus, but the inner knowing that is Neptune's. Neptune can also say that this quest doesn't matter, God takes care of all things. "You can go home, Sun in Leo, and enjoy your life. Forget your struggle here." Can the Sun do this? Is it true that none of this matters? These questions, clearly, are not just for our hero, but for all of us, for in each story there is also our own story.

The encounter with three such different characters can be confusing; we have the spirit of reform in Uranus, experience and commitment in Saturn, and dissolution in Neptune. What can a Leo Sun do with all of these? Is it even necessary to do anything? Uranus, Saturn, and Neptune represent three aspects of our hero's life which may be experienced as three different kinds of friends. You can ask the subject if she has different friends like these three and how they impact her life. Remember the point is to discover, to open, and to inquire. There are no right answers, no final interpretations of the natal chart; there is just the process of living with its innumerable possibilities.

Leaving the 11th House, we continue toward the 12th. At first, the land is similar (Capricorn on the cusp of the 12th), but then it changes as we enter Aquarius. What does it feel like in the land of Aquarius? How does that operate in the 12th House? Is it a place where people are hooked up to dream machines, where the body loses its importance? The common elements of

Aquarius and the 12th House are ethereal, non-material, and ideal. Is this paradise, or simply a place where the mind escapes from reality? In any case your imagination can fill in as much detail as you like.

We then come to the Ascendant, where we meet the Moon's North Node. You may treat this as a planet, a character, if you want. What does the North Node in Aquarius look like? Is it a friendly Dragon's Head, kind of a hippie dragon? Maybe it's a computer from the future. Our hero/ine meets him-/herself in the mirror at the Ascendant. This is the point where we project our image into the world, and here she has a chance to see herself as others do. Is she surprised that they see her as just another citizen (Aquarius) rather than a member of the royal family (Leo)? Maybe she's happy that others see her in this way. How does she feel about the differences between Leo and Aquarius. This is a central theme of this chart with the Sun opposite the Ascendant and the Nodes of the Moon along this axis. Leo is the Sun, the sole star in our Solar System. Aquarius, though, is about constellations in which many stars are seen as part of a larger pattern. Leo is the heart, the center; Aquarius is the circulatory system. The two are complimentary, but in opposition at the same time. Our hero will meet this opposition many times throughout her life.

To speed matters along we jump to the Moon in Aries in the 2nd House. The 2nd House cusp, being occupied by Aries, shows that this is a hot region, an incendiary place where resources can be spontaneously created, and just as quickly burned up. Who is the Moon in Aries? We can see her as a woman warrior. She has fought the battles and understands the value (2nd House) of standing up for oneself (Aries). She can be a funny old gal, warm and caring (Moon), but sharp and impatient (Aries) at the same time. She has something very important for our hero—she has the sense of self worth. This comes from the meanings of the 2nd House and from the self-interests of Aries. A 7th House Sun, one who lives for others, needs this balance very much. The Moon tells our hero that she must learn how to live alone, how to be self-sufficient. This can upset the Sun, as she sees herself through the mirror of relationship (7th House). "But," says the Moon, "the only way to succeed in relationship is to know who you are. When you begin with a strong sense of who *you* are, you can negotiate with love. When you have fear of losing yourself, because you are not sure who you are, you can only manipulate. Strong partnerships require strong individuals."

You can make up other stories, of course, in which the Moon tries to take the Sun off her path, away from her goal. What happens if this is done, if self-interest overcomes collective interest? How many ways can you present this Moon? She can be young or old, she can even be a man. What kind of animal would she be? Every exploration can fill in color and meaning in the birth chart. Every turn of the imagination can show us something new or show something already known, but in a way that can be seen and assimilated by the client. If you think of the birth chart as a diamond with many facets, you can see how it can be approached from a hundred different angles, each one reflecting its own light on the heart within.

We can continue through the 3rd House and pass the IC, or 4th House cusp, which shows the very roots of the person. Here we find Gemini, which means that duality is the thread that connects her to this world. It can allow for the contradictions between Leo and Aquarius, between Aries and the 7th House, between Saturn and Uranus. You can personify Gemini if you like, even though it's not a planet. Whatever you want to do to use this point is acceptable within the game.

The last planet encountered is Jupiter in Cancer in the 5th House. Is this the fat, jolly child, or a priest (Jupiter) playing with children. Perhaps it's someone making music or art. What is interesting here is that Jupiter, a planet of meaning, is in the 5th, a house of play. Is this Einstein with his violin? In any case the gift may be that which teaches that learning comes through play. This play is personal (Cancer), comes from the inside, and is not dictated by outside rules. "Discover your own truth," says this Jupiter, "The truth that brings you joy and makes the child within you sing. All I ask is that you laugh openly, that you show your joy as it also brings joy to others."

In the ancient Indian language of Sanskrit, the Jupiter is called "guru" or teacher. What are the gifts of Jupiter in Cancer? What does it ask of our Sun and what can our Sun give it in return? Jupiter asks the Sun to be ethical, to add meaning to experience. The Sun brings heart and life to Jupiter's principles, turning concept into experience, and belief into action. That is what you can do with astrology, as well. Turning interpretations, ideas, and even games like this one into a living experience.

Finally the Sun returns home. Has she fulfilled her quest? Has she met the king along the way, disguised as another planet, or is it really the king within her with which she has come to terms? What really matters, though, is the voyage itself. Using astrology in this manner allows an endless field for discovery and play. You can use transits, progressions, asteroids, midpoints, whatever you like. The goal in every case is the same: to go where the planets take you so that you may use them to find your way home. Have a great trip.

This creative method of managing astrology's symbolisms enriches client involvement with personal life-drama. It excites potentials of understanding and gives clear value to productive rapport between astrologer and client.

Wendy Z. Ashley

Wendy Ashley has been an astrologer since 1963, and has had an international practice in mythic astrology since 1985. She is also a ground-breaking teacher, synthesizing myth and astrology, restoring to astrology those symbolic elements lost when myth was deleted in the interests of modern religions and rationalism.

Her unique perspective arose from formal studies in myth, dreams, and symbols for 10 years with Charles Ponce, and informal studies with Marcia Moore and Joseph Campbell. She has a B.A. in Cultural Anthropology with concentrations in the Cross-Cultural Studies of Women and in Observational Astronomy from the University of Maine.

Wendy has conducted her School of Mythic Astrology every August since 1988, on the coast of Maine. Her counseling practice and lecture/seminar work take her to cities in North America and England. When she is not traveling, she at her home on Peak's Island, writing and seeing her clients.

Wendy Z. Ashley

Working with Measurement, Memory, and Myth

 Every individual is "living" a myth which has motifs and elements that are trans-personal, divine, and "fated" armor for their life's experiences. As a mythic astrologer, it is my task to reveal the specific myth and identify its motifs as fundamental elements threaded in and through my client's most significant experiences, relationships, and drives.

The whole purpose of the mythic approach I use is to discover and understand the myth each of my clients is "living." This is the way of the modern Jungian, Neo-Jungian, and Archetypal psychologists. C. G. Jung, himself, said that "to know one's myth is the task of tasks." Just identifying the myth is the first stage of this "task of tasks." The second stage is discovering just how it is that one *does live* a myth. As a mythic astrologer, I believe that one's horoscope can reveal one's myth, and it is my task first to identify the myth through the horoscope, and then to assist my client on the journey of self-discovery that the myth unfolds.

Horoscopes: Maps of Mythology
and Maps of the Self

How do we find the myth through the horoscope? It is patently obvious that astrology and mythology are related. The fact is that we have inherited an ancient system wherein the planets carry the names of Gods and Goddesses. We have continued that tradition by naming the newly discovered planets after the old Gods and Goddesses, as well. When we read myths, we find that the constellations, themselves are described as having been placed in the sky to immortalize Gods and Goddesses, Heroes and Nymphs. As astrologers, we should not find it difficult to understand that the mythic and divine associations are at the root or very basis of all astrological traditions. However, as Westerners we are now separated from the mythological basis of those traditions by more than 2,000 years.

Our first movement away from a mythic awareness was by an increasing turn toward a rationalism in which the inquiring mind sought to understand our world through logical systems and laws. The second way in which we lost mythic consciousness was through the new monotheism of this millennium, which made any reference to the old polytheistic divinities amount to heresy. We retained astrology, but we *de*volved the planets to be carriers of qualities or ideas, or abstractions, rather than of the archetypes of the Gods, or even as differentiations of the ultimate God. In these two ways, astrology became something of a schematized symbolic code or language, instead of a lens into a system of divine order, understood in myth through metaphor.

Myth is the language of the unconscious. It is the best means available to bring to light the contents of the unconscious, whether the "collective" unconscious or the "personal" unconscious. If mythology stands at the root of astrology—and we *are* beginning to use and see myth as a language of the unconscious—then it is tempting to see the mythic" dimensions of a horoscope only as another sort of psychological map in which the images are amplified and romanticized as myth and archetypes. Psychology proposes that we live in a dimension of the unconscious, but is our psychological unconscious all that there is of the unconscious? Is the psyche the only place for the operations of archetypes and myths?

Archetypal psychologist Dr. Charles Ponce, in speaking of the inadequacies of modern astrological practice in "Saturn and the Art of Seeing" (pp. 29–55 in *Working the Soul*), says that a psychological or spiritual use of planetary indicators in the horoscope is *counter to* the very thing the planets ultimately stand for.

> I specifically refer to the fact that the planets of astrology were once understood as Gods—not psychological co-ordinates. Our present inability to accept such an idea grows out of our failure to experience myth. [pp. 38]

The Gods are manifestations of the archetypal sort. Ponce reminds us that the archetypes are *not* creations of logos, nor are they symbols of Psyche:

> ... the human mind on the one hand, heaven or the suprapersonal on the other—the archetypes, as Jung has pointed out, "are not found exclusively in the psychic sphere," but manifest themselves throughout the world. [Ponce, p. 30]

> But if we remind ourselves of what Jung said concerning the archetypes—that they pass through, include and affect soul, but are not its property—then we are left with the fact that the archetypes not only work on something else, but also perform this work somewhere else. The first and most apparent place is in nature itself. .... What all of this implies is that the person is not the center of the cosmos: that the person is, in fact, something that must be connected to the cosmos. [Ponce, p. 39]

My objective, then, is to identify a mythology which is a metaphoric counterpart to my client's life experiences ... inner and outer; past, present, and future. This is an associative approach that brings us much closer to a consciousness which is at once archaic and lost, to all intents, from modern Western paradigms, as well as closer to a realization of the expanded dimensions of the personal unconscious in a modern archetypal psychology. It means to discover the Self in a transpersonal and Divine context, not in any etherialized or philosophized place, but rather specifically to a place in the world (of nature.)

Joseph Campbell, in *Yoga Journal* (Nov./Dec. 87), is quoted by interviewer Joan Marler as saying, "The fundamental aim of the great early and archaic mythologies is to put the nature of the

204 / Communicating the Horoscope

individual and society in accord with the nature of the world." He goes on to describe how we have come to view ourselves, as human beings, as outside, above, or beyond nature. In this he is saying that the myth of the expulsion of Adam and Eve from Paradise is our expulsion from a "paradise," or lost world. We have left a consciousness in which "the Garden," nature, knowledge, and ourselves were all one—before a separation of consciousness of ourselves as one with nature and God occurred. Campbell says we have to make a "Great Return" by rediscovering our place in the scheme of the natural world. He thinks we are perhaps beginning to make this "Great Return" back from believing that we are above and outside nature. He says, "Actually, we are of one life with the animal world, and I see that [understanding] coming back, as well as [a trend toward] going into nature and being refreshed by it. That's the beginning of the discovery of the wonder of what life really is."

It was not until the twentieth century that the West rediscovered the unconscious as psychology, and began to appreciate its value, and, of course psychology does make use of mythic associations to elements of the unconscious. Although we all recognize the value of looking into the unconscious in the psyche, only a few Westerners are beginning to rediscover the unconscious as the vast spiritual and natural symbolic world of myth and synchronicity manifesting in and through experience itself.

Unlike cultures where people are taught to think mythically, we Westerners are very carefully taught to think rationally. Unless we can educate ourselves in "mythic" thinking, we miss a whole perspective that could vastly enrich our lives.

We first need to know what a myth is and does. Most of us have been taught that a myth is a "made-up" story. In an attempt to get a definition of what myth is from a number of experts, one will assert that it is a naive scientific explanation of phenomena, another that it is the poetry of primitive religion, another that it is forgotten actual history, another that it is a projection of human concerns onto an imagined divinity, and yet another that it is primitive thought. Finally in recent years, we have been introduced to myth as psychology.

All the definitions of "myth" are right, but they are all inadequate as well. The experts are like the nine blind men asked to feel an elephant and to describe it. One says it is long and thick and snakelike, another that it is like a great broad wall, another that it is like a great sail or fan, another that it is curved, smooth and hard, etc. The elephant is too big to be comprehended in its entirety by such as a single blind man, and a myth in its multiple layers of meaning is too big to be reduced to a single element of itself, even as a complex or psychological structure.

Myth is layered in a multiplicity of functions and meanings. It is first of all a good story. Below that level is its association with nature . . . as the cosmos, the seasons, and the plants, animals, and landscape of the four seasons or directions. Out of this arise the divinities or powers that animate all of these as personifications. In each of these are specific capacities or capabilities to support or destroy life forms. This they do in unique ways and in a tension with one another. These tensions are substantially akin to the tensions of human interactions. All together, these layers are descriptive of all manifestations in the life and in the world. A mythology is a cosmology that explains and organizes every element of the world that produces it. We might say it is a way of understanding the world through the language of the unconscious, just as science strives to understand the world through the language of the conscious. I will want my client to see all of the layers of his or her mythology in his life.

In living religions, God is unencompassable in form, although depicted as a man. In the older myths the gods may likewise be anthropomorphic, but they are also theriomorphic, having the forms and capacities of animals, not as bestial powers but as metaphors. As metaphor, their zoomorphic associations are seen in antiquity when an animal accompanies the humanized form, as when Athene is depicted with her owl, Poseidon sits astride a bull and so forth. It must be understood in such images that Athene *is* an owl, Poseidon *is* a bull, despite the fact that the Greeks, as we do, preferred philosophically to dissociate their Gods and Goddesses from their animal counterparts, even when it served well to illustrate them for associative religious meaning.

Now, what has all of this to do with astrology and the relationship of astrologer to client? As astrologers, we can first of all keep in mind that the zodiac is a zoo-diac, a circle of life, a "zoe" (ζωη) in which the "life" is most frequently represented as an animal life. Those constellations which are representations of animals, plants, or landscapes are theriomorphic or zoomorphic forms of Gods and Goddesses no less than those whose images have anthropomorphic or human form. It is most probable that these animals (as God forms) were projected onto the sphere of heaven long before humanity was writing its own history, in the paleolithic period. They are far older than they are credited with being. They are the old, old source of the collective unconscious, as projection, and astrologically and archetypally as introjection.

To re-mythologize astrology, and to work from its compass, I have to know the correlations among myths, calendars, the phenomena of the seasons, naked-eye astronomy, and archeo-astronomy. I must go back to a pre-modern re-mythologized sky, a pre-Ptolemaic astrology. By staying true to the original associations made when the myths were first projected onto the sky aeons ago, I will stay true to the fundamental humanity in myths, disregarding the temptation to impose contemporary meanings onto them. I must work through an anthropological perspective, understanding the place of each element of the story in the economy, religion, and geography of that culture. Only then can I understand the myth's references. Only then can I interpret the myth in modern terms for modern men and women.

For any of us to understand myth and archetype, we must learn to "think" mythically. This is a leap of consciousness for Western minds, trained to rationalistic explanation. We disassociate the mythical from our experiences. It is only in the work of psychology that we Westerners have any practice with myth and thought. It is much harder for us to see the mythic in the world we live in—the landscape, people, places, creations, animals, weather and sky. To integrate the mythic dimension into psychology is insufficient—we must enlarge this psychological self *out* into the world of our personal experiences. When we can consistently do this, we then find ourselves in a world which "speaks" to us, through synchronicities that are in the ordinary course of things only occasional, accidental experiences or are the disturbing visions of the psychotic. It is through an understanding of our personal mythos that we can exist both in a sane and rational ordinary life and in a constant access to the deeper Self through the unconscious. The purpose of my relationship to my client is to foster that understanding, that sanity, and access to Self.

Working with Clients Using Mythology

Ordinarily counselors have a chance to assess clients at the first visit, to determine whether they can be of help and whether they are the right person for clients to see. As an astrologer, my first encounter with a client will be the principal or even the *only* encounter. In order to ensure that I can be useful, I see only those clients who are referred to me either by a client who has already seen me, or by a professional referral from their analyst, astrologer, or therapist. Usually this ensures that my client will be able to follow the metaphoric nature of the presentation. They must also be self-exploring, with an interest sufficient to follow-up our session with research and reflection to get full value for their time.

An astrologer can usually expect that the majority of their clients will be coming for consultation because they are "in crisis." Ordinarily, only a small percentage will make an appointment out of a desire for self-understanding, or because they want to do deep work in figuring out personal patterns or behavior. In my work the percentages are reversed: the majority of individuals are interested in uncovering deep underlying patterns and issues, and it is the minority who are in crisis.

That's as it should be. The material revealed in a mythic interpretation of a horoscope is from the deep psyche and strongly connected to the collective unconscious in that its images are personal and universal at the same time. In the ordinary course of counseling, one addresses material from the awareness level of the client. In astrology generally, and even more specifically in the mythic approach, the awareness level of the astrologer governs the proceedings. In counseling, you talk, I listen; in astrology, I talk, you listen. When this process is reversed, particularly when any kind of predictive work is done, the will and desire of the client who wants you to foresee specific outcomes colors the reading.

I do predictive readings so long as the client understands that the manifestation of the archetype is best understood as metaphor. It is wise to advise a client not only of the limitations of predictability in general, but especially how it is that the very nature of revelation brings forward for consideration the unthought-of, the stuff you don't expect to hear. The very nature of prediction should, I think, bring up the unforeseeable. Encountering resistance is frequent. The client will push to hear the hoped-for future, with the hoped-for timetable. This is an area requiring absolute integrity and a constant reference to the metaphoric nature of the material.

In general, this material demands that my clients be intelligent, self-aware, and emotionally healthy. When they are seeing a therapist, I can rely on there being a supportive vehicle to process what we uncover in our session. I also will not do a reading if I believe that awakening a dialogue with the unconscious would be dangerous, which it can be. This approach reveals the archetypal underpinnings to a person's life and drives, which lie in the unconscious. In some personality disorders, or with those individuals who appear to be already living in the realm of the unconscious, the material can not be grounded for reflection. Instead, it only serves to escalate erratic behavior by feeding the unconsciousness. If I can not present the material to someone who can stay in a conscious reflective relationship to it, on the one hand, or if it is apparent that they are unable to understand the material as metaphor, I must refer them elsewhere.

I must pay careful attention to my delivery so that I will not be misunderstood. To ensure that a client "hears" what I have said, I require that all readings be tape recorded. Astrology, coming as it appears to do, from a cosmic source, tends to amplify the client's *hopes and fears*. I emphasize that the presentation is interpretation and is therefore subject to all sorts of misinterpretation on both my part and theirs, and I outline the symbolic factors that are the basis of this interpretation. My readings are also, in consequence, very lengthy—at least three hours for a new client.

One side result of this rich approach, however, is that it builds trust between us, as they perceive the integrity of the interpretive effort and understand where it comes from. This is best described through illustration later in this chapter, using an actual chart and a dialogue with one client.

In describing the mythos of the chart, and in any presentation of its implications, I must be very careful of the way the material is expressed. Every astrological structure is only consistently "true" on the symbolic level, and incidentally "true" on the manifestational level. This is because any archetype has hundreds of possible manifestations.

This is why oracular statements are valid: they are true to their symbol-context. That is why they are best delivered as metaphor. That is why the priests at Delphi gave the oracle's pronouncement in such obscure terms, and why Nostradamus wrote his quatrains in the form that he did. Like a scientific theorem which must be expressed in a very specific way to be true, so an astrological indication is true when expressed in a way that is first and foremost true to the symbols (in other words, not interpreted, or more often, reinterpreted, to suit the projected desires, hopes, or fears of the client). One friend has described this method of expressing the material as "omenclature."

Example 1, "Toronto Apollo,"

Example 1, "Toronto Apollo," shows the ruler of my client's 6th House conjoined with his Sun, Saturn, and Mercury late in the 3rd House. That Pluto at the consultation time was by transit conjoining the ruler of his 3rd, the Moon. When he asked me to comment upon his health concerns, I could only say: "Current issues of health are tied to the way in which you and your brother were related in issues of health as children." In phrasing my response in this fashion, I was taking into account as many of the symbolic indicators as possible: the focus built up to the "house" angle through the Sun, the 6th House ruler, the epitome of Mercury ruling the Ascendant, the Moon's square with Saturn, the Moon's rulership of the 3rd House, etc.

This client responded to my statement this way: "My brother was very ill as a child; he had a major mastoid infection and lost his hearing in one ear." In my reaction, I first asked him; "How is *your* hearing?" followed by "Tell me about the time when your brother was ill." The actual reply to this exchange was "My hearing is just fine, but it's funny you should bring this other up because what I am worried about is my heart. I had a mild heart attack this spring. My mother died when we were boys; in fact it was during my brother's hospitalization. She had a weak heart." This of course brings to light a whole complex of related issues, which derive from the archetypal base of the angular Sun and Mercury in his horoscope. The archetype of the brothers dominates the chart (Gemini Ascendant), but in a specific context that associates health, the lost mother/feminine (Moon square Saturn), grief, fear of losing one's life, the theater, medicine, teaching, inventions, and on and on. The period of the brother's ill health in the context of the mythology is the central archetypal experience that had a formative impact on both of the brothers' lives. From this material we continue on to use the mythology to associate his teaching career in the theater, his brother's deafness and subsequent career in pharmaceuticals, their mother's death, their father's grief and remoteness, to his own fears reawakened at a time when his own son reached the age he was when his mother died.

This client's myth is a mythology of Apollo in a context in which it is Hermes who stands as his "opposite." Part of their tension in Greek myth is the story of the invention of the lyre and

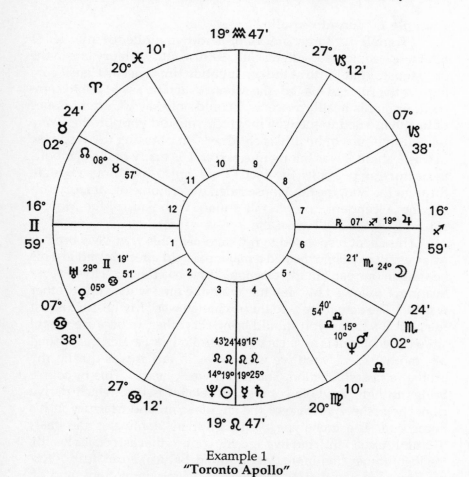

Example 1
"Toronto Apollo"

its gift to Apollo by Hermes. These two are expanded through the story of Orpheus and Euridice, and so forth. Each bit of these myths has relevance in his experiences. Unless you know the elements and motifs in the myths of the above mentioned Gods and mythic persons, you will not know how it is that any of the issues are "of one piece." It is not that the story as a whole is lived out, but that the motifs and their implications are like a fundamental structure that replicates itself on every scale in the fabric of his life.

Locating and Conveying the Specific Mythos

In light of the fact that we astrologers do counsel, Ponce proposes a new approach by astrologers to the horoscope . . . one that could reintegrate the archetypal into our work:

> But this type of counselor would have to be a peculiar blend of empiricist and metaphysician, having at his or her disposal a system whose very structure is archetypally given. In addition, the system would have to have as its structural base a clear-cut connection to archetypal images, if not myths themselves, and it would have to derive its information solely from those images or symbols. Furthermore, it could not be recent, with origins far removed from the created ideographic realm of modern persons. In short, its authority would have to be a given, derived in much the manner that an archetype expresses itself. Admittedly, these qualifications could in part answer certain schools of psychological thought, and almost all religious counseling. But neither one of these forms of counseling rely solely on the archetypes for seeing. Both demand that a human story be told, each then seeking to fit that story within the mold of the image they believe the story fits. And, furthermore, neither one of them can claim to see an entire life as an archetypal structure which from moment to moment is effected by archetypes that can be specifically named.

> The form of counselling that appears to fit all of the above requirements is astrology." [Ponce, p. 31]

This approach makes no attempt to "correct" the individual described astrologically—no attempt to discover the psychic or karmic maladjustments, no attempt to "normalize" the client.

Rather it attempts to *uncover* the archetypal ground of his or her being. Ponce says:

> The involvement with *what has been given* is the stuff of souls. I change nothing, attempt to make nothing better, but perceive "it" as it is in the hope of discerning in it an archetypal meaning that will deepen my perception of life. This would imply that one of the functions of astrology (as well as of psychology) would be involved not with the art of counseling but with the art of seeing, or with the art of revealing—for no other purpose than to see myself clearly as I am. The objective would be not to correct, but literally to objectify; not to expand but to deepen. What is now counselling would become witnessing. [Ponce, p. 43]

However, the mythic approach to an understanding of the archetypal dimensions of one's life is, in itself, profoundly *healing*. Furthermore "knowing" where and how one is affected by an archetype changes the power of the archetype to affect. We might say the unconscious becomes conscious as I witness myself in its context. Hillman writes that "any transformation of the images affects the patterns of behavior." [Ponce, p. 44]

Using a mythic means of locating and understanding destiny archetypally through the horoscope, we witness our own journey. In fact, the myth becomes the means of witnessing the journey. Ponce expresses the potential of our archetypal approach this way:

> This journey can be achieved only by insighting, by an archetypal imagining that allows the unconscious easy access to consciousness. It is a way of seeing, of visioning, that our culture describes as pathological—but which we find so attractive in Eastern cultures.
>
> The horoscope of the individual is still a way for this vision to be achieved *if* the counselor realizes that everything in a chart need not be interpreted but rather can be experienced and imagined." [Ponce, p. 53]

The Methodology Used in Mythic Astrology

In reading for a client, I will tell the story of the myth and explain its elements as metaphor for the elements and experiences of the client's life. The childhood story or memory that I have asked my client to bring to our session I will use to corroborate that I am on the right track, after locating the myth. The story may have elements that suggest a specific culture for the mythology. If the elements in the story do *not* correspond to the elements in the myth, it may be suggest that another myth is more appropriate. These stories serve to demonstrate that the myth is descriptive of the divine force behind the events, feelings and "fate" or circumstances in his/her life.

The method used to locate a myth in a horoscope differs from more conventional methods used today. Techniques usually thought to be important in our accustomed practice are not of much use in locating a myth. Instead the method used is through a synthesis by stages, as follows:

1) Locate the planets nearest the angles. I use an orb of about twenty degrees on either side of the angle. *These planets carry the identity of the archetype that participates in the destiny marked at the moment of birth.*

2) Locate the most dramatic or rare astral events or those emphasized by unusual position or configuration. Mythic astrology does not take the significators as qualities one by one, each qualifying the other but rather uses the *image* of the conjunction or whatever is present to identify a myth. It will be the myth itself which suggests the issues and elements of all the facets of a life.

3) Take note of conjunctions of planets and angles to fixed stars by parallel and longitude. The fixed stars, themselves, have mythic associations, attributable to their name and constellation.

4) Using the archetypal and mythic associations of the planets (and stars) and their observed behavior in the sky, express their behavior in the chart.

5) Identify the Zodiac Signs and *the other constellations* aligned with those planets. Mythic astrology uses the whole sky for the location of myths, not just the signs of the zodiac. The constellations above and below a sign and surrounding that sign are mythically associated to it. The constellations are *all* representations of myths.

6) Select by emphasis and synthesis the predominant myth. The methodology and its illustrations could take up pages of explanation. Instead the explanation is by demonstration, as you will see in the example chosen.

7) Check the correctness of the mythology through correlations from the client's (archetypal) stories. I ask for the story only after following all of the above steps, and already have some idea of the probable mythology which I will have already begun to relate to my client. It is through the story told me that I can check the validity of the myth I've selected and see its correlations continuously operating in the elements of my client's life.

Presenting the Material as a Mythos

The horoscope is a map of a mythic drama. As a map of an individual's life, it is a transpersonal one in which the planets, or divine powers, are the actors in that drama. The signs and constellations in which the planets reside are the stage or the sets. The houses, angles, and aspects are the script. Furthermore, as R. D. Laing said, "We are all born into the second act."

So you see: the myth is not something I can impose upon my client through psychological analysis or similitude to a psychological understanding or analysis. Instead it must be located in the chart itself through a knowledge of which myths were long ago associated with which signs and constellations, and which planets are the "carriers" of which Gods or archetypes. Then the chart becomes a map of a "Fate," in a transpersonal dimension and as metaphor.

I have to be able to communicate to my client the place and meaning of the myth in her or his life in such a way that it will facilitate my client's being able to continue to discover the correlations between the myth and her life when I am not present to do it myself. The myth itself then becomes a means to a constant reflection on one's place and experience in the world which is a continual affirmation of Self.

Ponce says of this process of discovery of self through myth and the horoscope:

My horoscope shows me exactly where and how the imaginal has become enmeshed with me, where the gods have taken on new characteristics, new problems. My horoscope is the continuation of written myth, it is the tale not only of myself, but of the Gods in their evolution in imaginal time and space, their individuation.

The horoscope might therefore be thought of as an active imagination performed by the Gods, or the planets, or whatever you wish to call these powers that shape us. The new function of the astrologer would be to engage me at this archetypal level by having me perform an archetypal imagination on my horoscope. This would entail not an hour of understanding or interpretation, but an hour of story-telling. The astrologer would tell me the story of the particular God-planets, and then point out exactly where my horoscope coincides with the original tale. {Ponce, p. 45] In short, the only way we can release ourselves from Saturn's tendency to spiritualize and intellectualize the cosmos and the imaginal is by in-sighting, or seeing into the imaginal through the mirror of the horoscope. [Ponce, p. 46]

It would be a great pity if astrology were to become just another psychology of consciousness, for it is only in astrology where we find the Classical representations of the Gods and of the soul unabashedly presented as powers residing beyond the control of ego, as mysteries whose movements and effects might be clocked and predicted, but whose ulterior motives may never be understood. To lose this sense of mystery in favor of respectable acceptance [of astrology] would be the final insult the modern person could offer to the archetypal ground that daily affects us. [Ponce, p. 54].

The Method and the Myth Illustrated

One early client of mine was Elisabeth Y. Fitzhugh, whom I saw in 1985. I first met her when she had a metaphysical bookstore in Washington DC called "Synchronicity Bookshop." She is a channel, and the "entity" she channels is called "Orion." Some of the "Orion" material is presented in her book, *The Orion Material*, published by Synchronicity Press in Takoma Park, Maryland in 1989, and available through New Leaf Distributors. When I first saw her, the book had not yet been written, I did not know she was a channel, or that the name of the entities she channels is

"Orion." She is married to an artist and is herself also an artist, and they have one child of their own. Her husband has three children from former marriages.

Elisabeth Fitzhugh was born with 20 degrees of Cancer rising. The fixed stars Castor and Pollux straddle the degree of her Ascendant. At 10:10 P.M., the night before her birth, there had been a Full Moon. At the hour of her birth, near noon, the Sun was on the local meridian in Aries. The Moon, the ruler of her Ascendant, still opposite the Sun, was closely conjoined with Neptune, in the 4th House, near the I.C. The planet Uranus is opposite Jupiter. Venus and Mercury are each a Sign away from the Sun on either side, and there is a rare conjunction of Pluto, Saturn and Mars. These are the principle factors which, in synthesis, will enable us to identify her myth.

Following below is some of the transcript of my dialogue with Elisabeth about her mythology, as she and I have worked with it over the last few years.

WA: I first read your chart when I was just beginning to shift to reading charts using mythology. The first time I saw you I talked with you about having a mythology of Artemis through the mythology of Orion. Right away you had a sort of shocked reaction and you said, "You know I channel Orion!" And I didn't know it at the time.

EYF: It was 1985. You didn't know at that time about my channeling work. That's very important. You didn't know at that time about my connection with "Orion." You knew I had a metaphysical bookstore. The reason we asked you to do our chart together, is that Michael Gritz and I had just gone public with our Orion work. I also need to say that we did not "choose" the name Orion consciously, and the group I channel did not say their name was "Orion." We asked them for a name. They said that we don't really have a name *per se*, but we understand that you want a symbolic name and they told Michael one would come to him in meditation. We came to a follow-up session, and nothing had come to Michael about a name, and he questioned that. They said, "Well, what comes to you now. To which Michael pops out with "Orion" and they said, "Oh yes, that will be a very fine name to use."

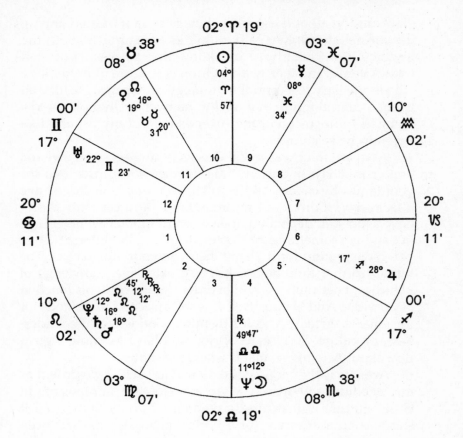

Example 2
Elisabeth Y. Fitzhugh
Mar. 25, 1948, 11:57 A.M. EST
Philadelphia, PA
75W11   39N57
Placidus Houses

We later did find out that the constellation Orion had just risen in the sky at that time, and synchronistically two weeks later I got a book in the mail on myths of Giants, and Orion was the cover of the book and the cover story.

WA: The myth of Orion is of enormous antiquity. There are many myths of "the giant" man. In China, Egypt, Europe, the Arab countries, and in the Mediterranean there are myths of the giant, and in all of these areas there is a giant located among the constellations. I actually didn't know as much about the mythic Orion then, but I did know that he was associated with Artemis. In other words, Orion is a figure in mythology who is ancillary to a central mythology of Artemis. He himself is not a central figure, not one of the twelve Olympian gods. So he is a dimension of the Artemis field of myths, and like Artemis, he is a hunter.

What a hunter was to the Greeks is not necessarily what a hunter is today. In ancient times, it meant you provided for your family by chance. You didn't have a shop, you didn't have a farm, you didn't have an inheritance. You certainly didn't have a job! You depended upon a serendipitous event. "I'll go out and get something for dinner, dear" is a lot different when you have to hunt for it, than when you go to the market. The hunter in that time had to have an extensive knowledge of nature and the animal world in order to succeed in his function as provider. And Nature itself was still an access to the gods for the Greeks. Artemis was for them the Goddess of the wilderness, or nature. To research Orion you have to know a great deal about Artemis, so that is where we start.

Artemis is the Moon goddess and as such, is described as not needing any man, a "virgin"—forever adolescent. In Greek culture at that time, a woman was only unmarried if she was an adolescent (or a widow who already had been married.) Very, very few women could choose to remain single. Some were not marriageable because of infirmity. Otherwise all Greek women married after adolescence. Marriage for Greek women represented a chattel-like status, but they had a considerable amount of freedom *before* marrying.

In a Greek context, Artemis represents the freedom available to an unmarried (hence, adolescent) girl, and also came to stand for the coming of age and marriageability of girls between 9 and about 13 years of age. In Greek myth, Artemis also hangs out with a bunch of dogs. The dogs represent the hunter as provider for the family, the protection of the vulnerable, and the guardian of the family. These are, in Greece, the masculine functions of a (female) divinity, the "warrior" side of the archetype of Artemis, functioning in the figure of Orion. On the feminine side of function, Artemis shows up in Greece as tremendously interested in the issue of having babies, associated with midwifery.

To modern individuals it seems incongruous that this Goddess could represent feminine independence, plus childbirth, plus virginity, plus hunting. But it all becomes understandable when we know her archaic underpinnings, which we can see in her animal forms. The animal forms Artemis is associated with were thought to be capable of parthenogenesis, the ability of a female to conceive on her own, without a male. Both the bear and the deer (her two principal animal forms) have delayed implantation of the ovum. Any examination of the uterus of these animals after copulation would fail to indicate that a pregnancy was the result. The animal only becomes pregnant (the ovum actually implants) months later. Seals also have delayed implantation, but in seals copulation occurs right after giving birth, so they are a special case in a Moon Goddess archetype. Hares (sacred to the Moon Goddess) are also associated with anomalous forms of pregnancy. In whatever form, Artemis is always a protector of babies and small children, and she always favors women.

WA: I want you to tell me what your reaction was to that reading, although I believe your mythology is more connected with Lepus (or Eostra), but I didn't bring the hare into the picture until two years later.

EYF: The Artemis aspect was very, very powerful for me. First of all, when you did the first reading, you did it on Michael Gritz and me. We told you we had formed a partnership. You didn't really know I was channeling, and I remember being so overwhelmed because you said that Michael and I very much shared Artemis and Apollo. Michael was my partner in the channeling mode and we had this incredible bond (and still do) that other people did find rather disconcerting, trying to place it. Because I had a husband, Michael wasn't my lover, and what was this whole thing? And when you said Artemis and Apollo, we said "Yes!"

You told me that I had an aspect in my chart that represented "the window between worlds" and at the time you weren't quite sure what that meant in "real" life. Michael and

I started laughing because we knew *exactly* what it meant! At the same time, you told Michael that he very much had an element of "the keeper of the oracle of Delphi," which of course was hysterical to us because he was my "grounder" and energizer during the channeling sessions.

WA: The symbol of the "window between the worlds" in your chart is from the fact that in archetypology the Sun and Moon represent eyes. The eyes are associated with "seeing" hence "windows." I also said it because you have 20 degrees of Cancer rising and the two stars (Castor and Pollux) conjunct your Ascendant were often associated with the motif of two eyes. The ruler of Cancer, the Moon, "The Eye of Night" is conjoined to Neptune. It is Neptune that is the veil between the worlds. With the two "eyes" of consciousness (the Sun and the Moon, called "The Eye of Day" and "The Eye of Night") so emphasized in your chart, it is as if there is an eye next to the veil.

EYF: Well it was very powerful, and Michael and I were familiar with the basic Greek mythology, and once you sparked it—the whole thing of Artemis and Apollo kept growing and growing in our lives. I could see all the Artemis stuff right there in my life. I have three step-daughters. I've always had a lot of women in my life. I've always worked with young teenagers. The whole thing of women as mentor. I have a younger sister; I was a "Big Sister" volunteer. I see my mothering as more mentoring than the kind of housewifely, lovey-dovey mothering. I sometimes feel I'm a bit of the warrior mom, the advocate mom. All that to me keeps representing Artemis.

As a girl I grew up on a "block" with a group of kids; we all grew up together, we were a "crowd" and I was usually the "single" one. As we got older, around 12 or so, and people started to pair off and for a period I was the unpaired one. They used to call me the "Dear Abby of Milne Street" because my friends would come and talk to me; and that confidant role, which I don't know if it is exactly Artemis, sort of the mediator role, was always mine. It was mine in my primary family, and it was mine with all of my friends. Often I was the anchor point of a group of friends, and that is still true, where

WORKING WITH MEASUREMENT, MEMORY, AND MYTH / 221

I am the anchor point to bring diverse people together. On the whole, it works, and sometimes it doesn't. To me, Artemis has always this aspect of unrelated people that feel kinship; a redefining of what kinship is.

WA: Artemis was the goddess of clan lineage and when a person has an Artemis mythology, they often want either tremendous independence from family and any ties, or conversely are absolutely tied to home and family. Cancer is usually interpreted as a homebody and a mommy and all that. Artemis as the Moon goddess wants to be free, and you don't put this stuff on her. On the other hand, Artemis is *the* goddess of clan lineage, belonging to this group of people, or this culture, or this location.

When you were talking about the warrior woman, in including this dimension of her in your chart, Artemis was the principal Goddess of the fabled Amazons. They were reported to have worshiped just two divinities—Ares and Artemis. Many people falsely assume Athena to be the Goddess of every warrior impulse. As principle divinity of Greek pride, Athena is the divinity of the *male* warrior, and in the mythology of Greek history, the followers of Athena defeat the pre-Greek Amazons. There is also a function of Athena as mentor, tutor, teacher, which is totally unrelated to her political function. Although your mythology is not about Athena, Libra is Athena's sign, and you have the Moon in Libra, although you don't have Athena dominating your chart. You have, instead, Artemis functioning in this tutorial or teaching or mediating kind of way, which is the opposite side of the warrior—peace, conciliation, and activation—the polarity of Aries and Libra. Any astrologer would look at this Aries/Libra polarity and talk about how you are an activist on the one hand, and a peace-maker on the other hand.

However, whenever I think of your personal life, a lot of discussion about what has been your history that continues on today is based on the fact that you have two clans in your household. Perry is from the Fitzhugh clan which is a sort of magical-mystery-tour of one kind, and then you are from the Yannucci clan which is a whole other story!

EYF: Yes, the "Y" energy in my life, Elisabeth Y. Fitzhugh, is very powerful and present.

WA: I'm becoming very interested in nomenclature. "I," the eye, is a motif associated with both Orion and with Lepus the hare. In the mythology and folklore of these two, the ability to "see"or "not see" is very emphasized. Furthermore, both are *also* related to the two stars (of Castor and Pollux) who are depicted in some cultures' skies as two eyes. In one Native American tradition, the constellation of Gemini is called "the parting of the ways" symbolizing a place where one path diverges into two paths, which when it is drawn out in diagram as the "I," then becomes the "Y." Even the word "eye" and the word "why," and "I," all have a thread of connection. A child will say, "How come *I* and *eye* sound the same?" and an adult will say it is because there are two different things. In fact, "I" is the word for "eye." It would be a bit of work to uncover the connections in all of this material in its etymology and symbolic history.

EYF: And to follow along: "Yannucci" is incorrect. it should be "Iannucci" which would be pronounced though with the "Ya" sound. When they came from Italy to Ellis Island, the clerk wrote down "Yannucci" because that's what it sounded like.

WA: The thing about Gemini is that it is in the place in the sky (where you have Uranus) where the one becomes two. Uranus itself in his myth is connected with the idea of a primal pit where what was originally "one" becomes separated into "two." That is, Uranus was once eternally joined to Gaia, and then they came to be cut apart, separated into heaven and earth, this is where the "I" becomes the "Y." It is very interesting to me that in language "Y" can replace "I." That is very common.

And this brings me back to the archetype of Artemis and the issue of duality. Artemis is normally not associated with men, but there are three or four stories in which she is. The Artemis archetype is nowadays popularly associated with women who are content to be on their own. Even so, in Greek myth, the Gods and Goddesses are best understood through their opposites, as well as their alliances. Artemis is most opposite to her brother Apollo, and also most allied to him. As astral twins, they are the Moon and Sun, and of course the Moon and Sun *are* experienced by us when we see them in the sky as "beings" of the same size: we observe them as equals. Still, neither Apollo nor Artemis are described as marrying. They are themselves an alliance, as a male and female-twin pair. We have spoken of how you relate to the Artemis/Apollo pair, through your relationship with Michael. But there are two other stories where Artemis has a relationship of some sort to a man. One is the connection with Orion, which has a whole slew of versions.

The other situation in Greek myth in which there is a connection of the Moon goddess to a man, is Selene (simply the word for the Moon), who falls in love with a sleeping shepherd, whose name is Endymion. As long as he sleeps, he is her lover. The Moon Goddess loves the dreaming man, the unconscious man, one might say.

EYF: And the one that I identify with my work with Orion is none of those.

WA: But I think the original versions have probably a more profound meaning which people simply haven't bothered to look into. One of the things about Orion is that he symbolizes a kind of issue of conscious-unconscious behavior and conscious-unconscious realization. For example, he lives in the woods, the place of the unconscious. Artemis meets him on the beach, a joint place between the conscious world and the unconscious world, the deeps of the waters. When she shoots him, he is just offshore in the water. Artemis, herself, represents the unconscious. She is night; her brother Apollo is day, so there is this issue of the conscious-unconscious meeting together in the form of a man. After Orion loses his sight, becomes blind, he is told he must swim to the east, to dawn, where the sun rises, and his blindness will be cured. Blindness, by the way was often in Greek times the sign or mark of the prophet or oracle. Apollo, the Sun God, is called by the epithets, "all seeing" or "all knowing" because, of course, sunlight makes everything visible.

The dreaming man, the unconscious man (and I want it to be understood that the word unconscious is not a negative term), stands for the realm of the unconscious as night, or as the consciousness which comes from the Moon at night, the realm of dreams, as well as what we would call intuition, Artemis's consciousness. In the story of Selene and Endymion, the Moon is in love, even though Artemis is not depicted as a "marrying" Goddess. So we have to see Artemis-Orion and Artemis-Apollo, or even Selene-Endymion, in terms which bring out the issues of the conscious-unconscious polarity which is, I think, not only central to your work, but has its place in other areas of your life as well. It is central to the work of being a channel, of allowing what is otherwise unconscious to come into consciousness.

Addressing another dimension of Artemis, we must look at her as an archetype of the Great Mother. When a person has a lunar mythology, the archetype of the mother—good, bad, single, married, poor, or blessed mother—can become enormous. Two of the animals that represent Artemis, the bear and the deer, are first overwhelmingly, crushingly good mothers, and then they abandon their children. The hare, however, is only so-so as a mother because of how they raise their children. The little leveret, (about three at a birthing) is bedded in a separate place, or form, and the mother hare only visits them now and then throughout the day. But whichever of the animals forms of Artemis, the issue of the mother archetype is a central element in her mythologies.

Because the bear, deer, and seal have delayed implantation of the ovum, and because they raise their offspring alone, they represent the archetype of the single mother. So there is a single-motherness in your life. I know that you are not a single mother, but Perry, your husband, had a single mother. He was adopted by an extraordinary woman who was not and never had been married, was he not? That was a very unique situation in the 1940s when he was an infant. You are also a working mother, and Perry works at home. So both in your family history, and in your personal history, the idea of the single mother is an enormity.

EYF: I see myself as all those things. I have a child who was adopted, so I have been the abandoning mother. It was what needed to be done at the time. There was a clarity in that. She needed to go off into the world and she may return. Then I waited a long time to have my son, Alexander. I was 32 when he was born, and I was at home and working at home in the art studio when he was little. But life started to shift when he was three. He grew up in rural Virginia, in a very art-oriented world. Our friends were artists and craftspeople, and we were working as artists and craftspeople. Although I was also exploring the mystic world, I was doing that pretty much with myself and my sister, and not so much with my circle of friends.

When it came to me in 1982 to open a metaphysical bookstore, we tried to do it in Virginia and it didn't work. We ended up in Washington, DC, in 1983, by finding an affordable space through incredible synchronistic events of money and timing, which surprised us. (It was called "Synchronicity Bookshop!") Alexander was three when we moved up here and opened the bookstore. So when he became more conscious, if you will, the world of people, of adults, this clan, changed. Although we still had contact with the artists and craftspeople, and the living in the country and the woods, which he still has a deep affinity for, his everyday world became filled with astrologers and healers and bodyworkers and mystics and tarot and psychics and channels—the entire mystic world.

WA: If we correlate the two children you have had to the Apollo-Artemis polarity, you have had a boy and a girl—Sun and Moon. Of one, you are very conscious, conscientious, and the other is unconscious, has grown up entirely separate from you, so that you do not "know" who or where she is. The duality of the conscious and unconscious materialized here as well. That is really interesting because the full Moon in your horoscope conjoined to Neptune is an amplification of the Greek association of the Moon with mythos—the world of night, dreams, the occult, and the world of magic. Your Sun, on the other hand, in this Artemisian mythology, represents the Apollonian world of creativity, of bringing the imaginal into consciousness, the world of the muses, the artists' world.

The Apollo-Artemis dichotomy in your chart has any number of manifestations, replicates itself in any number of situations.

The polarized part of it means probably you lived in the Artemis side as a child; only when you left home to have a child did you find your individuality through separation and independence. At that point you began to live fully in the artist's Apollonian world of the intellect and creativity. Then, when you had your second child, Alexander, you started moving into another dimension of the Artemis cycle, the lunar, "mystic" side. I suspect that when your son is grown you will move back into a more Apollonian life.

EYF: To follow up on my teenage pregnancy: my family required great caretaking by me. I was very much the mother of my primary family and, in retrospect, after counseling and other things, my first pregnancy was the only thing that let me give myself permission to "abandon" my primary family. So the child let me take care of me and move me away from my primary family. One side effect is that my younger sister did feel abandoned by me. I would say to her "but I left home because I was pregnant and I didn't abandon you," but maybe I did do that. A therapist once said to me from his psychological view of it, by getting pregnant I did the healthiest thing I could do to bring the focus back to myself. He said someone else could have made a suicidal gesture, could have gone into drugs or alcohol. What he felt was that people often endanger themselves to separate.

This pregnancy was very Artemis. First, I resisted marrying the father, second by not keeping the baby, I returned to "adolescence." Also I did marry after that pregnancy and that worked for quite a while. In retrospect, I see that it worked as long as it was an Artemis-type marriage. When I was about 24 my husband really starting pushing for me to "stop going through this phase," and act "married." I felt I was acting "married," at least for me, and we divorced.

WA: You did the Artemis thing, which was to become pregnant. By the way, when people read about Artemis, it is totally incongruous to them that the symbol of freedom in women could also have something to do with pregnancy—it doesn't seem apropos. It may speak, in fact, of women's experience and realization of themselves in communion with another being. I have said before that, in myth, Artemis is consistently involved with birthing and pregnancy.

EYF: In most cultures, a girl who becomes a mother is allowed a cultural shift and you are even given a certain authority in things if you are a mother as opposed to just a young girl or woman.

. . . Now we add the hare as an even truer mythology for Elizabeth . . .

WA: I must keep in mind that you were born near the full Moon, with an emphasis upon the Moon and Sun just three days after the Spring Equinox. Your mythology is *most* represented in this particular astronomical situation. And even though Artemis and Apollo seemed to fit really well, there were some clues I mulled over that caused me to begin to shift the central archetypal motif in your horoscope to Lepus, a constellation which stands directly below that of Orion in the sky. As the figure of a hare, it is still a Moon mythology connected to Artemis and other Moon Goddesses around the world. What led me to it was, in part, the fact that the planet Uranus at your birth was conjoined to the stars in the belt of Orion. In Northern Europe, the three stars in the belt of Orion are the three Wyrd Sisters, and their names essentially mean Yesterday, Today, and Tomorrow. The belt was called the Spindle of Fate, and the Saxons and Celts saw in these stars three women making time happen, spinning it out like a thread. They were crones and also known as the three Fates. Shakespeare put them in "Macbeth" and they pronounce what has happened, what is happening, and what will happen in the opening to the play. This is where people have an unexamined exposure to myth.

I don't speak of them because they are necessarily represented by hares, but because both hares and the Wyrd Sisters are connected to the motif of wisdom (or witchcraft) from those Pagan times. Because you have Uranus there in Gemini, *and* you have the degree rising of the two stars of Gemini, these would suggest that your mythology could well date from an era which pre-dates Polaris as the Pole star. I believe the three "Fates" date back to the Age of Gemini; 8,000 years ago these stars rose at the Spring Equinox.

Although we have no texts from that long ago, we can infer that yet another goddess of that age was Eostra, (Easter) which means "from the east." There are, by the way, multitudes of images from this age in Old Europe, depicting a goddess with a bird's head! Such an image would be a representation of a *springtime* Goddess, as the birds would have returned in the spring, or as they more probably saw it "with" the spring or "bringing" the new life that returns in the springtime. Since the Sun rises due east at the Vernal Equinox, bringing the blessing of warmer days and more light, the east itself became a sacred space that symbolized the return of life. Even Christianity celebrates Easter with services at sunrise, facing the East to symbolize the Resurrected God.

In ancient times, the year was measured by both the sun and the moon together. The first day of a month or a new year was measured from either the New or the Full Moon. Some peoples began the year at one of the equinoxes, others at one of the solstices. (Our tradition is from a beginning at winter solstice.) In this very archaic period, the return of the birds meant the return of new life in the spring, but it also meant a chance to gather eggs. Eggs would only have been available at this time of the year. (There was no domestication of poultry till about 6,000 years ago.) The birds would have been associated with the "easting" Sun, the Solar side of the springtime. The Hare, on the other hand is invariably a lunar animal, the Lunar symbol of a springtime New Year. The New Year was cause for rejoicing in the new life, which was symbolized by the March Hare, whose name was Eostra. The constellation of the Hare is right under the feet of Orion, who is literally standing on the little creature. Both have associations to the motif of the "eye" and both with Artemisian mythology: one is the giant Orion (who becomes blind) and the other is the hare, Lepus (who never shuts its eyes).

So when I came back a couple years later I wanted to add Lepus to your mythology (Lepus-Libby)! Lepus is a word which means "I rise." In the modern Christian mythos, it is the crucified Son of God, of whom it is declared at Easter that "He is risen." The Egyptian Osiris was also dying and resurrecting God and his cartouche contained the image of the hare. What is there about a hare that represents resurrection? We talked about this as your mythology, and you said, "Yuck, no thanks, no cute bunnies!" Artemis, Orion, you could understand and work with.

EYF: Well, there is the fact that I was born on the Thursday before Easter, which in the Catholic tradition is Holy Thursday. My mother had a horrible and terrible delivery, and we didn't go home for almost a month. When we did go home, my aunt (who is the person who gave me my childhood nickname of Libby), carried me and my mother carried the giant, stuffed bunny (about 3 or 4 feet tall) toy given to her in the hospital as a gift at my birth!

WA: One thing I must interject here is that your mother's difficult birth experience in the context of this mythology may betray her own difficulty with the Artemis archetype.

EYF: But in many ways I have come to think that the "separation" from my mother, was in fact, the hidden gift, because it allowed me really to be my own person. The dynamic, the struggle my mother always had with me, was that I was this little person, that didn't "need her." I'm not sure that it was about control, it was just that I was too separated from her.

In fact, one of the things that people still say about me (and it came up at first, when I started to do the mystic work more consciously)—friends of mine—their fear always was as one friend said it, "I'm always afraid you'll go around some corner and I won't be able to follow you and you won't come back for me or stay here with me." And my response to that was, "Well, I can't promise you I would stay." I do have that perhaps Artemis-quality that if need be, I will leave.

WA: It is also directly related to the hare. Where is the animal going to be next? They move in erratic movements, not in a straight path, which is why the rabbit's foot is lucky. Regarding your association of your nickname "Libby," Artemis represents liberty, so Libby is a word that could be associated with Liberty as well as with Lepus.

I spoke of the polarity of Orion and Lepus as figures associated with the motif of "sight." Orion, in the mythology, is made blind; the hare is an animal associated with being able to see in the dark. The hare also is symbolic of the return of spring and more sunshine, as well as the dawn, which daily brings forth the Sun. The term "I rise" is applicable to every kind of resurrection, as well as to every kind of enlightenment. I've talked about how the stars, Castor and Pollux, have to do with sight. Those two stars were, in ancient times, also depicted as two eyes. Just as one of the Gemini twins was mortal and the other was immortal, so the two eyes could be polarized, as one that sees in one way and the other that sees in another way or perhaps does not see at all. You know the word "gem" means "bud," but it also carries connotations of "bright" and "shiny." The bright and shiny organic manifestation of this—in the body—is the eyes; a very very archaic image. If, of Caster and Pollux, one were mortal and one were immortal, we can extend this to conclude that one could see into eternity and one saw into the temporal and immediate world.

And of course we have already described how it is that the Sun and Moon carry the motif of the two eyes in your horoscope as the eye of day and the eye of night. The eye of night in your chart is exaggeratedly nightly. It is exaggerated in its unconscious dimension because the Moon is next to Neptune, and Neptune is the planet of the unconscious. And furthermore, you have the eye of day at the very top of your chart—you are born three minutes before noon, so the Sun is exaggerated in its sunniness, at noon, and in Aries! At noon, the Sun reaches the pinnacle of its arc across the sky, as it is doing just that in your chart. This tells me that both solar and lunar consciousness are very exaggerated capacities in you. So this duality of seeing is in your horoscope in an archetypal image.

When I first talked to you about Lepus and Eostra and Easter, it was also because I realized that this pre-Christian Goddess' festival would not have been celebrated as we celebrate Easter, on the Sunday following the Full Moon nearest the equinox, but most probably would have been *on* the Full Moon. In essence, your chart is about the Full Moon at the Spring Equinox. In part of the major story of Orion and in every story of Orion, is the fact that he is struck blind. Tell the story you told me about babysitting and the blind boy and the rabbit's foot.

Elisabeth tells the story which is the archetypal form for Lepus

EYF: I was about 12 years old when this happened and there was a young family that lived next to us that had three children. The one little boy I was closest to, Luke, came to our house one day, and we had just rearranged the furniture, and he walked right into a table; it hit him right in the face. My mother said, "He didn't see that table" and went next door to his mother and told her to rearrange their living room. They did and then we took Luke home. He walked into things, and it became apparent that Luke had gone blind and no one had yet realized it! He was about three. It turned out that not only had Luke gone blind, but he had cancer and he ended up hav-

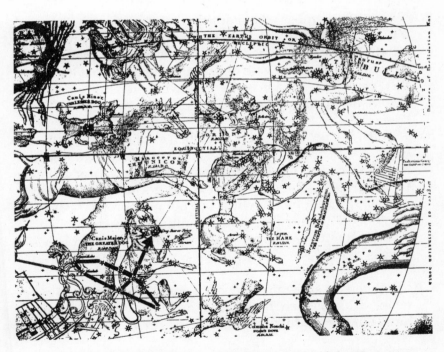

Atlas Designed to Illustrate The Geography of the Heavens
by Elijah H. Burritt, 1893

ing his eyes removed. It was very, very hard. I became Luke's buddy and I took care of him a lot, and we would do things. I was always trying to give him a sense of mobility in the world. We would go out together and I would sing to him in the park, in a big open field, so he could follow my voice without holding onto me, so he had some sense of moving in the world free. This was a favorite game of ours.

We had an old cat, and Luke was playing with the cat and touching him and pulling at him. My sister had a "good luck" rabbit's foot, and Luke got hold of this rabbit's foot, while holding the cat. He held it up screaming, because he thought he had ripped off the cat's foot. He was crying and there we were trying to explain to him that it wasn't the cat's foot. But of course, trying to explain that it was actually a rabbit's foot, and that that was good luck was just as hard! It was very intense. Actually, my whole relationship with Luke was very intense for me.

WA: Do you remember what happened at the time you first told me that story? Your son, who had been in the living room and I don't know what he had heard of this because I never could tell how big his ears were or how much he was paying attention, came into the kitchen where we were sitting and says "Mom, how come all your art is ladies' legs ripped off?"

EYF: Which is true! I like to do assemblages of found objects and I am very fascinated with doll's legs—actually I am fascinated with images that are cliches or archetypical for women: 1930s and 40s glamor women. I am not a very glamorous woman, I might be dramatic, but not glamorous. I basically like to work with arms and legs, multiples—I use Barbie-doll-type dolls with red fingernails and red high-heeled shoes—always red shoes.

WA: That goes to show that there is a mythic dimension of experience, which, when you judge it on the basis of "normalcy," turns out to have totally unrelated meanings.

EYF: To me, though, my art is not a protest. I use a lot of red—arms and legs, and red high heels—to me it is taking on these aspects and multiplying them. They all have multiples; it's many arms and many legs, and I am very attracted to using uneven, odd numbers. And I like the size difference because I use doll parts with either oversized images or regular-sized shoes.

WA: But when you cut apart the bride and groom dolls, when you put them with broken shards of glass in a bridal shoe with lipsticks, there is this trickster pose of protest. There is this cackle of power behind it. But I can also see the "duplication" function implied by the stars of Gemini conjunct your ascendant.

Back to the Luke story. When you first told it to me, you were prompted to tell me this story by my telling you that in Europe hares and cats were thought to breed together. Both of them were animals, familiars of witches. The idea of witches had association to you. Even though you wouldn't identify yourself religiously as Wiccan, as a channel you would have been so identified during the period of the persecution of witches, when Europe was trying to root out the pre-Christian beliefs and practices of Wiccan Paganism. It was only when I mentioned witches, hares, and cats in the same moment that your memory brought back Luke as an association between the cat and the hare.

EYF: The other thing that Luke and the hare is, and this is how he got to be playing with the cat and the rabbit's foot together, is that the first time I ever won anything at a carnival was when I was betting on a spinning game, betting Luke's birthday. I won a stuffed rabbit, which I gave to Luke, and my sister got the rabbit's foot as a consolation prize. The scene I just now crystallized was Luke sitting on the floor with the stuffed rabbit, (he may not have ever seen a real rabbit since he was blind from three), the pet cat, and the rabbit's foot.

WA: This memory is a nexus point, for seeing your mythos in an entirety, you understand, because all of the elements: blind Orion, the cat, the hare are all present, as is Artemis as the goddess of your coming of age, through the archetype of the wound. The motif of sacrifice is in many of the myths of the hare.

234/ Communicating the Horoscope

John Layard, the late great English analyst, in his book, *The Lady of the Hare* (Shambala, Boston, 1988) compiles the mythologies of the hare throughout the world. To fully understand the archetype, I had to become acquainted with the material. Only then did I have the material which would allow an understanding of all of the places and ways it permeates your life as outlined in your horoscope. He associates the hare to the motif of sacrifice at length, as well as its connections to lunar divinities.

In Greece the rites of Artemis were called the Brauronia, when little girls, and sometimes boys, dress up as little bears and carry small animals in a parade. This Artemis of the Brauronia is a Goddess of the young (girls) whose participants in her rites are celebrating the fact that their freedom is allied to their childhood. These little bear priestesses will shortly be leaving their mothers' sides as betrothed girls, they will soon menstruate. This is an Artemis whose rites predict a coming-of-age time. These rites and customs let us understand that as an Artemis woman, you are connected to your mother, yet you have to leave her. Your stepdaughter, who collects stuffed animals, is tied into this.

(EYF: And she came to live with us for a year when she was 12, leaving her mother's home.)

EYF: The other thing about being 12, is that 12 for me was a very powerful age. I felt like a very powerful person at 12 years old. I reached my mature height at 12. I was as tall as I am now at 12. I'm not really tall, 5'5", but then I was much taller than my mother.

I told you that I broke my pelvis at 12, but as I tell you this I remember that I really wasn't 12, I was 13, going on 14, because it happened in the beginning of 8th grade! But there is a parallel story because, when I *was* 12, my mother fell off the front porch and broke several ribs and I had to stay home from school for two weeks or so and take care of her. It was at that time she told me about menstruation and sex (such that she did), but it parallels my staying home the next year with my broken pelvis, and staying up all night with her watching the late shows (which is probably when I got all those "glamor" images fixed in my psyche). Both incidents happened in January or February, and are the two times we really enjoyed ourselves together.

WA: The coming of age rites of Artemis are through the experience of "blooding" or wounding. For the little priestesses of Artemis, it will be through their first menstruation. You have described a whole series of experiences of wounding, your wounding, your mother's wounding, and Luke's wounding. The archetypal animal in this wounding element of the mythology is the hare. You said you didn't really understand the hare mythology until you read *The Bunny Book* (by John D'Hondt, GOB Publishers, San Francisco, 1991) just last year, yet that bunny was already in Luke's hands 25 years ago.

EYF: And by the way, I never had stuffed animals. That is probably the only stuffed animal I had as a child, and I gave it to him.

WA: These literal wounds are your initiation experiences, even though two of them are vicarious. You had a coming-of-age realization wounding that is probably appropriate to your Aries Sun, Cancer Rising. The two planets of initiation into an adult identity are Venus and Mars. The Venus mode of initiation is through sexuality or love. The Mars or warrior mode is through an ordeal as initiation, or through the wound. You have Venus square Mars (see chart, page 241), but since you are an Aries I would expect a Mars mode of initiation. We no longer have ritual forms for these, instead they are experienced through the vicissitudes of life itself.

In your Mars/Saturn/Pluto conjunction square to Venus there is the image of an horrific dimension of experience. This was Luke's experience, not your own, but a vicarious experience.

EYF: Then, when I was 16, I essentially lost my father through his massive wound to the head.

WA: Which is very Orion-ish.

EYF: And my father basically went into the underworld because he had a brain injury in which he was in a coma for five months. By the way, Wendy, he had the accident while working on the *night shift*! They told us that he would die, and we were prepared for that. When this happened with my father, we went to the hospital every day.

WA: Which is the unconscious man who is loved by the moon.

EYF: After he had been in a coma state for almost five months, we get a telegram at 3:00 A.M., saying that he had awakened from the coma. We had prepared that he would die, so not only had my father come back, greatly damaged; we had already mourned him.

WA: He came back from the dead: Orion, Osiris, resurrection. "I rise."

EYF: He did rise and was this brain-damaged person, but he did recover. It was a great anomaly and unexpected. He did recover after many years. He was in and out of the hospital for two years. In fact the hospital was my home in my teenaged years, from 16-18. If you met him in later years, you would think he had had a stroke.

WA: Here we see the implications of this whole, intense emphasis with Mars, Saturn, and Pluto in your 2nd House opposite the 8th (page 217). In 1959–60, Uranus, the ruler of your 8th House passed over these three strong planets in your 2nd House. This was the time of Luke's "wounding." Uranus as "awakener" was the archetypal "opener of the way." All of these woundings underlie your work today as a channel, and your involvement in "the underworld," whether in your work with psychology, or in the time you spent on archeological digs, somehow. Mars, in fact, is the ruler of your 10th House, the father, and Mars conjoins Saturn, the planet of the father. So essentially, this journey through the underworld was undertaken by two men in your life when you were a child, Luke and your father.

EYF: The other thing that happened between the age of 12 and 14 is that I found out about Sigmund Freud, and I started reading Freud; not just "about" Freud, I was reading Freud's writings. And for me, the most pivotal thing of this time—I can't tell you how unbelievably powerful it was for me—was Freud. It opened up the concept of the unconscious. It opened up the concept that my mother's actions may not have had anything to do with me. Because my mother was a very erratic person, and if you are trying to base yourself on someone where if you did something on Monday it was okay, and if you did the exact thing on Wednesday and she went nuts, it was very hard to figure out how to figure it out. Freud, for me, meant that it didn't have anything to do with what *I* was doing on Monday and Wednesday, it had to do with my mother. I started to realize that I wasn't going to be able to figure the world out through her. Her actions were not exactly following the world, which was part of what I loved about intellectual stuff and school, because you could follow the world. If they wanted a report on Thursday, they probably still wanted it on Wednesday. The idea of psychology, the idea of the unconscious, was very powerful for me personally.

WA: If we examine the actual chart for the Full Moon preceding your birth, on Mar 24, 1948, at 10:10 P.M. EST, at Philadelphia where you were born, we can see the dramatic evidence of a wounding "unto death" in its planetary positions. Scorpio was rising, its ruler Pluto, Lord of the Underworld, was near the MC, square the Nodes and conjoined to Mars and Saturn. Pluto, or Scorpio, is the field of the Underworld which includes the idea of psychology (chart, page 239).

EYF: When my father was in the hospital . . . like any tragedy, a normalcy develops around it. So I have all these positive memories of songs and things from hanging out in the cafeteria of the Naval Hospital. My father is upstairs in a coma, and my friends are early Viet Nam wounded (this is 1964-65-66). I went to my prom with a guy who was the guard at the hospital. I had a very nice life, except it was based upon visiting my wounded father.

And I had this little blind friend, who wasn't just blind, but really had brain cancer, and we would go off and create this normalcy about this strange situation. We called the railing Mr. Charlie and we named the steps. Since he was getting radiation treatment, he couldn't get false eyes because his sockets were horribly burned. He wore little dark glasses after awhile. I remember once hearing him tell other little kids his age, "Don't be afraid of my eyes, my eyes had a disease in them and if they didn't take my eyes out, I would have died." The parents didn't know that Luke knew this much about everything until I told them this. The other little kids said, "Oh, okay," because he did look like some horrible torture happened to him. After all that, when he was six he contracted meningitis and went into a coma until he was 12, when he finally died.

WA: I remember telling you that the hare was the animal of sacrifice, and you said "Sacrifice! No way!"

EYF: For me most of it has been around me, as opposed to myself.

WA: And of course you are not at all the martyr type, and anyone who knows you could testify to the fact you are very much responsible for yourself and your feelings. But the myth is not portraiture. It is *an image of the spiritual dimension*, the transpersonal dimension of an archetype you experience and ground. It doesn't mean you have to sacrifice or *be* sacrificed; it means that the issue of wounding has a context associated with a dimension of something *both* sacred and mysterious, and yet is the very stuff of your history and experiences. The experiences have an effect, perhaps even a formative effect on the course your life and your consciousness take. The myth behind it all is the path through which you come to a realization of Self and purpose or destiny.

The mythology is more like a thread that weaves through your life. It connects things, but it doesn't always explain things, it associates things. This happened in your life. You can make any rational sense out of it, or any psychological sense out of it, that you want.

My main intention here is to uncover a way to find that thread, and to demonstrate that it is a constant presence of a divine (archetypal) energy that stands in and behind one's life. When I think about the hare, I understand it as an animal of enormous strength and enormous generosity, because, in mythology, hares sacrificed themselves for the gods. When we think of sacrifice, we think of the Catholic tradition, and that is your heritage; when you make a sacrifice you give something you love up, like at Lent. That is not what it meant once upon a time. It might mean you did cut off a piece of your flesh and offered it to the gods.

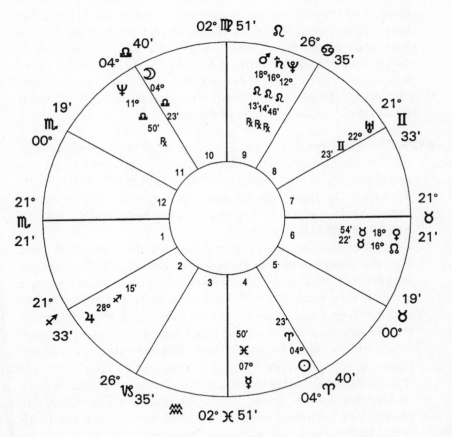

Full Moon
Mar. 24, 1948, 10:10 A.M. EST
Philadelphia, PA
75W11 39N57
Placidus Houses

EYF: Wasn't sacrifice to celebrate, to offer up celebration?

WA: Yes, and certainly not all sacrifices were bloody.

EYF: But you certainly gave food, wine, time.

WA: You sang. It wasn't always about being devoured, but in the case of the hare there is that element. On the other hand, although the hare and the bunny, even in *The Bunny Book*, represent the tremendous fragility of human life and the hope for peace and love and security on the one hand, the bunny; the hare symbolizes eternal life, because in hare mythology the hare goes to the Moon and the Moon cycles, it dies and is reborn every month. In the Moon is the hare. Then I came back and you told me that you didn't understand the hare mythology, Easter and all that, until you had read *The Bunny Book*. I really need you to explain that.

EYF: It's a good book. It's an awkward book in a literary sense. It's not that I didn't understand the hare. It's that I had not made peace with the *bunny* part of the hare myth. When I saw the title, "The Bunny Book" and someone else had written to me and told me it who knew about my hare myth, I knew I had to read this book.

It is a story about a guy whose lover dies of AIDS. And they collected bunnies. He would tell his lover the bunnies are watching over you, the bunnies are with you. And as his lover got sicker, he started to tell him stories about the bunny world and he offered the bunny as the idea of health and protection. People gave him bunnies, and other people began to give people bunnies. When his lover died, this man decides that the bunny thing was so present that he was going to find out what is there about bunnies. So he starts a search of the mythology of bunnies and of course, starts to discover this incredible plethora of information about bunnies from all different cultures. In this book, he relates all these little anecdotes and he has wonderful drawings of mythic bunnies from all over the world. He also shares this myth story about a woman who goes to the bunny world. He says it is the ongoing story he told his friend, but I'm not quite sure if that is a literary device or not. In the book he goes back and forth between this mythic bunny story and his friend's struggle with AIDS, and the stories about bunnies. Somehow it opened up the whole bunny things for me. It was then that I bought myself a stuffed bunny that is still pretty hare-like, but it was as bunny as I could get.

WA: The myth on some level has a constant presence, it is the divine, I think, continually putting things into your life, totally accidentally and synchronistically. You didn't create the child's blindness. This issue of the blindness came up. Later you said "Orion" told us that giants were far-seeing. It was interesting that in Greek myth, for example, Prometheus was a giant, and Prometheus is a word which means "far seeing." A giant is a being of enormous height, who can therefore see a long way off.

EYF: There is also a bringing of an awareness to people. The metaphor "Orion" gave was of the giant who came to the village. The village thought they were "the People," the only people there were, and the giant told them of the places they couldn't see, over the mountains.

WA: The smaller you are, the closer your horizon is. I wanted to get to the reaction to Lepus and the hare. After your reading, you dreamt of being dressed as a hare woman with a hare man.

EYF: We were humans, sort of. Our eyes were very strange, very large. I had long braided, multi-braided hair, with fur and nature things, flowers, small pine cones, etc., all braided through it. The clothes were all skins of hares. He also had long multi-braided hair with nature things, shells, pine cones and things. I had two long lop-eared ears attached to my headband, hanging on either side of my face. He had upright rabbit ears on his headband.

WA: You have moved into a shamanistic dimension of working with your myth.

EYF: When you brought this whole mythic work into my world, coming into consciousness about Artemis, coming into consciousness, even resistantly, about hares and eventually bunnies, it flung open portals. You said something earlier about mythic work being associative. Once you get this key, the associativeness becomes an active principle in my life and an active principle of enrichment. I can't tell you enough: there is this vitality about recognizing and feeling and experiencing your connections beyond your conscious self. Sometimes you can recognize these connections or you can sense connections, and you can feel the vitality, and you can feel the vibration, and you don't know yet what it is, but it is *tangible*. Often, either an insight comes back, or an interpreter comes back, or an interpretation from some other part of your life will come in, and it becomes known.

It really is exciting, there is a vitality, when you open the door to your myth and your totem, or when you let just the concept in. If you don't have someone like a mythic astrologer bringing it into the light, if you were reading this article and you even started to think about: "Is there a myth present in my life?" as people are doing now, starting with that simply "Could there be myths in life?" as neutral as you can get, it opens up all these portals. Maybe they're little peek-a-boo portals or big giant doorways, to further connections. Then you have a kind of guide. People are always looking for guides.

WA: The myth becomes inner guide to your experience.

EYF: Like the rabbit in *Alice in Wonderland*, because it sort of appears, pops up. Look, look. It attracts your attention.

WA: I don't know how you came to say that! Because that is what I say to those people whose mythos includes the hare—that the hare is conscious in the underworld, just like the White Rabbit in *Alice in Wonderland!* When I started working with myth, I discovered more about myself in knowing what my myth was and was able to connect things that before had no connection. They were so dissociated, and suddenly the thread they started to form said, "Oh that's why my mother married my father!" . . . It wasn't even the psychological things; what happened was this commonality on this deep level that made them have to be a part of each other. Furthermore, some of that commonality was negative, some was positive. If you choose your myth, like most people you would choose something you would like, but the myth also includes your shadow. It includes both substance and shadow. So most people won't choose their shadow; they'll reject it.

EYF: The other thing you were saying, about the big picture, that's it. It's back to those giants again. If you are standing right here you can see the addresses on the house. If you get up above in a plane, you can see the lay of the land and how the houses are all connected. I do think that when you start working with your myth, you see the bigger picture. I also think you keep expanding it. You go from the personal eventually to the transpersonal; and you start to look at the bigger myths, those of people close to you, your culture. And that is what keeps building *awareness*.

I still find that people who are working with mythology or archetypes are really unwilling to be mystics. They are afraid to let the energy be "real," not just conceptual. To me, these archetypes are not "archetypes," they are primal energies.

WA: That can only be *described* by an archetypal "projection."

EYF: It is an energy. It's like black holes or vortexes. It exists, it is not just in our minds, or thoughts, or even feelings. But people are afraid of that. If you touch into these energies, it's not just in your mind. It can happen in your body. It can be experienced.

I think our work really leads us to working with the "all," working with Unity, the interconnectedness of all things. But most people can not come to that; it is too much. It is sort of frustrating sometimes because they don't know what we are talking about or they can't touch it except in the small sense.

WA: It may seem inflated to say that this material is "advanced." And you and I have spent a number of sessions clarifying and associating the mythic motifs with elements of your life. But it is not because people are stupid that it is so hard to get. It is because we have so little education in an understanding of the "unconscious" symbolic world in general. So it is a big leap for us to see and know mythically.

It does take some effort to shift one's point of view, and I send my clients away with instructions to locate written sources for their mythology and then to start a journal for associations to the motifs. You dutifully read Layard's book and informed me that it didn't affect you. Then it fell together when you read *The Bunny Book*. The insight often comes like that, it falls into place like a keystone. When it does, the rewards are phenomenal in the increased connections made in psychological work, in the expanded awareness acquired, and in the increased level of synchronistic occurrences as revelation. To put it in the simplest terms; it increases the "Wows!" in your life. Thank you, Elisabeth, for sharing this with us.

Bibliography

Ashley, Wendy Z. "The Revelation of Mystery." *Mountain Astrologer*, October 1993, pp. 82-89.

Evans, George Ewart and David Thomson. *The Leaping Hare*. London: Faber and Faber Ltd., 1972.

Fitzhugh, Elisabeth Y. *The Orion Material*. Takoma Park, MD: Synchronicity Press, 1989.

Graves, Robert. *The Greek Myths*, 2 vols. Middlesex, England: Penguin Books, 1960.

D' Hondt, John. *The Bunny Book*. San Francisco: GOB Publishers, 1991.

Keen, Sam. "Personal Mythology." *Psychology Today*, Dec 1988, pp. 44-47.

Layard, John. *The Lady of the Hare*, Boston: Shambala, 1988.

Marler, Joan. "Joseph Campbell, The Mythic Journey," *Yoga Journal*, Nov/Dec 1987, pp. 58-61.

Ponce, Dr. Charles. "Saturn and the Art of Seeing," in *Working the Soul*, Berkeley CA: North Atlantic Books, 1988, pp. 29-56.

Seltman, Charles. *The Twelve Olympians*. New York: Thomas Y. Crowell Company, 1960.

Sesti, Giuseppe Maria. *The Glorious Constellations: History and Mythology*. New York: Harry Abrams, 1991.

Stashower, Daniel and Donia Ann Steel, and Editors of Time-Life Books. *Giants and Ogres; The Enchanted World*. Alexandria, VA: Time-Life Series, 1985, pp. 9, 14 and 15.

STAY IN TOUCH

On the following pages you will find some of the books now available on related subjects. Your book dealer stocks most of these and will stock new titles in the Llewellyn series as they become available. We urge your patronage.

To obtain our full catalog, to keep informed about new titles as they are released, and to benefit from informative articles and helpful news, you are invited to write for our bimonthly news magazine/catalog, *Llewellyn's New Worlds of Mind and Spirit*. A sample copy is free, and it will continue coming to you at no cost as long as you are an active mail customer. Or you may subscribe for just $10.00 in the U.S.A. and Canada ($20.00 overseas, first class mail). Many bookstores also have *New Worlds* available to their customers. Ask for it.

Llewellyn's New Worlds of Mind and Spirit
P.O. Box 64383-K866, St. Paul, MN 55164-0383, U.S.A.

* * *

TO ORDER BOOKS AND TAPES

If your book dealer does not have the books described, you may order them directly from the publisher by sending the full price in U.S. funds, plus $3.00 for postage and handling for orders *under* $10.00; $4.00 for orders *over* $10.00. There are no postage and handling charges for orders over $50.00. Postage and handling rates are subject to change. We ship UPS whenever possible. Delivery guaranteed. Provide your street address as UPS does not deliver to P.O. boxes. Allow 4-6 weeks for delivery. UPS to Canada requires a $50.00 minimum order. Orders outside the U.S.A. and Canada: Airmail—add retail price of book; add $5.00 for each non-book item (tapes, etc.); add $1.00 per item for surface mail.

FOR GROUP STUDY AND PURCHASE

Because there is a great deal of interest in group discussion and study of the subject matter of this book, we offer a special quantity price to group leaders or agents. Our special quantity price for a minimum order of five copies of *Communicating the Horoscope* is $36.00 cash-with-order. This price includes postage and handling within the United States. Minnesota residents must add 6.5% sales tax. For additional quantities, please order in multiples of five. For Canadian and foreign orders, add postage and handling charges as above. Credit card (VISA, MasterCard, American Express) orders are accepted. Charge card orders only ($15.00 minimum order) may be phoned in free within the U.S.A. or Canada by dialing 1-800-THE-MOON. For customer service, call 1-612-291-1970. Mail orders to:

LLEWELLYN PUBLICATIONS
P.O. Box 64383-K866, St. Paul, MN 55164-0383, U.S.A.

ASTROLOGY'S SPECIAL MEASUREMENTS
How to Expand the Meaning of the Horoscope
Edited by Noel Tyl

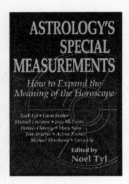

Every new student of astrology looks with bewilderment at that first horoscope and asks, "What's it mean when there's nothing in my 7th house? Won't I ever get married?" The student feels the strong need to *measure*. He needs something to define the space in the house and give meaning to the picture. Measurements are the lenses that help us see nearer, farther, and with greater contrast and clarity. In the process of analysis, measurement becomes diagnosis.

In this volume, ten experts discuss the finer points of measurement and meaning, analysis and diagnosis. How many measurements do you need? How many should fortify you for meaningful conversations with clients? Not all measurements work in every horoscope or for every astrologer—and too many can present so much data that you lose confidence within the multiplicity of options. Furthermore, no matter how precise the measurements, they still rely on the astrologer to adapt them to the human condition. *Astrology's Special Measurements* will be a tremendous resource for putting those special measurements to work easily and without fear.

ISBN: 1-56718-864-8, 6 x 9, 352 pgs., charts, tables, softbound $12.00

HOW TO PERSONALIZE THE
OUTER PLANETS
The Astrology of Uranus, Neptune & Pluto
Edited by Noel Tyl

Since their discoveries, the three outer planets have been symbols of the modern era. Representing great social change on a global scale, they also take us as individuals to higher levels of consciousness and new possibilities of experience. Explored individually, each outer planet offers tremendous promise for growth. But when taken as a group, as they are in *Personalizing the Outer Planets*, the potential exists to recognize *accelerated* development.

As never done before, the seven prominent astrologers in *Personalizing the Outer Planets* bring these revolutionary forces down to earth in practical ways.

0-87542-389-2, 288 pgs., 6 x 9, illus., softcover $12.00

SEXUALITY IN THE HOROSCOPE
Edited by Noel Tyl

To empower clients to be more successful and satisfied in every area of life is the astrologer's legitimate aim. You might specialize in relationships or finance, but you cannot ignore the rest of a client's life if you intend to enhance the whole person. You must be willing and able to deal with the private and the often painful, the repressed as well as the blissful.

Sex is a biological drive with a chemical basis, physiological parameters, physical manifestations, emotional and psychological dimensions, and sociological implications. It involves our states of self-awareness and self-esteem, our capacity for communications, and parental influence. At the most basic physical level, it is friction. At the most spiritual level, it is merging into transcendental oneness.

The experience of sexuality is complex in its manifestation in life and in its occurrence in the horoscope. As they explore charts of the famous, infamous, and everyday persons, ten well-known astrologers share insights into the following intriguing topics:

ISBN: 1-56718-865-6, 6 x 9, 336 pp., softbound **$14.95**

HOW TO USE VOCATIONAL ASTROLOGY FOR SUCCESS IN THE WORKPLACE
Edited by Noel Tyl

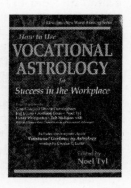

Announcing the most practical examination of Vocational Astrology in five decades! Improve your astrological skills with these revolutionary NEW tools for vocational and business analysis! Now, in *How to Use Vocational Astrology for Success in the Workplace,* edited by Noel Tyl, seven respected astrologers provide their well-seasoned modern views on that great issue of personal life—Work. Their expert advice will prepare you well for those tricky questions clients often ask: "Am I in the right job?" "Will I get promoted?" or "When is the best time to make a career move?" With an introduction by Noel Tyl in which he discusses the startling research of the Gauquelins, this ninth volume in Llewellyn's New World Astrology Series features enlightening counsel from the following experts: Jayj Jacobs, Gina Ceaglio, Donna Cunningham, Anthony Louis, Noel Tyl, Henry Weingarten, and Bob Mulligan. Read *How to Use Vocational Astrology* today, and add "Vocational Counselor" to *your* resume tomorrow! Includes the complete 1942 classic by Charles E. Luntz *Vocational Guidance by Astrology.*

0-87542-387-6, 384 pgs., 6 x 9, illus., softcover **$14.95**

Prices subject to change without notice.

EXPLORING CONSCIOUSNESS IN THE HOROSCOPE
edited by Noel Tyl

When Llewellyn asked astrologers across the country which themes to include in its "New World Astrology Series," most specified at the top of their lists themes that explore consciousness! From shallow pipedreaming to ecstatic transcendence, "consciousness" has come to envelop realms of emotion, imagination, dreams, mystical experiences, previous lives and lives to come—aspects of the mind which defy scientific explanation. For most, consciousness means self-realization, the "having it all together" to function individualistically, freely, and confidently.

There are many ways to pursue consciousness, to "get it all together." Astrology is an exciting tool for finding the meaning of life and our part within it, to bring our inner selves together with our external realities, in appreciation of the spirit. Here, then, ten fine thinkers in astrology come together to share reflections on the elusive quicksilver of consciousness. They embrace the spiritual—and the practical. All are aware that consciousness feeds our awareness of existence; that, while it defies scientific method, it is vital for life.

0-87542-391-4, 256 pgs., 6 x 9, tables, charts, softcover $12.00

HOW TO MANAGE THE ASTROLOGY OF CRISIS
edited by Noel Tyl

More often than not, a person will consult an astrologer during those times when life has become difficult, uncertain or distressing. While crisis of any type is really a turning point, not a disaster, the client's crisis of growth becomes the astrologer's challenge. By coming to the astrologer, the client has come to an oracle. At the very best, there is hope for a miracle; at the very least, there is hope for reinforcement through companionship and information. How do you as an astrological counselor balance a sober discussion of the realities with enthusiastic efforts to leave the client feeling empowered and optimistic?

In this, the eleventh title in Llewellyn's New World Astrology Series, eight renowned astrologers provide answers this question as it applies to a variety of life crises. *How to Manage the Astrology of Crisis* begins with a discussion of the birth-crisis, the first major transition crisis in everybody's life—their confrontation with the world. It then discusses significant family crises in childhood and healing of the inner child . . . mental crises including head injuries, psychological breakdown, psychic experiences, multiple personalities . . . career turning points and crises of life direction and action . . . astrological triggers of financial crisis and recent advances in financial astrology . . . astrological maxims for relationship crises . . . and the mid-life crises of creative space, idealism, and consciousness.

0-87542-390-6, 224 pgs., 6 x 9, charts, softcover $12.00

Prices subject to change without notice.